'Tickling the Palate'

GU00982741

Reimagining Ireland

Volume 57

Edited by Dr Eamon Maher
Institute of Technology, Tallaght

PETER LANG

Oxford • Bern • Berlin • Bruxelles • Frankfurt am Main • New York • Wien

Máirtín Mac Con Iomaire
and Eamon Maher (eds)

'Tickling the Palate'

Gastronomy in Irish Literature
and Culture

PETER LANG

Oxford • Bern • Berlin • Bruxelles • Frankfurt am Main • New York • Wien

Bibliographic information published by Die Deutsche Nationalbibliothek.
Die Deutsche Nationalbibliothek lists this publication in the Deutsche
Nationalbibliografie; detailed bibliographic data is available on the Internet at
http://dnb.d-nb.de.

A catalogue record for this book is available from the British Library.

Library of Congress Control Number: 2014934464

ISSN 1662-9094
ISBN 978-3-0343-1769-6

Cover image: The Jammet Hotel and Restaurant (Andrew Street) by Harry
Kernoff. Source: Restaurant Patrick Guilbaud – The Merrion Hotel, Dublin.

© Peter Lang AG, International Academic Publishers, Bern 2014
Hochfeldstrasse 32, CH-3012 Bern, Switzerland
info@peterlang.com, www.peterlang.com, www.peterlang.net

This publication has been peer reviewed.

Printed in Germany

Contents

vi

Acknowledgements

The editors would like to acknowledge the funding provided by the School of Culinary Arts and Food Technology (Dublin Institute of Technology) and the National Centre for Franco-Irish Studies (Institute of Technology Tallaght) towards this publication. Given that our two institutions are coming closer in a bid to gain Technological University status, this collaboration is as timely as it is welcome.

We also wish to thank all the contributors for supplying such an original and varied array of essays and for their professionalism and courteousness throughout the editing process.

The editorial team of Dorothy Cashman, Yvonne Desmond, Tara McConnell, Brian Murphy and Elaine Mahon invested great care and energy in reading through the manuscript, for which we are most grateful.

Since the genesis of this book arose from the inaugural Dublin Gastronomy Symposium in 2012, we would like to thank all who attended, both as presenters and as symposiasts. A special thanks to Darra Goldstein who gave the keynote address and also for contributing the Foreword to this volume. Thanks also to all in DIT Cathal Brugha Street who ensured that the Symposium ran seamlessly, particularly Frank Cullen, John Clancy, Pauline Danaher, Tony Campbell, Dermot Seberry, Tony Conlon, Sean Hogan and Mike O'Connor.

Finally, we are deeply indebted to all the staff at Peter Lang, especially the commissioning editor Christabel Scaife and the ever-efficient Mary Critchley.

Foreword

Ireland, until recently, appeared as only the smallest of dots on the map of high gastronomy. Too many self-avowed connoisseurs were convinced that Irish food began and ended with cabbage and potatoes – or the lack thereof. True, Irish soda bread had transcended the country's borders to become a bread-baking beginner's staple, but the lilting names of dishes like colcannon and fadge beckoning from the pages of cookbooks held, for many readers, more linguistic than actual appeal. The prevailing idea of Irish food as limited and monotonous – the result of want and famine – could not, it seemed, be dispelled. Even as food studies came into its own as an academic discipline, Irish foodways failed to receive their due. In *Hungering for America: Italian, Irish and Jewish Foodways in an Age of Migration* (2001, p. 85), Hasia Diner maintained that only the Irish – unlike the Italians and Jews who are also subjects of her book – did not have a richly developed food culture. She averred that 'Irish writers of memoir, poems, stories, political tracts, or songs rarely included the details of food in describing daily life'. And yet, any reader who delves deeper than *Angela's Ashes*, Frank McCourt's memoir of poverty so desperate that he subsisted largely on bread and tea, discovers that in fact Irish literature is replete with descriptions of food. This food claims a beautiful simplicity as an elemental expression of the land and the sea – natural delights such as smoked mussels and salmon, rock lobster and dulse, fennel-scented soda bread and floury potatoes.

To realise the meaningfulness of these essential flavours we need only turn to the first stanza of Seamus Heaney's 'Oysters', the opening poem of his 1979 collection *Field Work*:

> Our shells clacked on the plates.
> My tongue was a filling estuary,
> My palate hung with starlight:
> As I tasted the salty Pleiades
> Orion dipped his foot into the water
> (Heaney 1979, p. 3)

The immediacy of taste at once unites the oyster eater with his environment, with a very localised estuary, but as the poet continues to eat the
briny bivalve, his world expands, until he becomes one with history and,
ultimately, with the universe. Eamon Grennan's 'Food for Thought' similarly conjoins the poet with nature as a 'green butteriness' fills his mouth
when he chews on a blade of grass (2001, p. 9). From this simple gesture
the poem becomes a meditation on poetry and love, invoking the gods,
like Heaney's poem, to capture the sense of timelessness that a moment of
blissful experience can bring.

Ireland has suffered twice for its famines and food shortages: first due
to very real deprivations; and second because these deprivations present an
obstacle to the exploration of Irish food. All too often the story begins and
ends with potatoes or famine. But again, literature can be revelatory. Two
particular passages expressing opposite poles of Irish practice have stayed
with me over the years, one featuring the refined, French-inflected dishes
of the Anglo-Irish elite, as described in Molly Keane's *Good Behaviour*; the
other presenting the earthy, gutsy food of the common folk, celebrated by
James Joyce in *Ulysses*.

Good Behaviour begins with food, in a scene that juxtaposes the
restrained sensibility of the Anglo-Irish gentry (down-in-the-heels as they
may be) with the vibrant sensuousness of the Irish Catholic world, here represented by the servant, Rose. Aroon, the daughter of the manor, complains:

> Rose smelt the air, considering what she smelt; a miasma of unspoken criticism
> and disparagement fogged the distance between us. I knew she ached to censure
> my cooking, but through the years I have subdued her. Those wide shoulders and
> swinging hips were once parts of a winged quality she had – a quality reduced and
> corrected now, I am glad to say.
>
> (Keane 2001, p. 3)

Although Aroon knows that her invalid mother detests rabbit – the mother
has, in fact, a pathological fear of the meat due to a virus infecting Irish
rabbits – she decides nevertheless to prepare rabbit quenelles and present
them as her offering:

The tray did look charming: bright, with a crisp clean cloth and a shine on everything. I lifted the silver lid off the hot plate to smell those quenelles in a cream
sauce. There was just a hint of bay leaf and black pepper, not a breath of the rabbit
foundation. Anyhow, what could be more delicious and delicate than a baby rabbit?
Especially after it has been forced through a fine sieve and whizzed for ten minutes
in a Moulinex blender.

(Keane 2000, pp. 3–4)

Aroon pretends that she has prepared chicken mousse. Her mother is not
fooled, however, and her indignation is so great that she suddenly dies,
without having taken a bite.

Food in this introductory scene emblematises the strife between
mother and daughter and, even more significantly, the differences between
the Anglo-Irish gentry and the Catholics who serve them. Food, in the form
of a French dish strained through the tastes of the English, also provides
the arena, the metaphorical bones of contention, for a three-way battle of
wills among a former oppressor, a current oppressor – both Anglo-Irish
– and Rose, the Catholic servant, whose healthy, unconstrained move-
ments literally throw open the window to fresh air. Rose's 'wide shoulders
and swinging hips' threaten Aroon, who has been raised to keep herself
restrained, girdled, and controlled.

Such blowsy lack of containment is, by contrast, celebrated in *Ulysses*,
where sensuality rules. In the 'Calypso' episode, early in the novel, we see
how one appetite inspires another when Bloom goes into a butcher shop
to buy a kidney for breakfast and encounters the girl who lives next door:
'A kidney oozed bloodgouts on the willowpatterned dish: the last. He
stood by the nextdoor girl at the counter … His eyes rested on her vigorous
hips … Strong pair of arms … Mr. Bloom pointed quickly. To catch up and
walk behind her if she went slowly, behind her moving hams. Pleasant to
see first thing in the morning' (Joyce 1934, pp. 58–59).

Rabbit quenelles from French *haute cuisine* and raw kidneys with their
potent reek of uric acid – these foods, and the context in which they are
presented, tell a more complex story of Irish cuisine, one that goes beyond
the potatoes and cabbage of common perception. And it is this other story
that the volume at hand, a study of gastronomy in Irish culture, seeks to tell.
Here, at last, is a serious consideration of Ireland through its food, drink,

and language: a corrective to the false impression that Irish foodways are unworthy of attention.

To some degree this volume mirrors what has been happening in the world of Irish food outside of academia. Thanks to changing tastes and to Ireland's beautiful fresh ingredients, the country has at last appeared on the world's culinary map, and its extraordinary natural produce and artisanal cheeses are now recognised as among the finest anywhere. While lacking the variety and refinements of cuisines from countries where both climate and politics were more conducive to developing a rich food culture, Ireland nevertheless sings with brilliant flavours based on the food of poverty and the preparations of necessity. Such products as salmon smoked over old whiskey casks, organic oatcakes and dandelion syrup are now construed as signs of Irish culinary revival. Perhaps most significant of all is the newfound pride in the Irish land and culture (its agri-culture, quite literally), and a sense of a valuable and specifically Irish contribution to the global marketplace. The blossoming of smallholder food production has been accompanied by a renewed awareness of Ireland's long tradition of hospitality – as we learn from Brian Murphy's essay on pub culture, the '*briugu* or hospitaller' was one of the most important roles in ancient Celtic society. Here, again, literature comes to mind. Joyce's great short story 'The Dead' celebrates Irish hospitality, repeating the word five times during Gabriel's speech at the lavish dinner party featuring two dozen deliciously described enticements, floury potatoes among them (Joyce 2005, pp. 167–168).

Because the renaissance of artisanal food production in Ireland coincided with the burgeoning of food studies throughout Europe and North America, it is not surprising that a serious volume on the history of Irish gastronomy should appear. Indeed, as Máirtín Mac Con Iomaire and Eamon Maher, the editors of this volume, note in their introduction, even the Royal Irish Academy is getting in on the act, with a volume on food and drink in Ireland slated for publication in 2015. But it takes more than coincidence for such projects to come to fruition. Through the vision and tireless efforts of Máirtín Mac Con Iomaire, the first Dublin Gastronomy Symposium was held in June 2012, to great acclaim for its diversity of papers and for the many conversations stimulated by the confluence of presenters from vastly different spheres of culinary production, from academia to tourism to food purveying. The Symposium was marked not only by the broad range of its papers but by the depth of those papers' investigations. Thus it is a particular pleasure to introduce the resulting volume of essays. '*Tickling the Palate*' has much to offer both readers already familiar with Irish foodways and those who know little about them.

While the volume's focus on Ireland makes it the first of its kind, the strength of the collection lies also in its multidisciplinary approach. Quite beyond the new material they present, the essays open up questions for further investigation into other aspects of Irish culinary culture. Ranging across genres (literary criticism, semiotics, sociology, tourism studies) and time (from the eighteenth century up through the present and into the future), they consider the very nature of Irishness in relation to food and drink. As Brian Murphy asks in his exploration of the Irish pub abroad, 'How can the exportation of a gastronomic identity play a role in improving people's relationship with a place without it being perceived as false and inauthentic?' Meanwhile, within Ireland's borders, John Mulcahy has a vision for promoting all that is best about Irish food culture: 'So this is about creating, in Ireland, an imagined community of gastronomy that accommodates and balances innovation and tradition, individual creativity and time-honoured conventions, the singular and the collective.'

Such thoughts underlie Marjorie Deleuze's reflections on why Ireland is turning into a 'foodie nation'. She notes that as late as 1974 the Irish Tourist Board, in promoting Ireland as a destination to the French, defensively stated: 'Ireland is certainly not the country of gastronomy. But there's no need to denigrate Irish cuisine as a whole ... With modesty, we let those who know make complicated culinary preparations. What we serve is first and foremost simple.' By 1987, the Board's presentation was cautiously positive, revealing a growing self-confidence: 'It is obvious now, that over the last few years, Irish cuisine is getting better. Good restaurants are opening everywhere and for all pockets. Obviously, people are not coming for Irish cooking alone, but you never know ...'. Twenty-five years later, Fáilte Ireland (as the Irish Tourist Board is now known) is quite justifiably – and successfully – marketing Irish food to tourists as part of an 'authentic and local' experience.

The essays in this volume make clear that politics have been extraordinarily important in the construction of Irish cuisine, with a constant tension between the elite and the lower classes that did not lead to the sort of trickle-down effect so discernible in French cuisine. Yet here, again, this volume confounds expectations as it upends the upstairs/downstairs dichotomy. Tara McConnell's study of beer consumption in elite households in eighteenth-century Ireland demonstrates that the gentry and aristocrats enjoyed ale as well as beer and small beer, beverages commonly associated only with the working classes. And if we thought that *haute cuisine* was confined to the country manors of the Anglo-Irish elite, then it comes as a surprise to learn from Máirtín Mac Con Iomaire that in the mid-twentieth century, Dublin was home to what were named the finest restaurants in the world – even though the concept of the restaurant had entered the Irish lexicon only in the second half of the nineteenth century.

This volume's nuanced literary, cultural and sociological interpretations of Ireland and its food leave the reader with a sense of repletion. Even as we acknowledge the enforced sparseness of the Irish meal in the past, we can embrace the country's possibilities for Joycean excess and welcome the many iterations of Irish food practices that lie in between. Above all, *'Tickling the Palate'* conveys the wonderful richness of the Irish language and the traditions of Irish conviviality. I hope that this will be only the first of many volumes to explore Ireland's flavoursome gastronomy.

Darra Goldstein
Founding Editor, *Gastronomica: The Journal of Food and Culture*
Willcox B. and Harriet M. Adsit Professor of Russian,
Williams College, USA

Works cited

Grennan, E. (2001). 'Food for Thought', in *Gastronomica: The Journal of Food and Culture*, Vol. 1, no. 2 (Spring), p. 3.

Heaney, S. (1979). *Field Work Poems*. New York: Farrar, Straus and Giroux.

Joyce, J. (1934). *Ulysses*. New York: Random House.

Joyce, J. (2005). *Dubliners*. New York: Bantam Dell.

Keane, M. (2001). *Good Behaviour*. London: Virago.

Introduction

There has been a gradual but noticeable growth in scholarship concerning food globally, particularly in the last decade. One of the longest running and most influential forces behind this phenomenon is the Oxford Symposium on Food and Cookery (1981–present) which was originally founded and co-chaired by Alan Davidson, pre-eminent food historian, diplomat, and author of *The Oxford Companion to Food*, and Dr Theodore Zeldin, the celebrated social historian of France. This spawned a dedicated publishing house, Prospect Books, which published the conference proceedings and also the journal *Petits Propos Culinaires* (PPC), now approaching its 100th issue. Prospect Books boast an impressive catalogue of monographs, translations, conference proceedings and collections of essays around the subject of food and cookery. *Petits Propos Culinaires* was joined by other journals interested in food and culture including *Gastronomica: The Journal of Food and Culture* (University of California Press); *Food, Culture and Society: An International Journal of Multidisciplinary Research* (published on behalf of the Association for the Study of Food and Society (ASFS)); *Food and Foodways* (Taylor & Francis); *Food and History* (biannual scientific review of the Institut Européen d'Histoire et des Cultures de l'Alimentation/ European Institute for the History and Culture of Food (IEHCA)); *Journal of Culinary Science & Technology* (Taylor & Francis); and, most recently, the *International Journal of Gastronomy and Food Science* (AZTI-Tecnalia/ Elsevier).

A number of the University Presses (Oxford, Columbia, Chicago, California) have added food collections to their catalogues, and other publishing houses such as Bloomsbury, Berg, ABC-Clio, Greenwood Press, Altamira, Grub Street and Reaktion also have dedicated food series. Since the publication of *The Oxford Companion to Food* (Davidson 1999), there has been a surge in reference books and encyclopaedias around the topic (Kiple and Ornelas 2000; Smith 2004; Parasecoli and Scholliers

2011; Albala 2011; Kraig and Sen 2013). Food and cooking have become so visible in popular culture that many international journals have brought out special issues focusing on culinary materialism (*Collapse: Philosophical Research and Development*, Vol. VII, 2011), food history (*International Journal of Contemporary Hospitality Management*, Vol. 25, No. 2, 2013), cookbooks (*M/C Journal*, Vol. 16, No. 3, 2013) or food cultures (*Cultural Studies Review*, Vol. 19, No. 1, 2013).

The study of gastronomy in Ireland, equally, has shown steady growth in recent years, with doctoral research in particular casting new and much needed light on previous perceptions of Ireland's food heritage which traditionally had focused more on famines than on feasting. A number of individuals have laid the foundations for this work: scholars such as Anthony T. Lucas, Louis Michael Cullen, Kevin Danaher, Leslie Clarkson, Margaret Crawford, Fergus Kelly and Regina Sexton immediately come to mind. The Agricultural History Society of Ireland (AHSI) held a special conference in 2013 to discuss the veracity of Lucas's (1960) assertion that 'from prehistory to the close of the 17th century, corn and milk were the mainstay of the national food'. Scholars from the disciplines of food science, archaeology, history and folklore, using the most up-to-date analysis techniques, concluded that Lucas was broadly correct, but that a higher level of beef consumption than previously believed was evident from the osteo-archaeological data they unearthed. The prevalence of pig meat noted in written sources compared to the actual archaeological evidence was thus explained. Pig meat was a celebratory food, used at feasts and banquets, which made it more likely to be documented than other elements of the everyday diet.

One by-product of the intense road building programme of the 'Celtic Tiger' years (1995–2007) is the Archaeology and the National Roads Authority Monograph series, which includes the 2009 volume *Dining and Dwelling*, in which one can find a clearer picture of our culinary heritage based on archaeological evidence. Indeed, such is the current interest in gastronomy that the Royal Irish Academy has commissioned a special thematic volume of the journal *Proceedings of the Royal Irish Academy, Section C*, titled *Food and Drink in Ireland*, due to be published in 2015.

Areas of gastronomy have had dedicated core modules in the Culinary Arts programmes in the Dublin Institute of Technology for nearly fifteen years now. Gastronomy has been interpreted in its widest sense to include the history, sociology, anthropology, psychology and aesthetics of food and beverage, and not merely the narrow definitions of 'the culinary customs of a particular region' or 'the art or science of good eating' associated with the word in many dictionaries. It is this wider definition of gastronomy that is embraced by the Dublin Gastronomy Symposium (DGS), and indeed by this volume. Many of the chapters in this book stem from presentations at the inaugural DGS in 2012, while others arrived independently or by request in order to strengthen the Irish angle.

There are still some commentators, however, who argue that Ireland does not have a food culture and that the term 'Irish cuisine' is oxymoronic (Myers 2002; Cotter 1999). Diner (2001, p. 85) suggests that Ireland failed to develop an elaborate national food culture, and that, unlike other countries, 'Irish writers of memoir, poems, stories, political tracts, or songs rarely included the details of food in describing daily life'. She also notes that those who observed or recorded Irish voices seldom represented them as wanting to eat better or as craving exotic food items. Though there may be some truth in these arguments as they pertain to certain classes of migrants at a specific time and place in history, as a methodology this overlooks a long tradition of hospitality in Ireland. Indeed, one only needs to consider how the Middle Irish tale '*Aislinge Meic Con Glinne*' or Antaine Ó Raiftearaí's (1784–1835) poem '*Bainis an tS'leacháin Mhóir*' employ food to satirise a lack of hospitality to find illustrations of how prominently gastronomy features in Irish literary representations. Diner also ignores a long tradition described by Simms (1978, p. 78) as 'guesting and feasting', whereby the Brehon Law tracts outlined various legal rights to hospitality in Ireland, or where hosts voluntarily issued invitations to a feast. Cullen (1981, p. 141), writing about the early modern period, notes that butter consumption in Ireland was the highest in the world, that meat consumption per capita was also relatively high, and that the range of meat eaten was uniquely wide-ranging, making the Irish diet and cooking 'one of the most interesting culinary traditions in Europe'.

Terry Eagleton (1997) proposes that the most celebrated food-text of English literature is the work of an Anglo-Irish patriot, Jonathan Swift's *A Modest Proposal* (1729), in which he bitterly recommended munching babies as a solution to his country's economic ills. During the Great Famine, this may well have happened. As Swift's fellow Dubliner Oscar Wilde observed: 'life has a remarkable knack of imitating art'. Eagleton suggests that the starved words, gaunt bodies and sterile landscapes of Beckett's dramas may well carry within them a race memory of the Irish famine, and that it is possible to read Beckett's meticulously pared-down prose as a satirical smack at the blather and blarney of stage-Irish speech. Beckett, he argues, 'hoards his meagre clutch of words like a tight-fisted peasant, ringing pedantic changes on the same few signs or stage properties like someone eking out a scanty diet'. Eagleton continues that there is, perhaps, a Protestant suspicion of superfluity in evidence here, in contrast to the extravagant ebullience of James Joyce, the linguistic opulence of John Millington Synge or the verbal gluttony of Brendan Behan. Language in Irish culture, however, is associated less with food than with drink. The three main themes of this volume are language (literature), food and drink. As drink flows in, so words pour out, each fuelling the other in a self-sustaining process. In fact, despite our reputation for drunkenness and the close association with Guinness particularly, Eagleton points out that 'apart from the notoriously bibulous trinity of Behan, Flann O'Brien and Patrick Kavanagh, remarkably few Irish writers have been alcoholics – far fewer than American authors, for whom alcohol seems as much of a prerequisite as a typewriter' (Eagleton 1997).

Given the stereotypical propensity of Irish writers for the demon drink, it is logical that this volume should open with a section dealing with literary representations of Irish gastronomy. Dorothy Cashman's essay explores an aspect of the Anglo-Irish writer Maria Edgeworth's work that may not be widely known, namely her culinary sensibility. Elite households such as the one in which Edgeworth lived ate a strange mixture of Anglo-Irish cuisine and a native Irish diet. In Cashman's view, 'this co-existence would not be unusual in the culinary history of a country'. Archival research into the household accounts of the period produces fascinating findings as to what was being consumed by the elite classes, who looked to France and

England for examples of best practice, but evidence of what the ordinary Irish were consuming is less readily available. Then there is that other issue, particularly prominent in nineteenth-century Ireland when Edgeworth produced much of her literary work: the narrative of famine, a narrative that does not take in the whole story of food in Ireland. Cashman manages to make a strong case for a closer consideration of the way in which Irish eating habits in the period during which Edgeworth wrote offer an excellent insight as to the mores and mentality of the time. Venison, sweet plums, salmon, lobsters, game of all sorts – this was the fare that was served at the tables of the better-off members of the Anglo-Irish aristocracy, who saw themselves as the equal of their English counterparts at the time.

James Joyce was never one to see himself as being inferior to anyone, English or Irish. Flicka Small's chapter delves into the rich food compendium that is *Ulysses*, a novel that starts and ends with breakfast. Leopold Bloom's diet is rather exotic – he loves eating the inner organs of beasts and fowls – and, strangely enough for the time, his domain is the kitchen. Small points out the particular role that food plays in Joyce's novel: 'Bloom's memories of a more intimate time with Molly are related to food, and many of the happiest ones are of the two of them eating together'. 'Food memories' abound in *Ulysses* and the world is viewed very much in terms of food. Small notes how Bloom considers that 'a vegetable diet can make a person poetical. He can almost taste death, which he imagines tasting like raw turnips; he thinks that cheese is like the corpse of milk ....'.

Michael Flanagan's chapter deals with the prevalence of food in children's literature, a constantly recurring motif in that particular genre. The examples chosen come in the main from classic texts such as Lewis Carroll's *Alice's Adventures in Wonderland* (1866), Charles Dickens' *Oliver Twist* and *A Christmas Carol*, Kenneth Grahame's *The Wind in the Willows* (1908), and numerous fairytales such as *Little Red Riding Hood, Hansel and Gretel, Sleeping Beauty*, all of which would have been widely read in Ireland. These texts have a strong emphasis on food (or the lack thereof), which is viewed as being inseparable from the characters' other preoccupations. Enid Blyton's *Famous Five* books are interesting simply in terms of the amount of time which these intrepid young sleuths devote to eating. According to Flanagan, the five have a balanced diet: 'Sweets are eaten sparingly; hunks of crusty bread are accompanied by handfuls of radishes or fresh fruit. The children manage a structured approach to eating.'

Eamon Maher delves into the literary imagination of John McGahern and finds a treasure trove of references to food and drink. From pints of Guinness and ham sandwiches in Blake's Pub in Enniskillen, to the mandatory meal in The Royal Hotel that Mahoney offers as a reward to his son for getting a university scholarship in *The Dark*, or the sophisticated London restaurants described in *The Leavetaking* and *The Pornographer*, it can be seen that McGahern's literary universe revolved around the table or the bar counter. The most common culinary treat in the various fictional texts of the Leitrim writer is what would have been referred to as the mixed grill. Lamb chops, sausages, black pudding, tomatoes, eggs and fried bread were the main ingredients of this popular dish, celebrated in McGahern's texts, which also provide detailed descriptions of whiskey and Guinness that could only have been written by a connoisseur of these drinks. Gastronomic culture, for McGahern, was an indispensable component of the various social and religious rituals that punctuate the lives of his characters, which is undoubtedly why he spent so much time lovingly evoking them.

The first section of the book concludes with Rhona Richman Kenneally's discussion of Sebastian Barry's 2002 novel *Annie Dunne*, which, she argues, illustrates the extent to which food is a source of communal expression in Ireland. Set in the late 1950s, the novel 'devotes remarkable attention to growing, preparing, serving, eating, and even excreting food'. Food is also a source of empowerment for the eponymous heroine of the novel, who is an accomplished food provider. The contrast between eating habits in the city, Dublin and the more traditional rural areas evoked in the novel are quite stark: 'The transition to commercialised, standardised food production, and its increasing displacement from country to city, are sources of dissatisfaction to Annie, although it is true that she is also depicted as having missed Dublin life (and food) during her first years in the country ...'. Kenneally concludes that a fictional account like that contained in *Annie Dunne* confirms the view often made by historians like Joe Lee (1989, p. 384) that one must turn to its writers for insight into the 'larger truth' of Irish culture and society at any given moment in time.

Section II deals with culinary and dining traditions in Ireland, beginning with Tony Kiely's chapter which uses oral history as a tool to unlock the richness of the life experiences of Dublin Tenement mothers. He focuses on how these accomplished food providers 'managed', performing the daily miracle of putting food on the table for their families during the 1950s. The chapter reveals the various mechanisms used by these extraordinary women as they negotiated the power of the Catholic Church and of less than co-operative husbands. The food choices, purchasing and storage routines varied between households. Stews, for example, were 'your mother's stew' and, being gleaned from family tradition, 'never changed', often causing familial problems after marriage. One woman commented: 'He [her husband] spent the whole of his life longing for his mother's stew.' Oral history also forms the basis for Máirtín Mac Con Iomaire's chapter, which traces the influence of French *haute cuisine* on the development of Dublin restaurants. From the opening of Restaurant Jammet in 1901 to the continued success of Restaurant Patrick Guilbaud, the key milestones and individuals on this journey are identified and discussed. Despite the assertion by the editor of *Le Guide du Routard* in 2011 that 'the Irish dining experience was now as good, if not better, than anywhere in the world', few are aware that two Dublin restaurants in the 1950s were considered among the best in Europe, and that in 1965 Egon Ronay suggested that the Russell Restaurant must be among the best in the world. Mac Con Iomaire's chapter charts the rise, stagnation and gradual rebirth of fine-dining restaurants in Dublin over more than a century.

In her essay, Marjorie Deleuze asks 'why has Ireland turned into a nation of foodies?' She traces the term 'foodie' to Gael Greene in 1980 and notes how the pejorative connotation Paul Levy and Ann Barr attached to their *The Official Foodie Handbook* has progressively been lost, although it might still sometimes retain a 'mocking edge'. Deleuze charts the gradual growth of interest in food in the media from 'finger licking' Monica Sheridan in the early years of *Raidió Teilifís Éireann* (RTÉ) – the state broadcaster – to today's ubiquitous food programming, cookbooks and blogs. She suggests that the declining influence of the Catholic Church has resulted in the Irish regarding food less as an occasion of sin and more as a symbol of national pride, as we promote the consumption of local, ethical, artisan food. Taking examples from *Bord Fáilte* brochures over the years, this chapter outlines the role that both the tourism and food industries have played in promoting Irish food. It is this promotional process, and the influence wielded by each Irish citizen through their food choice, that concerns John Mulcahy's chapter. The Irish economy and society, he suggests, could be transformed through gastronomic nationalism. Giving examples from Singapore, New Zealand, Scotland and Norway, Mulcahy argues that a gastronomy-driven economy is realistic, viable and sustainable, as gastronomy offers a scalable, cost-effective means of local and regional development, with the potential to strengthen identity, enhance appreciation of the environment, and encourage the regeneration of local heritage and the local economy.

The final section of the book concerns itself with beverage consumption and the psychological melding of the pub with a certain sense of 'Irishness'. Tara McConnell's chapter details how 'beer and ale not only formed a necessary element of the daily nutritional intake of servants and workers, but also found a place on the sideboards of the privileged classes in this period'. Traditionally, it would have been wine, and claret in particular, that would have been associated with the nobility and gentry of Georgian Ireland. However, beer consumption was also common among this class, who, along with other groups, often considered it 'a nutritious and wholesome alternative to unsafe water supplies'. Beer formed part of the remuneration package of labouring men, in the form of a beer allowance. Some of the larger estates, such as Carton in Kildare, engaged the services of a full-time brewer, who was expected to produce high quality produce, which was often served at meals. McConnell concludes by remarking that beer was 'the most democratic of beverages', being employed equally in servants' halls and elite dining rooms.

Brian Murphy's chapter begins by quoting from a January 2012 edition of the *Lonely Planet* in which it was stated that the pub was the main attraction for visitors coming to Ireland. It is seen as the place which captures the real pulse of the Irish nation. In his examination of the lessons that can be learned from the success of the Irish pub abroad, Murphy argues that the general perception of Irish culture and society has ultimately been enhanced by this locale, which has become synonymous with 'craic', music and animation. The chapter concludes by noting that the Irish pub abroad acts as a type of 'cultural ambassador' that establishes strong ties to Ireland and ultimately brings more tourists to our shores.

Eugene O'Brien brings the section and the book to a conclusion with a lively discussion of how Bloomsday and Arthur's Day, two highly successful icons of Irish culture, have become what he refers to as 'secular sacraments'. Quoting the description of how to pull a pint of Guinness correctly available on the website of that famous company, O'Brien detects 'a ritualistic and almost sacramental aspect' to the instructions provided. He describes the process 'as a form of secular transubstantiation', something that might go some way towards explaining why Guinness has been so long associated with Ireland and Irishness. The emergence of Arthur's Day, which is akin to a 'Guinness feast day' – something that causes heated debate between the drinks groups and those concerned about the unacceptably high incidence of heavy drinking among all generations of Irish people – 'is an example of sacramental time being interfused into secular time', and it has begun to gain the same type of traction that one associates with Bloomsday. Social and cultural capital are linked with the two events, which leads O'Brien to conclude that, just as *Ulysses* is as much an event as a book, so too Guinness has become more than a black drink with a creamy head; it is now a cultural symbol with almost sacramental status.

Smoked salmon, lamb, beef, whiskey, Guinness, stew, the Irish breakfast, milk, potatoes, chocolate, a warm welcome, the pub, hotels, restaurants ... when one thinks of it, Ireland has a lot to offer visitors in terms of the quality and variety of the gastronomic experience they will encounter here. Long gone are the days where the potato was served with every meal and where sauces were a rarity. Wine consumption is increasing exponentially and the Irish, having become accustomed to eating out more regularly during the Celtic Tiger period, now continue to consume a greater variety of food and drink products, often in the home. More and more Irish people now have an intimate knowledge of their food and wine and are not content with a dreary, monotonous diet. For those who can afford it, there are an increasing number of places to sample various forms of cuisine. One could even go so far as to suggest that, in an era of technological sophistication and rapid communication, the good news story of Irish gastronomy might be transmitted to a broad audience in order to dispel the myth that one cannot enjoy reasonably priced and locally produced food and drink in this country. Clearly, it will take a long time to compete with the likes of France and Austria in this area, but it is possible that the world will soon come to appreciate that Ireland can tickle people's palate with the best of them.

What follows is by no means an exhaustive study of gastronomy in Irish culture and literature and in the Irish public imagination. Rather, it is a first step in what will be an ever-increasing preoccupation for anyone who is even remotely interested in how food and drink contribute in a singular fashion to the economy, identity and literature of the island nation that is Ireland. We hope that readers will find something with which to sate their appetite as they explore this fascinating subject.

Bon appétit!

Máirtín Mac Con Iomaire and Eamon Maher

Works cited

Albala, K. (ed.) (2011). *Food Cultures of the World Encyclopedia* (3 vols). Santa Barbara, California: Greenwood Press.

Cotter, D. (1999). *The Café Paradiso Cookbook*. Cork: Atrium Press.

Cullen, L. M. (1981). *The Emergence of Modern Ireland 1600–1900*. London: Batsford Academic.

Davidson, A. (1999). *The Oxford Companion to Food*. Oxford: Oxford University Press.

Diner, H. R. (2001). *Hungering for America: Italian, Irish and Jewish Foodways in the Age of Migration*. Cambridge, Mass.: Harvard University Press.

Eagleton, T. (1997). 'Edible ecriture'. *The Times Higher Education Supplement*, p. 25 (13 March).

Kiple, K. F. and K. Coneè Ornelas (eds) (2000). *The Cambridge World History of Food* (2 vols). Cambridge: Cambridge University Press.

Kraig, B. and C. T. Sen (eds) (2013). *Street Food around the World: An Encyclopedia of Food and Culture*. Santa Barbara California: ABC-CLIO.

Lee, J. J. (1989). *Ireland, 1912–1985: Politics and Society*. Cambridge: Cambridge University Press.

Lucas, A. T. (1960). 'Irish food before the potato'. *Gwerin 3*. 1960–1962, no. 2, pp. 8–63.

Myers, K. (2002). 'An Irishman's Diary'. *The Irish Times* (7 February).

Parasecoli, F. and P. Scholliers (eds) (2011). *A Cultural History of Food* (6 vols). Oxford: Berg.

Simms, K. (1978). 'Guesting and Feasting in Gaelic Ireland'. *Journal of the Royal Society of Antiquaries of Ireland*, vol. 108, pp. 67–100.

Smith, A. (ed.) (2004). *The Oxford Encyclopedia to Food and Drink in America*. Oxford: Oxford University Press.

Literary Representations of Irish Gastronomy

DOROTHY CASHMAN

'That delicate sweetmeat, the Irish plum': The Culinary World of Maria Edgeworth (1768–1849)

Introduction and background

In the scope and extent of literary criticism and discussion that Maria Edgeworth and her writing has occasioned there is possibly no more unlikely discussion than that of an exploration of her culinary sensibility. A landmark literary biography of Edgeworth by Marilyn Butler was published in 1972, and a twelve-volume edition of her novels and selected works, edited by Butler and Myers, was published in the years from 1999 to 2003. Edgeworth's writing straddles several different categories, including as it does educational and moral tales for children, drama and romantic novels. Her work has attracted particular attention as a result of the rise of feminist literary criticism in the aftermath of second wave feminism, as scholars seek to explore concepts of patriarchy and ideals of domestic fulfillment in and through her fiction (Kowalski-Wallace 1991; Narin 1998).

Castle Rackrent, published anonymously in 1800, has been critically acclaimed as a comic masterpiece (Butler 1992, p. 1). Popularly categorised as the first regional, Anglo-Irish and Big House novel in the English language, this is contested by Campbell Ross (1991, p. 682) who points out that for at least fifty years before it was published many Irish authors, male and female, had produced a substantial and varied body of work that was published on both sides of the Irish Sea, and most of these authors were from a similar background to Edgeworth. If she has overshadowed these earlier novelists such as Chaigneau (1709–1781), Amory (1691–1788), and, in an Irish context, Laurence Sterne (1713–1768), arguably this has strengthened her position as 'the central figure in Irish literary history between Swift and the modernist generation of Shaw and Yeats' (McCormack 1991, p. 1011). Her handling of the complexities surrounding the issues of nationality and nationhood has been somewhat obscured by the fact that she is identified with the Big House due to her background, in addition to her subject matter. Added to this, the troubles of the latter part of the twentieth century in Northern Ireland have resulted in some hostility towards her as an allegedly '"colonial" writer' (Mc Cormack 2008). Edgeworth was the most commercially successful novelist of her time but appears to have fallen from favour, if judged by modern reprints of their respective works, when compared with her contemporaries Jane Austen and Walter Scott. Her commercial success during her own lifetime may be gauged from her personal record of earnings, which by 1842 totalled £11,062.8.10 (Lawless 1905, p. 196).

Born in 1768 at Black Bourton, Oxfordshire, Maria was the third child of Richard Lovell Edgeworth (1744–1817) and his first wife, Anna Maria Elers (1743–1773). After Anna Maria's early death Richard Lovell Edgeworth married a further three times, fathering in total twenty-two children. Honora and Elizabeth Sneyd, his second and third wives respectively, were sisters, and his fourth wife, Fanny Beaufort (1769–1865), was the daughter of the cartographer Daniel Beaufort (1739–1821) and the sister of Admiral Francis Beaufort (1774–1857), deviser of the Beaufort wind scale. There was less than a year in age between Maria and Fanny. Francis Beaufort married Honora Sneyd Edgeworth (1791–1858) in 1838, Maria's stepsister. By virtue of this marriage Honora became both stepdaughter and sister-in-law to Fanny. All bar the first marriage of Richard Edgeworth, which was the result of an elopement, were happy. Although Maria's early life and schooling took place in England, by 1782 she was resident in Edgeworthstown with her father and his third wife and remained there for the rest of her life.

The Irish culinary landscape of the nineteenth century

By the time Maria Edgeworth was writing, a parallel Anglo-Irish cuisine co-existed with what could be termed the native Irish diet (Mac Con Iomaire 2009). In so far as this Anglo-Irish cuisine represents the foodways of elite culture, this co-existence would not be unusual in the culinary history of a country. However, attitudes towards the development of a culinary repertoire in Ireland are complicated by the fact that this elite class, looking to both the traditions of England and of France, functioned within a political and cultural structure that was not subscribed to by a significant majority of the populace.

Evidence of what was consumed in elite households can be found in the various household account books of the period. Evidence regarding what the non-elite classes consumed is more problematic. The story of food in Ireland is further complicated by the fact that much of the discussion takes place within a narrative of famine. However, it is well to bear in mind that this is not the whole story of food in Ireland, even in the nineteenth century. As Cullen indicates, much of the misunderstanding surrounding the question of cuisine in Ireland arises from 'the assumption that the bulk of the population has been degraded to the lowest social level' (Cullen 1981, p. 146). Discussion about cuisine and diet is frequently politicised within this dominant narrative.

In attempting to arrive at some comprehensive view of the culinary landscape for the period in question, two of the most valuable resources available are the literary writings and household manuscripts of the period. One avenue that is regrettably closed for Irish culinary historians is that of a study of cookbooks written by Irish authors in this early period. To date only three cookbooks of Irish, or Anglo-Irish, authorship are available for discussion. *The Lady's Companion: or Accomplish'd Director In the whole Art of Cookery* was published in 1767 by John Mitchell in Skinner-row, under the pseudonym '*Ceres*', while the Countess of Caledon's *Cheap receipts and hints on cookery: collected for distribution amongst the Irish Peasantry* was printed in Armagh by J. M. Watters, for private circulation, in 1847. The much more modern sounding *Dinners at Home*, published in London in 1878, under the pseudonym Short, would appear to be of Irish authorship as a review in *The Irish Times* describes it as being written by a lady from Dublin, the inference being that she was known to the reviewer (Farmar 2011).

Maria Edgeworth: culinary interlocutrice

As previously noted there has been scarcely any discussion of the culinary aspects or the role of food in Maria Edgeworth's novels. However, like her contemporary Jane Austen, Edgeworth was adroit in her use of culinary detail. *Castle Rackrent* has occasioned some commentary in respect of her arguably ironic use of the phrase 'a raking pot of tea' (Edgeworth 1992, pp. 95, 135) and the longstanding tradition of anxiety surrounding its consumption (O'Connell 2012, p. 34). This authorial commentary on the association of tea with tongue loosening is fascinating to observe, for example William Congreve's (1670–1729) lines in *The Double-Dealer* (1694):

> CARE, 'No, faith, but your fools grow noisy; and if a man must endure the noise of words without sense, I think the women have more musical voices, and become nonsense better'.
> MEL, 'Why, they are at the end of the gallery; retired to their tea and scandal, according to their ancient custom, after dinner ...'
> (Congreve 1694, p. 8. Act 1, Sc. 1.)

The theme reappears in the work of Richard Brinsley Sheridan (1751–1816), with Lady Wormwood exclaiming in *The School for Scandal* (1777) 'Strong tea and scandal! Bless me how refreshing' (Sheridan 2008, p. 208, Prologue). The exact phrase used by Edgeworth is repeated by the Irish diarist Dorothea Herbert (c.1767–1829) in her poem *The Sea-Side Ball or the Humours of Bonmahon*: 'The Supper done the Dance renew'd, The

Morning's Rays at length intrude, About the Dawning of the Day, We make a Raking-Pot-of Tea ...'[1] (Finnegan 2011, p. 35).

Before turning to a detailed examination of *The Absentee* there is another aspect of *Castle Rackrent* that deserves mention and that is the way that the author uses the dietary precept regarding the eating of pork to display the cruelty of Sir Kit towards his Jewish wife:

> Her honey-moon, at least her Irish honey-moon, was scarcely over, when his honour one morning said to me, 'Thady, buy me a pig!' and then the sausages were ordered, and here was the first open breaking out of my lady's troubles ... and from that day forward always sausages, or bacon or pig meat in some shape or other, went up to table; upon which my lady shut herself up in her own room, and my master said she might stay there, with an oath.
>
> (Edgeworth 1992, p. 79)

The vignette has its equal in Molly Keane's *Good Behaviour* when Aroon kills her mother, Mrs St Charles, by forcing her to eat rabbit on her sickbed. Mrs St Charles has a fear of rabbits as a result of seeing the effects of the virus myxomatosis on them:

> 'Myxomotosis' she said. 'Remember that? – I can't.' I held on to my patience. 'It was far too young to have myxomotosis. Come on now, Mummie' – I tried to keep the firm note out of my voice – 'just one'.

Rose, the housekeeper, confronts Aroon with the accusation

> 'you can eat your bloody lunch and she lying there stiffening every minute. Rabbit – rabbit chokes her, rabbit sickens her, and rabbit killed her – call it rabbit if you like. Rabbit's a harmless word for it – if it was a smothering you couldn't have done it better.'
>
> (Keane 1999, p. 8)

---

1   There are two possible explanations of the term 'raking'. In Jonas Hanway's *An Essay on Tea* (1757), the term is used in a footnote and explained as being the original translation for the colicky disorder caused by green tea. The original source from which this is taken is not supplied. The other, more attractive, explanation is the Hiberno-English use of the word 'rake' meaning a large quantity, as in the phrase 'a rake of', meaning a large quantity of something (Dolan 2006).

It is the servant who attempts to intervene on behalf of the mistress in respect of Sir Kit and Aroon, and by making servants visible in her novels it has been argued that Edgeworth advanced her 'vision of a transformative paternalism infused with social rebellion' (Nash 2007, p. 2). In both cases the cruelty of the oppressor is in the exercise of control over that most fundamental of human needs, the need to nourish.

However, it was after a perceived anti-Semitic depiction of a character in *The Absentee* that a young American, Rachel Mordecai Lazarus, wrote to the author and posed the question: 'Can it be believed that this race of men are by nature mean, avaricious and unprincipled?' It was a question that was to lead to a long correspondence between the two ladies and to a deep and lasting friendship. A fuller exploration of anti-Semitism in Edgeworth is discussed in Schulkins (2011). However, it is to *The Absentee* that this discussion now turns, to examine how Edgeworth explores the ideas of conviviality and social behaviour that surround the table.

The Absentee (1812) was one volume of *Tales of Fashionable Life*, a series of six volumes published between 1809 and 1812. McCormack (1991, p. 1012) makes the argument that Edgeworth's fiction implicitly posits a westward flight: Dublin is favoured over London, the Irish midlands over Dublin, and 'the wholly imaginary Black Islands of *Ormond* are the ultimate resting place of this progression from metropolitan society towards nature'. This flight can be traced in *The Absentee* physically and Edgeworth uses culinary detail to mirror this flight in a different sphere.

The story operates on several levels. Lord and Lady Clonbrony are the absentees in question, absent from their estates in Ireland as landlords. In writing about absentees and the economic drain consequent on the remittal of rents out of the country, Edgeworth is reflecting the concern felt across several levels of Irish society. Cullen (2009, p. 172) observes that while Price's *List of the absentees of Ireland* became the most reprinted economic tract of the eighteenth century, the issue of absenteeism and the consequent problems with middlemen is not without complexity. It must be pointed out that Lord Clonbrony is not a happy absentee, facing ruination as a result of the expense of keeping up with the London *bon ton*, and the extravagant demands of his frivolous wife. This displacement to London was consequent on the Act of Union of Great Britain and Ireland of 1800, which had drawn fashionable society away from Dublin to London. Clonbrony's response to his situation is invariably to bemoan 'that there need, at all events, be none of this, if people would but live upon their own estates, and kill their own mutton' (Edgeworth 1988, p. 67). In an effort to understand what is happening on the Irish estates in question, Lord Colombre, Clonbrony's son and heir, decides to travel incognito to Ireland.

Before progressing, it is necessary to point out that for the purposes of this discussion the subplot of the novel regarding Grace Nugent, and the issues of alienation, identity and leadership identified by critics, are beyond the scope of this chapter. The intellectual complexity of Edgeworth's writing is frequently in danger of turning her work into didactic treatises, a quality noted by Deane (1986, p. 95) when he observes that the will to educate has the capacity to ruin 'brilliant stories' such as *Ennui* and *The Absentee*. What is proposed here is to turn the reader's attention to specific instances in *The Absentee* where Edgeworth uses domestic and culinary detail that carry less academic freight but which nonetheless progress the novel and flesh out her characters in a very accessible fashion. These instances of domesticity are also of immense interest to historians attempting to reconstruct the culinary life of the period.

The first remarkable reference to food takes place in London. A certain Lady St James is hosting a party to which Lady Clonbrony has not been invited. Desperate to be there, Lady Clonbrony's lady's maid, an odious toady appropriately named Miss Pratt, suggests that a salmon from Ireland might achieve the desired effect:

> At last Pratt suggested, that perhaps, though everything else had failed, dried salmon might be tried with success. Lord Clonbrony had just had some uncommonly good from Ireland, which Pratt knew Lady St. James would like to have at their supper, because a certain personage, whom she would not name, was particularly fond of it.
> (Edgeworth 1988, p. 56)

This is one of two references to fish in the book; the second specifies that the 'the dish of fish at the head of the table had been brought across the island from Sligo' (p. 90). While Ireland was renowned for fishing, there is nothing to suggest that Sligo was exceptional (Finlay 1827, p. 133). However, one of the many culinary manuscripts archived in the National Library of

Ireland (NLI) has a reference to 'pickling salmon the Sligo way' (Figure 1).
This reference occurs in MS 34,952, a manuscript compiled by Mrs Baker of
Ballaghtobin, County Kilkenny (Mac Con Iomaire and Cashman 2009).
This is the first volume of what was a two volume work, dated 1810. The
second volume is not known to be extant. Mrs Baker gives an index to the
second volume in the first volume and it is here that the recipe is refer-
enced. It is likely that Mrs Baker took this recipe from a Blunden family
manuscript of 1760 as referred to in *Analecta Hibernica* (McLysaght 1944).
The recipe, 'Sligo pickled salmon', has appeared in *Cookery and Cures of
Old Kilkenny* (St Canice's 1983, p. 24). Sligo and salmon also feature in the
Birr Castle manuscript, with a recipe for 'salmon done the Sligo way' from
the same period (Rosse 1993, p. 128).

It is appropriate to refer to Mrs Baker's manuscript with reference to
Maria Edgeworth. Mrs Baker was born Sophia Blunden, daughter of Sir
John Blunden of Castle Blunden (Nevin 1979). Her uncle, on the maternal
side, was Otway Desart, who resided near Ballaghtobin at Desart Court.
He was the spouse of Lady Anne Browne, daughter of the 2nd Earl of
Altamont and sister of the Marquess of Sligo (Herbert 1929, p. 6). The
link between Mrs Baker, Edgeworth and, tenuously, Sligo is a recipe in Mrs
Baker's manuscript for barm (ale yeast) from a Mrs Beaufort. That this is
Fanny Beaufort's mother, Maria's stepmother, may be deduced from the
preceding recipe from a Mrs Waller. Waller was Mrs Beaufort's maiden
name. A visit to Kilkenny by Maria and her father in the autumn of 1810 is
recorded where she attended the theatre and supper in the great gallery of
Kilkenny Castle: 'the superb hospitality, the number of beautiful women
and witty men, the gayety, the spirit, and the brilliancy of the whole, could
have been seen nowhere else' (Hare 1895, p. 185).

The next notable use of culinary detail is when Lord Colombre arrives
in Ireland. In an effort to understand what is happening on his estates, he
visits two of the agents employed by his family to manage them in their
absence. The village that bears his name, Colombre, is under the care of
Mr Burke. This estate has been managed in an exemplary fashion and all
is tidy and prosperous in the village and on the land. The way that this is
communicated to Lord Colombre and the reader is entirely through discussion surrounding food and provisioning. The inn that Colombre stays at

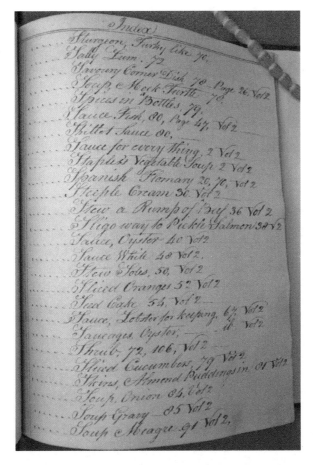

Figure 1: MS 34,952, Mrs Baker, Vol 1. Index, *Sligo Way to Pickle Salmon*.
Courtesy of the National Library of Ireland

is described as having 'a good supper', about which he remarks 'very good cutlets'. The innkeeper tells Colombre that indeed they have a right to be good, for Mrs Burke, the agent's wife, sent her own cook to teach his wife how to dress cutlets, and he continues: 'there's salad sir if you are partial to it. Very fine lettuce, Mrs. Burke sent us the plants herself' (Edgeworth 1988, p. 130). This reference to salad is not to salad in the sense of salad leaves; rather, it is to the vegetable known as cabbage lettuce.[2] Recipes for stewing cabbage lettuces, referred to as simply lettuces, are common in manuscripts of the time, including Mrs Baker's manuscript, as indeed are recipes for the cooking of lamb cutlets.

Colombre is informed by the innkeeper that the porter provided to drink is as good as any from Cork, and that it was Mr Burke who lent his own brewer to teach the innkeeper the art of brewing. As Colombre remarks, everything about Mr Burke is apparently entirely 'apropos' (Edgeworth 1988, p. 131). All this is in marked contrast to the other part of the estate, Nugent's Town, which is under the control of another agent, Nicholas Garaghty, the personification of all that is to be despised in middlemen. Here Edgeworth tells us that the beer is illegally stilled, the women head up the country to beg and the men go over to reap the harvest in England.

On his way back to Clonbrony, Colombre's carriage has a mishap and he spends the night in a local cottage. Again the scene is described in culinary terms. A stool is set by the fire for the stranger. He is bid 'kindly welcome' and the instruction is given 'put down some eggs, dear, there's plenty in the bowl ... I'll do the bacon' (Edgeworth 1988, p. 150). Edgeworth continues: 'the table was set; clean trenchers, hot potatoes, milk, eggs, bacon and "kindly welcome to all"'. Salt and butter are also set down. The foods listed here by Edgeworth are the staples of the Irish domestic diet of the time, the *bán bia* or white meats, which are all the permutations possible from milk and the meat of the pig.

The story turns from these rustic interiors to the dining rooms of Mrs Raferty and Count O'Halloran. Mrs Raferty is the sister of the agent Nicholas Garaghty and wife of a Dublin tradesman, a grocer. She invites Colombre to dinner at her house, *Tusculum*. As a preamble to the dinner Edgeworth describes how Mrs Raferty's architectural aim was to have a little taste of everything in the design of the house:

2   Maggie Lane notes that Jane Austen does not use the term 'vegetable' until 1817 (Lane 1995, p. 65). There is evidence, however, that the term did co-exist with the other terms used for vegetables such as potherbs – herbs suitable for the pot (Willan 2012, p. 186) – garden stuff and garden things. Part VII of Mrs Rundell's (1745–1828) *A New System of Domestic Cookery* (1806) is devoted to 'Vegetables'.

So she led the way to a little conservatory and a little grapery, and a little aviary, and a little pheasantry, and a little dairy for show, and a little cottage for ditto, and a little hermitage full of earwigs, and a little ruin full of looking glass ...

(Edgeworth 1988, p. 89)

Tusculum is reputedly modelled on *Bellvue*, the La Touche house built by David La Touche and his son Peter at Bray, Co Wicklow (Edgeworth 1988, p. xix). Taking ten years to complete, from 1783–1793, the house is described as having matching vineries on either side of a glasshouse which reputedly measured 552 square feet, flanked by a pair of peach houses, an orangery and a cherry house (Lamb and Bowe 1995). Prior to this, in 1766, an octagon had been built with a panther on springs, which could be made to jump out at unwary visitors (Davies 2002).[3]

After this preamble it comes as no surprise that the dinner provided by Mrs Rafferty should offend every idea of good taste and conviviality that Edgeworth subscribes to. The final skewering of Mrs Rafferty is accomplished by Edgeworth's statement that 'the dinner had two great faults – profusion and pretension'. The dish of fish at the head of the table 'had been brought across the island from Sligo, and had cost five guineas; as the lady of the house failed not to make known' (Edgeworth 1988, p. 90). The unfortunate Colombre can see all too plainly the parallels with his own mother's pretensions: 'it was the same desire to appear what they were not, the same vain ambition to vie with superior rank and fortune, or fashion which actuated lady Clonbrony and Mrs Rafferty' (Edgeworth 1988, p. 91). Edgeworth commented in a letter subsequently regarding the dinner: 'I have been told that Larry the footboy and Mrs Rafferty's dinner are nothing to what has been seen at the dinners of *les nouveaux riches* at Liverpool and Manchester' (Colvin 1971, p. 15).

The dishes mentioned by Edgeworth here include sea kale and 'grass' or asparagus. Sea kale, native to Ireland and the northern coasts of Europe, was at the height of fashion as a table vegetable in the nineteenth century, as was asparagus. Thomas Jefferson planted seed of sea kale in 1809 at Monticello and the Prince Regent served it at the Royal Pavilion in

3   *Watson's Almanack* of 1799 notes: 'To the list of noted places, add Belviu, Bray'.

Brighton (Fowler 2005, p. 55). The Edgeworths were not impervious to its appeal, as seen in a letter from Maria's brother to his mother Elizabeth: 'I have a particular curiosity to know whether my Aunt Mary has produced any sea kale on the supper table yet – prey don't forget to answer me this important question' (MS 10,166 NLI). The false sophistication of Mrs Rafferty's table is in marked contrast to the hospitality and fare on view in the visit to Halloran Castle. The contrast in the names of the two abodes provides a framework within which Edgeworth works the theme of outward appearance reflecting inward reality.

The visit to the Count is in order to prevail upon him to give permission to hunt and shoot on his grounds in the next season, and Colombre is one of a party that includes two military men. The castle is described as 'a fine old building, part of it in ruins, and part repaired in great judgment and taste' and the Count variously described as 'a great oddity', 'singular', and 'a man of uncommon knowledge' (Edgeworth 1988, p. 113). The Count, standing for Gaelic Catholicism, may be partly based on Sylvester O'Halloran, a famous and eccentric surgeon from Limerick, and on Count Nugent, one of the 'wild geese', a member of the Jacobite army who fled to the continent after the defeat of Sarsfield and the end of the Williamite wars in Ireland (Edgeworth 1988, p. xxv).

In the Count's castle Edgeworth again raises the issues of Irish manufacture or provenance. Previously, Miss Pratt had been propitiated with the promise of a 'half a dozen pair of real Limerick gloves', 'wheel within wheel in the fine world, as well as in the political world! – Bribes for all occasions and for all ranks!' (Edgeworth 1988, p. 56); so in Halloran Castle the Count offers Major Williamson and Captain Benson a basket of fishing flies: 'gentlemen, you seem to value these ... Would you do me the honour to accept of them? They are all of my own making and consequently of Irish manufacture' (p. 120). This is a reference to another one of the strands of this highly complex novel that is beyond the scope of this chapter, namely that of Ireland's right to export commodities to England, a discussion that Swift (1667–1745) made the most memorable contribution to with his *Drapier Letters*, a series of pamphlets written in 1724 and 1725.

It is a theme that carries over to the handsome collation provided by the Count for his guests. '"Pon honour! Here's a good thing, which I hope we shall live to finish", said Heathcock, sitting down before the collation; and heartily did he eat of eel-pie, and of Irish ortolans' (Edgeworth 1988, p. 121). The military guests agree that it is worth being quartered in Ireland to enjoy the bird in question and the Count recommends to Lady Dashfort some of 'that delicate sweetmeat, the Irish plum'.

> 'Bless me, sir – count!' cried Williamson, 'it's by far the best thing of the kind I have ever tasted in my life: where could you get this?'
> 'In Dublin, at my dear Mrs Godey's; where *only*, in his majesty's dominions, it is to be had,' said the count.
> The whole vanished in a few seconds.
> ''Pon honour! I do believe this is the thing the queen's so fond of,' said Heathcock. Then heartily did he drink of the count's excellent Hungarian wines; and by the common bond of sympathy between those who have no other tastes but eating and drinking, the colonel, the major, and the captain, were now all the best companions possible for one another.
>
> (Edgeworth 1988, p. 121)

Of particular interest here are the references to the Irish ortolan and Mrs Godey's sweetmeats. Of note also is the conviviality engendered by good eating amongst unlikely bedfellows referred to at the end of the extract. This has a parallel in Bishop Stock's narrative of the French invasion of Mayo in 1798 where Bishop Stock, although held captive in his castle by French officers, found the French ways of easy sociability much more congenial then those of their English liberators. As Stock candidly admitted, 'during his captivity he had enjoyed fine food and excellent wine that the French had requisitioned from the cellars and larders of his loyal neighbours' (Kennedy 2009, p. 102).

Edgeworth footnotes the Irish ortolan, a bird of the bunting family, in the text. Referencing Smith (1756), she explains that this bird, known to the Irish as a gourder, is native to the Blasket Islands, off the coast of Kerry. She describes them as almost one lump of fat which, when roasted, is 'reckoned to exceed an ortolan; for which reason the gentry hereabouts call them the *Irish ortolan* [sic]' (Edgeworth 1988, p. 121). Chatterton (1839, p. 285) refers to Smith but remarks that ortolans 'are called by the people "Didleens", from their peculiar cry, which resembles the sound of that word'.

The reference to Mrs Godey is personal to Edgeworth herself. In 1812, the year *The Absentee* was published, John Godey, a confectioner, traded at 12 Sackville Street, now O'Connell Street, having previously traded at 9 Grafton Street (Edgeworth 1988, p. 307). In the 1813 edition of *The Tradesman*, described as a confectioner and cook, Godey is declared bankrupt, a not uncommon end for successful confectioners who were frequently left unpaid by their aristocratic clients (*The Tradesman* 1813). The Godeys had apparently bought out an existing business (Figure 2), that of Christopher Linde. Linde can be traced back, via *The Charter party of the Free annuity company of the City of Dublin records* (1770), as having operated from Blind Quay, one of the south quays constructed alongside the river Liffey in the 1700s. Writing from Edgeworthstown to a friend, Mrs Marcet, on 15 August 1813, the author explains that Mrs Godey was taken dangerously ill soon after the publication of the book. On her deathbed she asked her nephew 'to have packed up and sent to me a large box of the original Irish plums as a mark of her gratitude – Accordingly it was sent to me a few days after her death – Can I help being anxious to spread the fame of such a grateful sweetmeat?' (Hausermann 1952, p. 71).

Edgeworth tells Mrs Marcet that she is sending a box of the plums to her via a friend, Lord Carrington. In later correspondence she reveals that the plums were never delivered, only an accompanying letter. She continues:

> I meant that lord Carrington should have sent plums and note at one and the same time; and how it happened that His Lordship, whom I imagined to be one of the most punctual of men and of commission=doers [sic] could have made such a blunder I cannot conceive – I suppose the air of Ireland had operated upon him – I write to inquire from him how it is with him and his plums.
>
> (Hausermann 1952, p. 72)

That Mrs Godey was a well-known confectioner may be deduced from Edgeworth's relating that her portrait was painted for the Exhibition at Somerset House[4] in London that year. The Royal Academy held its

---

4   There is no reference to Mrs Godey by name or trade in the 1813 catalogue for the Royal Academy. Her portrait may be among one of the very many untraced 'Portrait(s) of a lady'.

Figure 2: MS 8040. Courtesy of the National Library of Ireland.

exhibitions at Somerset House, now the galleries of the Courtauld Institute, from 1780 to 1836. While no record has emerged of Mrs Godey's recipe for her 'delicate sweetmeat', many similar exist in the manuscripts of the period (Figure 3).

Given the connections between *The Absentee* and Mrs Baker's manuscript, it is appropriate to conclude with these recipes. At the outset it was noted that this was perhaps an unlikely topic for discussion. However,

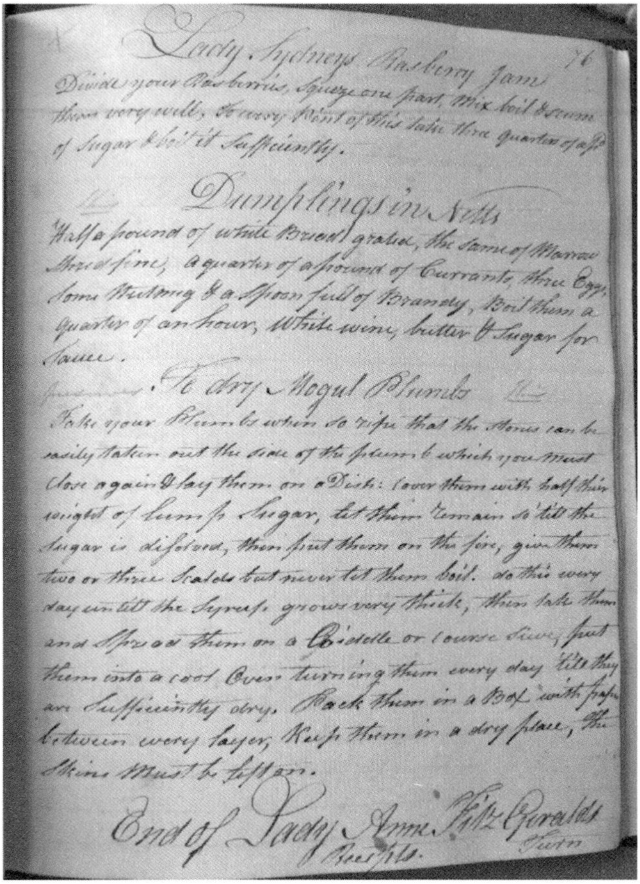

Lady Sydneys Rasberry Jam 76
Divide your Rasberries, Squeeze one part, Mix boil & scum them very well, to every Pint of this take three quarters of a pd of Sugar & boil it Sufficiently.

Dumplings in Netts
Half a pound of white Bread grated, the same of Marrow Shred fine, a quarter of a pound of Currants, three Eggs, some Nutmeg & a Spoon full of Brandy, Boil them a quarter of an hour, White wine, butter & Sugar for Sauce.

To dry Mogul Plumbs
Take your Plumbs when so ripe that the Stones can be easily taken out the side of the plumb which you must close again & lay them on a Dish: Cover them with half their weight of lump Sugar, let them remain so till the Sugar is dissolved, then put them on the fire, give them two or three Scalds but never let them boil. do this every day untill the Syrup grows very thick, then take them and Spread them on a Criddle or Course Sieve, put them into a cool Oven turning them every day till they are Sufficiently dry. Pack them in a Box with paper between every layer, Keep them in a dry place, the Skins must be left on.

End of Lady Anne Fitz Geralds Receipts Turn

Figure 3: MS 34,952. *To Dry Mogul Plumbs*.
Courtesy of the National Library of Ireland.

by looking at *The Absentee* through this lens a more accessible Maria Edgeworth emerges.

It is a thread that continues in her later work. In her novel *Patronage*, published in 1814, although begun five years previously, Edgeworth concludes with the felicitous detail that in the celebrations for the heroine's wedding, Mrs Harte, housekeeper to the Percy family for thirty years, was

constructing with infinite care, as directed by her *Complete English Housekeeper*, a
desert island for a wedding, in a deep china dish, with a mount in the middle, two
figures upon the mount, with crowns on their heads, a knot of rock candy at their
feet, and gravel walks of shot *comfits* judiciously intersecting in every direction their
dominions.

(Edgeworth 1814, p. 360)

The recipe Edgeworth is quoting is from Mrs Raffald's *Experienced English
Housekeeper: For the use and ease of Ladies, Housekeepers, Cooks*, first published in 1769. Recipe books seldom appear in household inventories and are
very rarely listed as present in a household library. It is, however, tempting
and quite probable to conclude that Edgeworth had a personal knowledge
of such a popular book and that, indeed, with her extensive experience of
stepmothers, this was perhaps a recipe used by the family when celebrating
the marriage of her father and Frances Beaufort.

In all the academic discussion that Maria Edgeworth's work has been
subjected to, it is sometimes seen as of minor concern that this was a woman
immersed in domestic detail in Edgeworthstown. It is in her letters that
this side of her life emerges, when she recounts domestic anecdotes with
pellucid simplicity, and she was known to exchange recipes herself, as can
be seen in her recording of the recipe for lemon cream 'eaten at J. Corry's
house at Shantonagh' in June 1808:

The rind of six lemons grated, and the juice – a pound of sugar in powder – mix them
together with a quart of sweet cream – whip it a little – let it lie – whip it again –
let it lie – whip it again – let it lie – whip it a third time [sic] till it is thick obs – if
made over night the better.
All eaten therefore approved by good judges at Chantinee [sic]

(MS 10,166/639, NLI)

In one of her most amusing letters she describes a visit to the Martins of
Ballinahinch in 1833 and in the narrative gives the detail of a dinner there,
reminiscent of the Count's, certainly not of Mrs Rafferty's:

London *bon vivants* might have blessed themselves! Venison such as Sir Culling
declared could not be found in England, except from one or two immense parks of
noblemen favoured above their peers; salmon, lobsters, oysters, game, all well cooked

and well served, and well placed upon the table: nothing loaded, all *in* good taste, as well as *to* the taste; wines, such as I was not worthy of, but Sir Culling knew how to praise them; champagne, and all manner of French wines.

(Hare 1894, vol. 2, p. 228)

When she was asked to write a biographical preface to her novels Edgeworth's reply was modest: 'as a woman, my life, wholly domestic, can offer nothing of interest to the public' (Hare 1894, p. v). To explore her regard and respect for the importance of culinary detail is in some measure to render tribute to this neglected side of a complex personality.

Works cited

Butler, M. (1972). *Maria Edgeworth: A Literary Biography*. Oxford: Clarendon Press.
Butler, M. and M. Myers (eds) (1999–2003). *The Novels and Selected Works of Maria Edgeworth in 12 volumes*. London: Pickering and Chatto.
Campbell Ross, I. (1991). 'Fiction to 1800'. In *The Field Day Anthology of Irish Writing Vol. 1.*, ed. S. Deane. Derry: Field Day Publications.
Chatterton, H. G. (1839). *Rambles in the South of Ireland During the Year 1838, Vol. 1*. London: Sunders and Otley.
Colvin, C. (ed.) (1971). *Maria Edgeworth: Letters from England 1813–1844*. Oxford: Clarendon Press.
Congreve, W. (1895) [1694]. *The Double-Dealer London:* Methuen and Co. <http://www.gutenberg.org/catalog/world/readfile?fk_files=1444878&pageno=8> [7 December 2012]
Cullen, L. M. (1981). *The Emergence of Modern Ireland 1600–1900*. London: Batsford.
Cullen, L. M. (2009) [1986]. 'Economic Development 1691–1750'. In *A New History of Ireland, IV, Eighteenth Century Ireland 1691–1800*, eds T. W. Moody and W. E. Vaughan. Oxford: Oxford University Press.
Davies, M. (2002). 'Paradise Lost', *Irish Arts Review*, Vol. 21. no. 2. pp. 104–109.
Deane, S. (1986). *A Short History of Irish Literature*. London: Hutchinson and Co.
Dolan, T. P. (2006). *A Dictionary of Hiberno-English*. Dublin: Gill and Macmillan.
Edgeworth, M. (1988) [1812]. *The Absentee*. Oxford: Oxford University Press.
Edgeworth, M. (1992) [1800]. *Castle Rackrent and Ennui*. Oxford: Oxford University Press.

Edgeworth, M. (1814). *Patronage*. London: J. Johnson and Co. <http://archive.org/ stream/patronageinfouro0edgegoog#page/n8/mode/2up> [12 August 2013]

Farmar, A. (2011). Email correspondence between Farmar, author of *Ordinary Lives: Three Generations of Irish Middle Class Experience*, and M. Mac Con Iomaire, 26 January 2011.

Finlay, J. (1827). *A Treatise on the Laws of Game and Inland Fisheries in Ireland*. Dublin: Cumming.

Finnegan, F. (2011). *Introspections, the Poetry and Private World of Dorothea Herbert*. Piltown: Congreve Press.

Fowler, D. L. (2010) [2005]. *Dining at Monticello. In Good Taste and Abundance*. North Carolina: The Thomas Jefferson Foundation, University of North Carolina Press.

Hanway, J. (1757). *A Journal of Eight Days Journey, to which is added, An Essay on Tea. Vol II*. London: H. Woodfall. <http://ia700408.us.archive.org/32/items/ JonasHanwayEssayOnTea/HanwayEssayOnTea.pdf> [7 September 2013]

Hare, A. (ed.) (1894). *The Life and Letters of Maria Edgeworth Vol. 1*. London: Edward Arnold. <http://archive.org/details/lifeandlettersmooharegoog> [7 August 2012]

Hare, A. (ed.) (1894). *The Life and Letters of Maria Edgeworth Vol. 2*. London: Edward Arnold. <http://archive.org/details/lifeandlettersmo1haregoog> [7 August 2012]

Hausermann, H. W. (1952). *The Genevese Background: Studies of Shelley, Francis Danby, Maria Edgeworth, Ruskin, Meredith, and Joseph Conrad in Geneva (with hitherto unpublished letters)*. London: Routledge and Kogan Paul.

Herbert, D. (1929). *Retrospections of Dorothea Herbert 1770–1789*. London: Gerald Howe.

Keane, M. (1999) [1981]. *Good Behaviour*. London: Virago Press.

Kennedy, C. (2009). 'Our Separate Rooms: Bishop Stock's Narrative of the French Invasion of Mayo 1798', *Field Day Review* 5, pp. 94–107. <http://www.jstor.org/ stable.25664528> [6 December 2011]

Kowaleski-Wallace, E. (1991). *Their Father's Daughters: Hannah More, Maria Edgeworth and Patriarchal Complicity*. New York: OUP.

Lamb, K. and P. Bowe (1995). *A History of Gardening in Ireland*. Dublin: National Botanic Gardens.

Lane, M. (1995). *Jane Austen and Food*. London: Hambledon Press.

Lawless, E. (1905). *Maria Edgeworth*. New York: Macmillan and Co. <http://digital. library.upenn.edu/women/lawless/edgeworth/edgeworth.html> [20 December 2012]

Mac Con Iomaire, M. (2009). *The Emergence, Development, and Influence of French Haute Cuisine on Public Dining in Dublin Restaurants 1900–2000: An Oral*

History (Doctoral Thesis). School of Culinary Arts and Food Technology, Dublin Institute of Technology. <http://arrow.dit.ie/tourdoc/12>.

Mac Con Iomaire, M. and D. Cashman (2011). 'Irish Culinary Manuscripts and Printed Books: A Discussion', *Petits Propos Culinaires* 94, pp. 81–101.

McCormack, W. J. (2008) [2004]. *Oxford Dictionary of National Biography* <http://www.oxforddnb.com/view/printable/8476> [12 February 2013]

McCormack, W. J. (1991). 'Maria Edgeworth'. In *The Field Day Anthology of Irish Writing Vol 1*, ed. S. Deane. Derry: Field Day Publications.

McLysaght, E. A. (1944). *Analecta Hibernica 15*. Dublin: Irish Manuscripts Commission.

Nash, J. (2007). *Servants and Paternalism in the works of Maria Edgeworth and Elizabeth Gaskell*. Aldershot: Ashgate.

Narain, M. (1998). 'A Prescription of Letters: Maria Edgeworth's *Letters for Literary Ladies* and the Ideologies of the Public Sphere', *The Journal of Narrative Technique*, vol. 28. no 3. pp. 266–286.

Narain, M. (2006). 'Not an Angel in the House: Intersections of the public and private in Maria Edgeworth's *Moral Tales* and *Practical education*' in *New Essays on Maria Edgeworth*, ed. J. Nash. Aldershot: Ashgate, pp. 57–72.

Nevin, M. (1979). 'A County Kilkenny Georgian Household Notebook', *The Journal of the Royal Society of Antiquaries of Ireland*, Vol. 109, pp. 5–19.

O'Connell, H. (2012). '"A Raking Pot of Tea": Consumption and Excess in Early Nineteenth-Century Ireland', *Literature and History*. vol. 21, no. 2. (2012), pp. 32–47.

Raffald, E. (1769). *The Experienced English Housekeeper*. Manchester: J. Harrap. Available to download on Google Books.

Rosse, I. (1993). 'Ireland, Birr Castle' in *Traditional Country House Cooking*, ed. C. Anne Wilson. London: Weidenfeld and Nicolson.

Schulkins, R. (2011). 'Imagining the Other: the Jew in Maria Edgeworth's Harrington', *European Romantic Review*. vol. 22, no. 4. (2011) pp. 477–499.

Sheridan, R. B. (2008) [1777]. *The School for Scandal and Other Plays*. Oxford: Oxford University Press.

Smith, C. (1774). *The Ancient and Present State of County of Kerry*. Dublin: Cater.

St. Canice's Cathedral. (1983). *Cookery and Cures of Old Kilkenny*. Kilkenny: Boethius Press.

The Tradesman; or commercial magazine. New Series Vol. 1. (1813). London: Sherwood Neely and Jones. <https://play.google.com/store/books/details?id=gDcaAQA AIAAJ&rdid=book-gDcaAQAAIAAJ&rdot=1> [10 December 2012]

Willan, A. (2012). *The Cookbook Library. Four Centuries of the Cooks, Writers, and Recipes That Made the Modern Cookbook*. Berkeley: University of California Press.

FLICKA SMALL

'Know Me Come Eat With Me':
What Food Says about Leopold Bloom

James Joyce's *Ulysses*[1] tells the story of a day in the life of a city. The city is Dublin in 1904 and the main protagonists are Leopold Bloom, an advertising canvasser with the *Freeman's Journal*; his wife Molly, a singer who is having an affair with concert promoter Blazes Boylan; and Stephen Dedalus, a young teacher and writer. Each chapter of the novel is represented by a bodily organ, which gives life to the city, and an allotted hour of the day. Meals chart the progress of time and the story of Leopold Bloom unfolds through the foods that he eats.

In 1904, Dublin had a population of 404,000, which was one tenth of the whole country at that time. Since the Great Famine in 1845, when thousands starved to death, many more emigrated, and many more again moved from rural areas into the city, the majority of the people were still hungry and lived crowded together in tenements with no facilities. Ireland was part of the British Empire and Dublin was also home to a militia that lived in barracks and frequented the city's many brothels (Somerville-Large 1979, p. 271), as well as being a major port en route from England to America and the Colonies.

At the same time, this was an era of intellectual change, and Leopold Bloom's constant questioning and theories reflect the world he lives in. On the one hand, transport and industrialisation had changed available commodities and employment, and on the other, there was political unrest in the air, in the whole of Europe as well as in Ireland. The shift in how food is obtained and presented impacts on Bloom and excites his appetite for

---

1   Joyce, J. (1998). *Ulysses*. Oxford: Oxford University Press. All further references made in parentheses in the text.

unusual tastes. Bloom's basic needs, in common with most people, are for food, water, sex, sleep and excretion, and in his thoughts they take on a lively and interactive exploration that enters into the inner reaches of his psyche, linking and blending his thoughts with his actions through the day.

In *Ulysses*, breakfasts bookend Bloom's waking and his falling asleep. At 8 o'clock on this particular Thursday morning in June, Bloom is preparing breakfast (p. 53). He talks to his cat as he lays up a tray for Molly's breakfast in bed, and as he does so he wonders what to eat for his own breakfast. The cat is his audience, but the cat is also the mirror in which he views himself. 'Wonder what I look like to her', he thinks. How others see him will concern him for the rest of the day. The fastidious preparation of the tray extends to his respect for food. He eats carefully, avoids waste, and never eats too fast or unthinkingly. The 'humpy' tray is arranged with precision and in his attention to detail he yields to Molly's requirements. What she wants and the way in which he provides it, indicates a symbiosis between them, that sometimes Bloom forgets. Despite her admonishments of 'scald the teapot' and 'something's burning', this is a scene of domestic understanding, where Bloom is happy to be near her bedwarmed flesh, to pick up her discarded undergarments and to answer her questions on metempsychosis. Only when she smells burning does he scuttle back to the kitchen (p. 60).

Bloom loves eating the 'inner organs of beasts and fowls', but first he contemplates eating eggs for breakfast; however, there has been a drought and the chickens are off-lay. He then thinks about buying a mutton kidney, because that is what he really likes best, with its fine tang of faintly scented urine, but there will be no fresh meat in the shops due to the religious observance of no meat on a Friday, the next day. Therefore buying a pork kidney is not his first choice, nor his second.

Bloom is happy when he is at home and paradoxically it is in its insularity where he is proven to be most sociable. The kitchen is his domain and, far from emasculating him, it is where he is able to exercise authority. Having the kitchen to himself is also a convenient way to have private time, and reflect on the day ahead. As he prepares to go to the butcher's shop he surveys his territory, banking up the fire and filling the kettle. He leaves the door on the latch, puts on his hat and steps out. He walks past milk and bread being delivered by horse-drawn vehicles and we learn later that he has been thinking of a scheme for using dog-vans and goat-vans for the delivery of early morning milk (p. 671). This is typical of Bloom, for his appetite for eating is not merely nutritive, but food thoughts tweak his curiosity and make him wonder about, for instance, the taste of exotic fruits or where they come from, or how they are grown and transported. Bloom engages in the economic culture of the time, and aware that colonisation has reached around the world in a drive to find new foods, he is eager to smell, touch and taste them all.

The smells that assail him as he passes shops on the street this particular morning are of food: 'ginger, tea dust, biscuit mush' alongside the 'flabby gush of porter' (p. 56). He would also be able to smell hops and barley from the Guinness factory at St James' Gate, and rich baking from Jacob's biscuit factory in Bishop Street, mingling with the smell of manure from the horse-drawn delivery vans (Farmar 2010, p. 87). It is only a step away to Dlugacz's, the Polish butcher who has 'sausage pink fingers' (p. 57). Admiring the buxom proportions of the 'next door girl', who is a customer in the shop, Bloom fantasises about her being a dominatrix, because he has watched her skirt swinging with each whack that she gives to the carpet on the clothes line. Bloom often associates edible meat, or animal parts, with people, especially in a sexual context. He waits to follow the girl home so he can watch her moving 'hams', and his erotic thoughts wander from the moist tender gland (the kidney), to the girl's courtship with a constable who has a 'prime sausage'. This physicality in his thinking will be fully realised during his dream and the hallucinatory-like experiences that take place in 'Circe', the brothel episode that occurs later on in the evening.

In the butcher's shop Bloom picks up a page from a pile of cut newspaper sheets used for wrapping meat. Reading an advertisement to invest in a communal farm venture in Kennereth in Palestine, he envisages a land to the East growing and exporting exotic citrus fruits such as oranges and lemons as well as melons, almonds and olives, reminding him what it must have been like in Szombathely in the Hungarian Empire, where his father was born (p. 58). Bloom has a genuine desire to know what these foreign lands are like. Would the people look different, he asks himself, and he imagines turbaned faces and carpet shops, mosques and awned streets, a violet night sky the colour of Molly's garters, but, being ever practical, he

dismisses it as the 'kind of stuff you read'. Possibly he is engaging with his
father's ancestral memory here. His imagination is so finely tuned, it is as
if he has a photograph in front of him. The very aura of the heat, and the
perfumes that fill his head, concentrate his mind's eye in infinitesimal detail.

Bloom is very conscientious in matters of personal hygiene and after
he has eaten breakfast he pays attention to defecating, and we accompany
him to the outside 'jakes' (p. 66). Bloom likes to read 'at stool', so that his
bowels can ease themselves slowly. Cascara Sagrada is a herbal remedy that
he has been taking as a laxative, and he wishes that all life's problems could
be so easily cured. His practical nature combined with his interest in excreta
leads him to think about the properties of manure from different types of
animal and how he could use it on his garden so that he might benefit from
growing peas or some lettuce, and thus having fresh greens to eat every day.

As Bloom leaves home for a second time this June morning, and walks
along the street, he sees a Christian Brother buying sweets; at the same time
he notices Dilly Dedalus (Stephen's sister), who is underfed and suffering
from malnutrition. It was not unusual to see children 'crawling in rags
along the pavement – whimpering with cold and hunger' (Somerville-
Large 1979, p. 264). Bloom reflects on the position of the church, which,
by condemning contraception, promotes large families that are difficult
to feed and support. He compares this to clergy who live alone and are
able to live off the 'fat of the land', while poor people have to live on not
much more than 'potatoes and margarine' (p. 145). The famine was still
in living memory and Bloom is cognisant of the personal and long-term
effects of hunger on society. For Bloom, taste and smell are a trigger to
appetite, and thereby to hunger that may or may not be satisfied. The smell
of 'newbaked jam-puffs' make him think of the ingredients for good pastry,
flakes of which are on Josie Powell's dress, when he meets her. He sees a
barefoot Arab standing over a grating so he can breathe in the fumes of
baking to deaden the gnaw of hunger. Bloom feels hungry himself, but
his hunger is linked to his memories, and a whimsical hunger for a time
when he and Josie were younger. He laments that the blossom of her youth
has been replaced by a shabby gentility, for she used to be a 'tasty' dresser,
and now wears an old dress and a dowdy little hat that is decorated with
'three old grapes' (p. 151). As he becomes hungrier, the sun slips behind a

cloud, sapping his energy and making him feel as if he has been 'eaten and spewed' (p. 157). His reaction is to recall his fondness for eating the inner organs of animals, and he looks forward to vanquishing his despondency by eating them again at his next meal. His feelings of melancholia are always counteracted by the need to eat familiar foods which give him solace, for Bloom recognises that hunger can give rise to many emotions: 'A hungry man is an angry man,' he says, and later makes the frightening suggestion that 'peace and war depend on some fellow's digestion' (p. 161). Ironically, the good luck talisman that was given to Bloom by his Irish mother, to ward off pestilence and plague, is a potato, the very crop that failed and caused so much misery.

Bloom pays more attention to the value of food, and how much money he spends on it, than he does to drink. His accounts at the end of the day list the smallest items of food and yet his day's expenditure exceeds the weekly wages of, for instance, a cart driver or a tailor at the time (O'Brien 1982, p. 165). The proprietor of Davy Byrne's says that he has never seen Bloom with too much drink taken, and indeed the customers in Barney Kiernan's say that he never buys a round. When he turns down a drink in favour of a cigar, it meets with disapproval. Nosey Flynn suggests that Bloom must be a freemason, because how else could he afford to buy cream for Molly's tea, but by this he is only drawing attention to Bloom's abstemiousness and careful allocation of his income (p. 169).

Passing the open backdoor of All Hallows church, Bloom enters (p. 77). The priest is distributing communion wafers to the congregation. Bloom watches keenly as the priest bends down to put the wafer in each mouth; 'shut eyes, open mouth, no chewing, swallow it down'. As he translates from the Latin he is taken aback by the words and thinks to himself, 'Corpus, body, corpse; like eating bits of corpse!' and he is intrigued. Bloom recognises that sharing is belonging, but is confused by the seemingly cannibalistic nature of believing that bread and wine can be converted by the ritual act of transubstantiation into the body and blood of Jesus Christ. This trajectory of thought about religion and cannibalism makes him think about missionaries who have allegedly encountered cannibals in 'primitive' cultures. A limerick about a Mr MacTrigger comes to his mind, in which the cannibal and his wives eat the missionary's genitals. This train

of thought is further developed when Bloom is at the funeral of his friend
Paddy Dignum, and he tries to imagine the taste of corpse, likening it to
raw white turnips (p. 110).

On the way to the funeral the carriage passes live cattle being driven in
the opposite direction, bringing to Bloom's mind the aphorism 'in the midst
of death we are in life', used during the funeral service. The supply of meat
in Dublin at this time was not very hygienic; much of it being slaughtered
in backyard abattoirs. Dilapidated sheds stained with offal, blood and guts
were evidence of the bloody business of killing, and amongst the smells that
came from the small huxter shops were unpleasant ones of tripe, crubeens
and black pudding being prepared for eating (Farmar 2010, pp. 86, 87).
Bloom, having worked in the cattle market at one time, empathises with
the inhumane killing of the cattle: 'Wretched brutes there at the cattlemar-
ket waiting for the polaxe to split their skulls open ... Pulp, Rawhead and
bloody bones. Flayed glasseyed sheep hung from their haunches' (p. 163).
The echo of the hooves of cattle permeates Bloom's thoughts, just as the
'flop and fall of dung' is for ever in his consciousness (Somerville-Large
1979, p. 260).

Although Bloom often conflates human and animal body parts in
his mind, during the day, death is the most obvious aspect of a human
being's animalness, and in consequence feelings of disgust are the defence
mechanism against thinking too deeply about death (Rozin 1997, p. 68).
When Bloom pushes open the door of the Burton eating establishment,
the stink that assails him is of 'pungent meat juice and slop of green' and
'men, men, men, [are] perched on high stools ... hats shoved back, swill-
ing, wolfing gobfuls of sloppy food' (p. 161) and he is reminded of animals
at feeding time. 'Am I like that?' he wonders. Feeling disgusted he is pro-
pelled out onto the street and into rejecting meat. He enters nearby Davy
Byrne's 'moral' pub and orders a Gorgonzola cheese sandwich with some
olives on the side. Cutting the sandwich into thin strips before eating it,
and holding the wine on his tongue to savour the taste before he swallows,
is in contrast to the bolted, half masticated, chewing he has just witnessed.

Bloom's thoughts about cattle being killed, and on cannibalism, and
his disgust at the men in the Burton, culminate in his consideration of AE
(George Russell), who he sees coming out of a vegetarian restaurant on

College Green.[2] Russell was an activist in rural matters as well as being a poet and the editor of *The Irish Homestead*. Wearing homespun clothes, he would bicycle miles into the country to address poor country people on agricultural and co-operative ideas (Colum 1947, p. 170). Bloom constantly returns to his reverie of how people see him and how he sees others, and never so often as in conjunction with food. The aphorism 'we are what we eat'[3] takes on a significance for Bloom when he wonders whether a vegetarian's brain patterns are different to a meat eater's. When he sees AE with Lizzie Twig it is the fact that they are vegetarians and that their brains might be formed differently that makes him irked at their physical appearance and intellectual conversation. Conversely, he cannot imagine that the sweating constables he saw earlier, who eat Irish stew, can write any poetry at all. So that when Bloom chooses to eat a cheese sandwich, he is temporarily endorsing a group that does not kill flesh and thereby feels superior.[4] Cannibals, such as those that ate Mr MacTrigger, believe they take on the attributes of the person they are eating (Fernandez-Armesto 2001, p. 33). Unless you eat 'weggiebobbles and fruit', says Bloom, 'the eyes of the cow will pursue you through all eternity' (p. 158).

Out of the home and the safe refuge of his kitchen, Bloom appears to be at the mercy of those eating around him. Eating meals with others pierces his vulnerability, as if the world is entering through his mouth (Rozin et al. 1997, p. 68). His reaction to public eating is not merely one of disgust, but the sight of the men in the Burton chewing and chomping genuinely terrifies him. The public space, and the 'smell of men', takes him out of his comfort zone. Some see meat eating as a 'primitive' occupation and turning to a vegetable diet as a sign of civilised behaviour (Lévi-Strauss 1997, p. 40). Primitiveness is at the very heart of Bloom's fear; when he says 'eat or be eaten', he is responding to the threat that Boylan is hunting his wife, and that being usurped in the home is akin to Boylan going in for the kill.

2   See advertisement for The College Cafe, *The Irish Times*, 25 March 1904.
3   The esteemed gourmand Jean Anthelme Brillat-Savarin coined this term. James Joyce had a copy of Brillat-Savarin's *Physiologie du Goût ou Méditations de Gastronomie Transcendante* in his Trieste library.
4   See Review of 'The Crank', *The Irish Times*, 24 September 1904.

Outside of his home Bloom has to internalise the offensive, or perceived danger, to which his senses have alerted him.

Bloom and Molly have not had conjugal relations since their son Rudy died nearly eleven years ago. Bloom's memories of a more intimate time with Molly are related to food, and many of the happiest ones are of the two of them eating together. He thinks fondly of the day of the Choir picnic at the Sugarloaf, when Molly was admired and they ate rabbit pie. '[I felt] happier then' (p. 148), he reflects. Another time, after one of Professor Goodwin's farewell concerts, Bloom remembers frying lap of mutton for Molly's supper with the chutney sauce that she liked (p. 149). Standing at the hearth he was able to watch her undressing in the bedroom, and he felt 'Happy. Happy.' His food memories have already linked him romantically to Josie Powell and her well-filled rhubarb tarts; and paternally to his daughter Milly, who once cooked him a cutlet and decorated it with a piece of parsley. However, his most significant memory and the one that reinforces his love for Molly is of their love-making on Howth Hill when she kissed him, putting warm and chewed seedcake into his mouth. 'I ate it,' he says, and it was 'Joy' (p. 167).

Bloom is acutely aware that as the clock hands turn, the hour of Molly's and Boylan's rendezvous approaches. 'Eat first. I want. Not yet. At four she said' (p. 250). Bloom's desire to eat becomes stronger, and so his appetite for eating inner organs returns. Eating is Bloom's defence and he hides behind it by ordering foods that he is familiar with. In the Ormond Hotel Bloom is invited to join business colleagues and dine with them. Thinking to himself, 'Sit tight there. See, not to be seen' (p. 254), he can hear the conversations of other people around him, but the words fail to keep out the thoughts that are inside his own head. He is within the group but outside it too. Seeing Boylan drinking a glass of sloe-gin at the bar, Bloom links his inner discourse to those of the other speakers. So desperately does he want the hour to be over, that he is surprised to see Boylan and wonders what he is doing there. 'Has he forgotten? Is it a trick?' he asks himself. The rising sense of melancholia that overtakes Bloom, first from the loss of his father, then the loss of his son, and now his wife, is symbolised by a lone sardine on a 'bier' of bread, underneath the sandwich cover. 'I feel so

lonely', he inwardly mourns, as Simon Dedalus, holding the attention of
the people in the bar, sings 'The Last Rose of Summer' (p. 277).

Twelve hours after his breakfast, as Bloom is standing on the strand,
tucking in his semen-moistened shirt, his thoughts return to the men
in the Burton, one of whom was 'eating off his cold plate' and 'spitting
back gumchewed gristle' (p. 354). These desolate images of rejection cause
Bloom's thoughts to follow a thread that leads from prostitutes, to other
men's wives and so to Molly. But when he thinks of Molly, and her lovers,
he remembers happier times such as the grand banquet they ate at the
'Glencree Dinner', ten years earlier. There, Molly was admired by other
men, such as the Lord Mayor Val Dillon, and Bloom basks in the reflected
admiration of how other men see his wife (p. 354).

Later in the night Bloom rescues Stephen from drunkenness and harm
in the Monto brothel area. As they wind their way back from Nighttown,
Bloom is concerned about Stephen's state of inebriation, and thinking that
it would do Stephen good to get some food inside him, they stop at a cab-
man's shelter, under the Loopline bridge. He relaxes in Stephen's company
and after a dismal cup of coffee and a stale bun they stroll on to Eccles
Street. The witching hour has passed, Boylan has come (literally) and gone,
and Bloom can return in safety to his private territory. Bloom's sociability
returns in his kitchen and he engages in his own ritual of 'communion' by
making Epp's soluble cocoa, carefully following the instructions on the
packet. He discusses with Stephen the possibilities for educating Molly,
and of renting him the bedroom vacated by Milly. Bloom considers how
appropriate it would be to exchange food and lodging for food for thought.
Stephen, still drunk, dissents, especially when Bloom starts to discuss the
importance of dietary and civic self-help. Host and guest drink in silence,
bringing about a unity Bloom has been seeking since he tried to grasp the
meaning of the Eucharist in All Hallows church earlier in the day.

When Stephen leaves, Bloom reviews the contents of his kitchen,
including the foods on the shelves of the dresser. Itemising and repeating,
he is able to take control and ground himself once more in reality and
safety; a reality that does not ignore the fact that Boylan has also made
himself at 'home' in this house. An empty bottle of port, an empty jar of
potted meat and some 'luscious' pears are signs of the invasion that has

taken place. At last the day is over and thinking over its events, and the lifetime of memories that he carries with him, Bloom feels complete. He kisses
'the plump mellow yellow smellow melons of [Molly's] rump' (p. 686).
Unbeknown to him (or maybe in his dreams), Molly is also thinking of
that day on Howth Hill, when she gave him the chewed seed cake in her
mouth and said 'yes!' By keeping jealousy in check, and staying away from
his own home, Bloom has transcended any 'take-over' that Boylan might
have tried to make.

Bloom invites us to 'know me come eat with me', and so we have
(p. 167). He has shown us that what we eat is linked to the way we think
and feel and that that is the way in which we should look at and understand him. Standing on the periphery of the society into which he was
born, Bloom feels different, but he does not always go out of his way to
conform in matters of eating, and he is not inhibited when defending what
he believes in. In the 'Lestrygonians' or 'eating' episode, the symbols of
social order are all around him and the military and authoritarian imagery
is aligned with food. Constables force food into their gullets like ammuni-
tion, they march with 'goose' steps and they have a 'good load of fat soup
under their belts', but Bloom undermines their authority by saying the
best moment to attack them is in 'pudding time' or to give one of them a
'punch in his dinner' (p. 155).

When Bloom views the world he sees it very much in terms of food.
When melancholia comes upon him, or he is deprived of sunshine, he
describes it as grey oils sliding along his veins. Sadness makes him feel as if
he has been chewed and spat out. He thinks that a vegetable diet can make
a person poetical. He can almost taste death, which he imagines tasting
like raw turnips; he thinks that cheese is like the corpse of milk; and his
penchant for inner organs symbolically makes him part of the city which
is described as being made up of bodily organs.

A discourse on food can be diverse. How we are affected by hunger,
what memories are resurrected by food, how we deal with taboos and fashions, our ethnic or social backgrounds, all influence our attitude to food
and our choices of food. We have to eat to stay alive, but over time we have
progressed from being hunter-gatherers to learning how to grow our own
food, how to cook it, and how to imbue it with social significance. In a

moment of exultation, Bloom welcomes us to the new 'Bloomusalem' in the 'Nova Hibernia of the future' (p. 457). This, he says, will be a colossal edifice, with a crystal roof, built in the shape of a huge pork kidney. Thus, from the half burnt kidney we shared with him for breakfast, we learn about Bloom through the foods he eats, and we celebrate with this man who has shown us, by his own interactions with food and eating, his particular humanity and compassion.

Works cited

Colum, M. (1947). *The Life and the Dream*. New York: Doubleday.
Farmar, T. (2010). *Privileged Lives: A Social History of Middle-Class Ireland 1882–1989*. Dublin: A & A Farmar.
Fernandez-Armesto, F. (2001). *Food: A History*. London: Macmillan.
Joyce, J. (1998). *Ulysses*. Oxford: Oxford University Press.
Lévi-Strauss, C. (1997). 'The Culinary Triangle'. In *Food and Culture: A Reader*, eds C. Counihan and P. Van Esterik, pp. 40–47. New York: Routledge.
O'Brien, J. V. (1982). *'Dear Dirty Dublin': A City in Distress, 1899–1916*. Berkeley LA: California University Press.
Rozin, P., Haidt, J., McCauley, C. and S. Imada (1997). 'Disgust: The Cultural Evolution of a Food-Based Emotion'. In *Food Preferences and Taste*, ed. H. Macbeth, pp. 65–82. Providence, Oxford: Berghahn Books.
Somerville-Large, P. (1979). *Dublin*. London: Hamish Hamilton.

MICHAEL FLANAGAN

Cowpie, Gruel and Midnight Feasts: The Representation of Food in Popular Children's Literature

If food is fundamental to life and a substance upon which civilisations and cultures have built themselves, then food is also fundamental to the imagination. Perhaps the deepest emotional exposure we have of imagination is that which we experience in childhood. Just as food studies is becoming important in the field of general literature, so too is it becoming important in the field of children's literature. Whether in memoir, fiction or poetry, writers continually hark back to childhood experiences of food, even when the intended audience is adults rather than children, as with Proust's *Remembrance of Things Past*. Food experiences form part of the daily texture of every child's life from birth onwards, as any adult who cares for children is highly aware; thus it is hardly surprising that food is a constantly recurring motif in literature written for children.

(Keeling and Pollard 2009, p. 10)

This chapter sets out to explore the representation of this 'constantly recurring motif' in children's literature with an emphasis on those aspects of the field which might be loosely termed 'popular' – folktales, the work of such classic children's writers as Kenneth Grahame and Enid Blyton, the school story (including examples of this genre from the pages of *Our Boys*, an indigenous paper produced by the Christian Brothers, a Catholic lay order)[1] and comics, for example. Although the majority of stories dis-

---

1   This magazine was first published in 1914 and survived until 1990. Its initial impetus sprung from a desire on the part of nationalists that Irish children might be offered a suitable alternative to the perceived imperial/colonial propaganda of the British *Boy's Own* genre (Flanagan 2011, p. 57). *Our Boys* proved to be massively successful, with a peak circulation in the 1920s of over 70,000 copies per issue (Cullen 1989, p. 232).

cussed in this chapter were published in England, these were all aspects of international children's popular culture that were hugely popular in Ireland also. Indeed, it could be argued that these books and comics assisted in breaking Irish cultural isolation at a time when cinema was censored and before the appearance of television. In the process I endeavour to explore the place of food in these genres from the perspectives of psychology, sociology and popular culture.

A common setting related to food in children's literature is teatime. Usually employed to dramatise states of harmony or disharmony, teatime is used to great effect in such works as Lewis Carroll's *Alice's Adventures in Wonderland* (1866), in which Alice learns to come to terms with the world around her via her experiences at the Mad Hatter's distinctly uncivilised tea party. Food and order images are also used liberally in such tales as Kenneth Grahame's *The Wind in the Willows* (1908), where food denotes coziness and plenty. In addition to reflecting social order and civilisation, food is often representative of the limitations imposed upon a child's world, blending well with the idea of excess as a key element of childhood fantasy. For example, Maurice Sendak's *In the Night Kitchen* (1963) uses food as a vehicle to express strong childhood emotions, and, like many other children's texts, uses rituals of eating as a metaphor for the power struggle inherent to family dynamics. Blackford (2009, p. 41) suggests the entire question of food in the early life of the child is perhaps a far more complex issue than we might realise, maintaining that the foundations of power are constructed and expressed by food consumption and production.

Very many types of families exist within children's literature, their behaviours becoming homogenised by their need to adhere to the models established by those further up the social scale. The family at table is a strong cultural signifier representing stability and prosperity and the fact that those in power have used this image to reassure the nation only emphasises its influence. The overriding image of a happy family round the table has remained static, fixed in culture, as something that should happen, something that is essential to the wellbeing of the family and the nation. This is prevalent in all kinds of different media. *Many Happy Returns of the Day* (1856), for example, an iconic Victorian painting by William Powell

Frith, demonstrates the importance of ritual and celebration in family life, gathered together and marking occasions of private meaning. Such imagery plays a crucial part in naturalising the family meal in the same way as certain types of meals or recipes are handed down the generations and thus create tradition, nostalgia and a sense of belonging (Alston 2008, p. 125).

Wendy Katz would maintain that to understand the relationship between children and food is to understand the world of the young. Citing such varied examples of children's literature as *Alice in Wonderland, The Wind in the Willows* and *The Adventures of Huckleberry Finn* she identifies a number of themes as they apply to these texts: civilisation, community, identity, emotional stability, meals and food events, empowerment (Katz cited in Keeling and Pollard 2009, p. 10).

Perhaps the first exposure children experience to the cultural codes of society is contained in the tradition of fairy stories. Bruno Bettelheim has undertaken an extensive study of the crucial role of this genre in the process of the psychological development of childhood. In his seminal book *The Uses of Enchantment: The Meaning and Importance of Fairy Tales* (1976) Bettelheim considers the significance of food in these stories. He maintains that the threat of being devoured is the central theme of *Little Red Riding Hood*, as it is of *Hansel and Gretel*. The same basic psychological constellations which recur in every person's development can lead to the most diverse human fates and personalities, depending on what the individual's other experiences are and how he interprets them to himself. Similarly, a limited number of basic themes depict in fairy stories quite different aspects of the human experience; all depends on how such a motif is elaborated and in what context events happen. *Hansel and Gretel* deals with the difficulties and anxieties of the child who is forced to give up his dependent attachment to the mother and free himself of his oral fixation. *Little Red Riding Hood* takes up some crucial problems the school-age girl has to solve if oedipal attachments linger on in the unconscious, which may drive her to expose herself dangerously to the possibility of seduction.

Hansel and Gretel, subjects of their oral fixation, think nothing of eating the house that symbolically stands for the bad mother who has deserted them (forced them to leave home), and they do not hesitate to burn the witch to death in an oven as if she were food to be cooked for eating. Little Red Riding Hood, who has outgrown her oral fixation, no longer has any destructive oral desires. Psychologically, the distance is enormous between oral fixation symbolically turned into cannibalism, which is the central theme of *Hansel and Gretel*, and how Little Red Riding Hood punishes the wolf. The wolf is the seducer, but as far as the overt content of the story goes, the wolf doesn't do anything that does not come naturally, it devours to feed itself. And it is common for man to kill a wolf, although the method used in this story is unusual. Little Red Riding Hood's home is one of abundance, which, since she is way beyond oral anxiety, she gladly shares with her grandmother by bringing her food. To Little Red Riding Hood the world beyond the parental home is not a threatening wilderness through which the child cannot find a path. Outside Little Red Riding Hood's home there is a well-known road, from which, her mother warns, one must not stray (Bettelheim 1976, pp. 159–183).

Another fairy story that deals with food, more specifically, fruit, is *Sleeping Beauty*. Bettelheim describes how, in many myths as well as fairy tales, the apple stands for love and sex, in both its benevolent and its dangerous aspect. An apple given to Aphrodite, the goddess of love, showing she was preferred to chaste goddesses, led to the Trojan War. It was the biblical apple with which man was seduced to forswear his innocence in order to gain knowledge and sexuality. While it was Eve who was tempted by male masculinity, as represented by the snake, not even the snake could do it all by itself – the apple, which in religious iconography also symbolises the mother's breast, was also required. On our mother's breast we were all first attracted to form a relationship, and find satisfaction in it. In *Snow White* mother and daughter share the apple. That which is symbolised by the apple in *Snow White* is something mother and daughter have in common which runs even deeper than their jealousy of each other – their mature sexual desires. To overcome Snow White's suspicion of her, the queen cuts the apple in half, eating the white part herself, while Snow White accepts the red, 'poisonous' half. Repeatedly we have been told of Snow White's double nature: she was as white as snow and as red as blood – that is, her being has both its asexual and its erotic aspect. Eating the red (erotic) part of the apple is the end of Snow White's 'innocence.' The dwarfs, the companions of her latent existence, can no longer bring her back to life; Snow White has made her choice, which is as necessary as it is fateful. The redness of the apple evokes sexual associations like the three drops of blood which led to Snow White's birth (Bettelheim 1976, pp. 199–215).

One of the most iconic images of food and childhood is that of Oliver Twist 'asking for more' in the workhouse scene of Charles Dickens's eponymous book. Dickens described Oliver's typical workhouse diet as consisting of three meals of 'thin' gruel a day, an onion twice a week, half a bread roll on a Sunday. However, researchers say that while the typical workhouse diet would have been plain it would have been 'nutritionally sufficient' for a growing nine-year-old. They accuse Dickens of exaggerating the sparsity of the food on offer to make his case against the Poor Laws, which said that poor people should work in workhouses. Dr Sue Thornton, a senior paediatric dietician at Northampton General Hospital, who led a team which looked at the reality of workhouse diets in the mid-1800s, argues that Dickens reminds us that fictional 'truth' does not always coincide with the true facts. They compared Dickens' claim with Dr Jonathan Pereira's 'workhouse dietaries', published in 1843 and adopted by poorhouses throughout England (Devlin 2008, p. 6).

In the novel, Oliver leaves the workhouse after committing the sin of asking for more food. But research into the workhouse diet of the era reveals a very different idea of what would have been eaten. The real workhouse diet would often have contained meat, including beef and mutton, potato, cheese and rice pudding. Even the gruel would not have been the 'thin' meal that Dickens described, and would have contained one and a quarter ounces of the 'best' Berwick oatmeal, according to Pereira's diet book. The team who led the research say that the Pereira diet would have sustained the growth of a nine-year-old child, like Oliver, unless they were forced to do very physical activity every day:

Oliver Twist's diet:
Three meals of 'thin' gruel a day
An onion twice a week
Half a bread roll on a Sunday
An extra two and a quarter ounces (60 g) of bread on religious holidays

The 'real' workhouse diet:
Thick gruel containing one and a quarter ounces of 'best' Berwick oatmeal
Meat – including beef and mutton
Potato; Cheese; Rice Pudding
Bread

(Devlin 2008)

Charles Dickens's great fable of Christmas, *A Christmas Carol*, emphasises the contrast between poverty and wealth, a contrast which was of great concern to the Victorian middle class. The consumption of food plays a critical role in the representation of this distinction. When it comes to culinary delights Charles Dickens is a master of description. *A Christmas Carol* is full of delicious Christmas food: geese and game, mince pies and oysters, apples and oranges, raisins and figs are laid out before the reader in such a way as to evoke the Christmas cheer of Victorian London from the street markets to the poor man's humble festive dinner. Dickens' writing on Christmas food also serves as a way to contrast the rich colours, textures and smells of the culinary delights with the mean, cold and dark life of the main character, Ebenezer Scrooge; Scrooge who takes his 'melancholy dinner in his usual melancholy tavern' and returns to his gloomy, dark, cold rooms where a little saucepan of gruel lies on the bare table.

When the Spirit of Christmas Present visits Ebenezer Scrooge, a feast of gastronomic delights takes place. It is a feast for the eyes and the senses: a mighty blaze is roaring in the hearth, holly, ivy and mistletoe hanging from the walls and ceiling and on the floor forming a kind of throne is such Christmas food as Scrooge's home had never known: 'turkeys, geese, game, poultry, brawn, great joints of meat, suckling-pigs, long wreathes of sausages, mince pies, plum puddings, barrels of oysters, red hot chestnuts, cherry-cheeked apples, juicy oranges, luscious pears, immense twelfth-cakes and seething bowls of punch that made the chamber dim with their delicious steam'.

Dickens emphasises the bounty, despite their poverty, of the Christmas dinner of the Cratchit family, and some of his references to food in this episode of *A Christmas Carol* are particularly cinematic. Christmas food in the home of Scrooge's employee consisted of goose, gravy, mashed potatoes, apple sauce and pudding, apples, oranges and chestnuts.

'There never was such a goose. Its tenderness and flavour, size and cheapness, were
the themes of universal admiration'.
'A great deal of steam! The pudding was out of the copper. A smell like a washing-
day! That was the cloth. A smell like an eating-house, and a pastry cook's next to each
other, with a laundress's next door to that! That was the pudding'.
The pudding: 'like a speckled cannon-ball, so hard and firm, blazing in half of a half-
a-quartern of ignited brandy, and bedight with Christmas holly stuck into the top'.
(Dickens 2012, p. 55)

Commentators have emphasised the link between sex and oral gratification that comes from food in children's literature. Certainly the gluttony
and lack of resistance to temptation emphasised in the literature points
towards the expression of the sexual as does the fact that these slips often
occur outside family control, when the child is in the company of the ever-
threatening other, as in the symbolic role that food plays in fairy stories,
as outlined earlier. But the cosy food-related images prevalent in the texts
of Blyton and Grahame suggest a sense of self-indulgent desire, albeit one
that is socially controlled (Alston 2008, p. 111).

The family in children's fiction is all about control and adherence to a
certain way of life, and it directs children to the conservative even when it
seems at its most sensual, for the literature and the food it features remain
policed by custom and tradition. Food signifies a sense of belonging and the
need to belong is intrinsic to children's literature and of course to family,
but belonging also entails loyalty to family and nation and it is noticeable
that children's literature is often very conservative about the type of food
which it promotes. The children in the *Famous Five* series, *Swallows and
Amazons*, *The Wind in the Willows* and countless others all eat what seems
to the modern eye vast amounts but they are never construed as gluttons
and this is because they eat very traditional British food, the type of food
that is considered wholesome, that mothers are supposed to put on the
table. The children in these texts consume ginger beer, tea, sandwiches,
fried breakfasts, potatoes, roast dinners, fish and fruit pies and they avoid
foreign food such as Turkish Delight (Alston 2008, p. 119).

Wullschlager (1995) describes Kenneth Grahame's ability to identify
the association between food, nostalgia and the longing for home in his
'great pastoral drama of the changing seasons,' the Edwardian children's

classic *The Wind in the Willows*, as a technique of 'imbuing food with a precisely evoked nostalgia for time, place and English tradition':

> When the girl returned, some hours later, she carried a tray, with a cup of fragrant tea steaming on it; and a plate piled up with very hot buttered toast, cut thick, very brown on both sides, with the butter running through the holes in it in great golden drops, like honey from the honeycomb. The smell of that buttered toast simply talked to Toad, and with no uncertain voice; talked of warm kitchens, of breakfasts on bright frosty mornings, of cosy parlour firesides on winter evenings, when one's ramble was over and slippered feet were propped on the fender; of the purring of contented cats, and the twitter of sleepy canaries. Toad sat up on end once more, dried his eyes, sipped his tea and munched his toast, and soon began talking freely about himself, and the house he lived in, and his doings there, and how important he was, and what a lot his friends thought of him.
>
> (Wullschlager 1995, p. 163)

The boom in children's comics began in the 1930s with the arrival in the marketplace of Scottish company DC Thomson. This company, based in Dundee, had previously published story papers but now took a fresh approach with *The Dandy* (1937) and *The Beano* (1938). The circulation of the *Dandy* and *Beano* comics reached a combined peak of four million copies a week in the 1950s (Carpenter 1983, p. 103). They were, along with other examples of the genre such as *Victor* and *Hotspur* (for boys) and *Bunty* and *Judy* (for girls), extremely popular and widely distributed in Ireland, along with all other 'acceptable' British-produced daily newspapers and popular weekly titles. These comics will be familiar to successive generations of Irish and British children and they, more than any others, have defined modern perceptions of a comic in this part of the world and it is a testament of their phenomenal success that they survived for so long, only ceasing publication in 2013. They were published on cheap paper and had brightly coloured covers that were to prove irresistible to children. The real secret of the comics' success was their fluent style of joke telling and the illusion of movement the picture panels achieved through dispensing with the previous use of captions beneath the pictures. These papers had what has been described as a 'Depression sensibility' insofar as the mood in the early issues (and since) reflected the place of their origin, Dundee, in the midst of the 1930s Great Depression. This was a world where social inequalities were pronounced and where everybody was hungry: hence the strips about relationships between 'toffs' and the working class, typically ending with a reward of a plate of 'grub' (such as a huge plate of mashed potatoes with sausages sticking out at odd angles). Curiously, this formula has changed little over the years (Sabin 1996, pp. 28–29).

One of the most enduring features of these papers was Desperate Dan, a character in *The Dandy*. Dan was American, living in the Wild West, in the town of Cactusville, a curious place that, whilst unmistakeably in the Wild West, nevertheless had British street lamps and was policed by British bobbies. Starting before the Second World War, this series has been described as a kind of British comedic indigenisation of Americana. Dan is so tough that he shaves with a blow torch and his appetite is so huge that he famously consumes huge portions of cowpie (Stratton 2010, p. 53).

Enid Blyton wrote twenty-one *Famous Five* books, the first of which, *Five on a Treasure Island*, was published in 1942.[2] As Ransley (cited in Sutton 2012) notes: 'the food eaten in the books anchors the Famous Five to a definite period in dietary history. During and immediately after the Second World War British children ate well but austerely and Blyton is true to this.' In other words, they ate healthily but not heartily. Well over half of the books were written during food rationing, as Ransley points out and wonders if perhaps Blyton is consciously tantalising her readers with elaborate descriptions of food beyond that of ration book allowances.

Sutton (2012, p. 10) suggests that in Blyton's first book, a simple spread of cold ham, salad, bacon and eggs, plums and a ginger cake fuelled the discovery of gold ingots on Kirrin Island. But over the years, as the five go off in a caravan, or camping on Billycock Hill, Blyton discovered the

2   Enid Blyton was voted Britain's best-loved author in a 2008 British nationwide poll of adult readers (Anita Singh, *The Telegraph*, 18 August). Also a perennial favourite of Irish children, Blyton was chosen ahead of such other children's authors as Roald Dahl and J. K. Rowling. She also proved more popular than Jane Austen, William Shakespeare and Charles Dickens. Eight million Blyton books are still sold worldwide every year, including more than one million *Famous Five* tales.

importance of food in recounting a good yarn: 'A large ham sat on the table, and there were crusty loaves of new bread. Crisp lettuces, dewy and cool, and red radishes were side by side in a big glass dish, great slabs of butter and jugs of creamy milk' – simple descriptive skills which make the food hugely appealing.

Staples are found throughout: ham, bacon, eggs, the ubiquitous ginger beer and lemonade, together with loaves of crusty bread and cakes and buns. But Sutton (2012) points out that luxuries – chocolate, for example – don't find their way onto the menu until the post-war years. Blyton doesn't goad us with unobtainable 'exotics' as Elizabeth David did in the 1950s, rather she describes familiar foodstuffs, albeit available to her readers in much reduced quantities through the rationing system. The five eat a balanced diet. Despite an abundance of humbugs, toffees and ginger pop, when grouped into the five main food categories (fruit and vegetable; meat and fish; dairy; starchy foods; high fat/sugar foods), no one group outweighs another. This comes naturally to the children rather than by diktat. Sweets are eaten sparingly; hunks of crusty bread are accompanied by handfuls of radishes or fresh fruit. The children manage a structured approach to eating. Breakfast, lunch, dinner and supper all mark out the day. Even while cavorting across the moors in search of spook trains, the five will stop and sit down so that a meal becomes an enjoyable social interaction. Mealtimes provide an opportunity for the children to share thoughts and to take in all that is happening to them (Sutton 2012, p. 10).

It may be useful to help us to understand the immediate post-war obsession in British literature for children (and adults – as in Ian Fleming's lovingly composed descriptions of James Bond's meals – an early 1950s version of product placement) by examining the wartime (and immediate post-war era) diet:[3]

---

3   It should be understood that though Ireland was not immediately affected by the war and did not endure rationing into the late 1940s, Irish children were as much deprived of treats as their British counterparts in the austere economic and social conditions of 1950s Ireland. For a detailed analysis of this period, see Lee 1989, pp. 271–329.

1oz cheese (Roughly about 2 inch by 1 inch by half-inch cube, barely enough to fill one sandwich)
2oz tea (Equivalent to about twenty teabags today)
2oz jam spread
4oz bacon or ham
8oz sugar
1 shilling's worth of meat
8oz fats of which only 2oz could be butter

Later sweets and tinned goods could be had on a points system. Bread was not rationed until after the war in 1946. Rationing was harder for many after the war in the late 1940s and early 1950s rather than during the war. Gardiner (1999, p. 60) outlines how rationing did not actually end until 1954, fourteen years after its introduction and nine years after the end of the war.

The many references in children's popular literature to food and eating might, along with the tantalising fantasy resulting from deprivation (as in Dickens) or restricted diet (Blyton's post-war children's books), as has been discussed above, be considered as expressions of sexuality. This carnal association is all the more pointed in that quintessential setting of British popular literature for girls – the school story. The constancy of these references has been noted by McClelland (1996) and others in their commentary on the *Chalet School* series, written by Elinor Brent-Dyer. Helen McClelland quotes one twenty-six-year-old Australian fan who wrote 'Why, oh why, are they always eating?' These descriptions in the main fall into one of two categories: specifically 'foreign' food; and festive meals at school. 'Foreign' food is often eaten on excursions. For example, in the first of the Swiss books, *The Chalet School and Barbara* (1954), the girls have a 'typically Bernese' lunch:

> They began with a thick vegetable soup, and followed it up with Bernerplatte which turned out to be cabbage boiled together with thin strips of smoked ham, smoked sausages, potatoes and carrot. It was good, but so very filling that it was just as well that the sweet was of the lightest – meringues, blanketed in whipped cream and adorned with glacé cherries.
>
> (Brent-Dyer 1954, p. 153)

Later 'they went to a patisserie where they had the sort of luscious tea with cakes of cream and nuts and honey and chocolate that everyone enjoys once in a way' (Brent-Dyer 1954, p. 154). A typical description of a festive meal is: 'A gorgeous meal was spread. Jellies, creams, fruit, sweets, chocolates, cakes and sandwiches of all kinds covered the table; and there were [sic] frothing chocolate with whipped cream, and iced lemonade to drink' (Brent-Dyer 1954, p. 98). It is noticeable that most of the food on offer at this latter meal is sweet, with the only savoury items – sandwiches – listed last although normally consumed first. As the majority of Brent-Dyer's readers were pre-adolescent, it is probable that many readers derived a sensual pleasure from reading these descriptions of mainly very sweet foods, both 'foreign' and British. However, unlike many of the authors of 'girls' schools stories', Brent-Dyer did not portray midnight feasts as desirable, and used the only midnight feast mentioned in the series to illustrate the consequences of greed (McClelland 1981, p. 174).

Other authors such as Enid Blyton kept their portrayals of sweet food for descriptions of midnight feasts, where an association with an enjoyable, forbidden night-time activity made its erotic function more overt: '"Golly! Pork-pie and chocolate cake, sardines and Nestlé's milk, chocolate and peppermint creams, tinned pineapple and ginger-beer!" said Janet. "Talk about a feast! I bet this beats the upper third's feast hollow! Come on – let's begin!"' (Blyton 1953, 2005 edition).

The conventional hero of the Boys' Paper genre was very much associated with the project of empire. In turn, the genre of the boys' school story was a central aspect of the imperial narrative, one feeding into the other in the creation of that essential moral and physical structure of 'Muscular Christianity'. By implication the antithetical characters (those who cannot rise to such heroism) are physically limited, and thus 'space' was created for those characters that were not physically proficient and athletic to be stereotyped with a range of negative personality traits. The 'Muscular Christian' model of heroism aggressively continued – and does so today – setting up oppositional stereotypes. Billy Bunter is perhaps the most well-known of these, who centrally filled the space left in opposition to the muscular hero. First featuring in *The Magnet* paper in 1908 (in *The Greyfriars School Stories* by Frank Richards), Bunter went on to become a principal character in thirty-eight books written between 1947 and 1965. He also featured in several comic strips in the 1950s and 1960s. Billy Bunter, although one of the main characters in these tales, is a 'hero' with distinctly antiheroic qualities who is set up as a comic character and is the butt of jokes. He is decidedly overweight, greedy, a spy, lazy and cowardly. In all, he demonstrates negative qualities in opposition to the ideal qualities of the Muscular Christian hero. He is described as 'The Fat Owl of the Remove' – his food choices are invariably unhealthy, sweet highly calorific foods, as with the sticky buns which he lovingly devours in such great quantities.

Food becomes sexualised because Bunter is often portrayed with an almost lascivious, sly expression as he is about to consume that which he loves. Iced buns themselves are almost sexual objects, sweet, soft, moist and sensuously satisfying to the mouth. The image of Bunter could not be more different from that of the typical imperial hero – he is effeminised with the emphasis placed on his overly coiffured hair, the curls more befitting a girl than an aspiring hero in the mode of Muscular Christianity. In short, his food choices are in accord with the demasculinisation of the obese figure (Webb cited in Keeling and Pollard 2009, pp. 109–110).

Bessie Bunter, Billy's sister, a boarder in the Cliff House School, was a character created by Charles Hamilton in the comic *School Friend* in 1919. She also appeared in prose in *The Schoolgirl* and then reappeared in comic form in the revived *School Friend* (1964), *June* (1964–1974) and *Tammy* (1974–1981) (Gifford 1987, p. 21). All of these girls' comics were widely read in Ireland, particularly in the cities and small towns. Billy Bunter had an Irish counterpart in the equally portly shape of 'Fatty Fagan', a boarder at St Sylvester's, whose adventures in pursuit of 'tuck' and seemingly never-ending search for that elusive invitation to a midnight feast graced the pages of *Our Boys* from the 1930s. Many of the stories in the boy's papers, both in this Irish version and its British counterparts were recycled by the publishers from one school-boy generation to the next.

Food can also be employed, as Wullschlager (1996) outlines, to contrast the predictability of the culinary conventions of home with the exotic as in this iconic scene from *The Wind in the Willows*, the encounter between Ratty and the grizzled, old and much travelled Sea Rat:

'That is indeed an excellent suggestion,' said the Water Rat, and hurried off home. There he got out the luncheon-basket and packed a simple meal, in which, remembering the stranger's origin and preferences, he took care to include a yard of long French bread, a sausage out of which the garlic sang, some cheese which lay down and cried, and a long-necked straw-covered flask wherein lay bottled sunshine shed and garnered on far Southern slopes. Thus laden, he returned with all speed, and blushed for pleasure at the old seaman's commendations of his taste and judgment, as together they unpacked the basket and laid out the contents on the grass by the roadside.

(Wullschlager 1996, p. 165)

Childhood literature is essentially concerned with adventure – and the recurring desire for the security of home, that place of safety to which we all, in one form or another, long to return, as in the example of *The Wind in the Willows*, but also in the stories of Enid Blyton and such children's classics as Ransome's *Swallows and Amazons*. P. L. Travers, the author of *Mary Poppins*, spent her childhood yearning for the England she imagined from her own reading and from the stories of her father. In her compelling portrayals of middle class English childhood, the world of 17 Cherry Tree Lane is one of sensible shoes and nannies, teatime and nursery food – gingerbread, raspberry jam, thin bread and butter slices and crumpets. Its sensory preoccupation with traditional foods and an ordered existence punctuated with magical adventures was English to its core. In our sense of place, our desire to orient ourselves in the world, home is a central preoccupation. Food is, literally, a vital component of our understanding of the essential meaning of home (Knuth 2012, p. 181).

There are few more poignant descriptions of the pull of home, of its place in our memory and the central importance of mealtime routine in the process of nostalgia than Rupert Brooke's recollection of his childhood as expressed in his 1912 poem, *The Old Vicarage, Grantchester* written in Germany as he recovered from a breakdown and forever engraved in our collective cultural consciousness by the poet's untimely death in 1915, at the tragically young age of twenty-eight, in transit with his regiment to the ill-fated Dardanelles campaign:

> Say, is there Beauty yet to find?
> And Certainty? and Quiet kind?
> Deep meadows yet, for to forget

> The lies, and truths, and pain?... oh! yet
> Stands the Church clock at ten to three?
> And is there honey still for tea?
>
> (Giles and Middleton 1995, p. 210)

George Orwell's seminal piece, 'Boys' Weeklies', first published in 1939, encapsulates much of the significance of the various aspect of food in popular children's literature discussed in this paper:

> The year is 1910 – or 1940, but it is all the same. You are at Greyfriars, a rosy-cheeked boy of fourteen in posh tailor-made clothes, sitting down to tea in your study on the Remove passage after an exciting game of football which was won by an odd goal in the last half-minute. There is a cosy fire in the study, and outside the wind is whistling. The ivy clusters thickly round the old grey stones. The King is on his throne and the pound is worth a pound. Over in Europe the comic foreigners are jabbering and gesticulating, but the grim grey battleships of the British Fleet are steaming up the Channel and at the outposts of Empire the monocled Englishmen are holding the niggers at bay. Lord Mauleverer has just got another fiver and we are all settling down to a tremendous tea of sausages, sardines, crumpets, potted meat, jam and doughnuts. After tea we shall sit round the study fire having a good laugh at Billy Bunter and discussing the team for next week's match against Rook-wood. Everything is safe, solid and unquestionable. Everything will be the same for ever and ever.
>
> (Orwell 1977, pp. 189–190)

Works cited

Alston, A. (2008). *The Family in English Children's Literature*. Abingdon: Routledge.

Bennett, A. and J. Stratton (2010). *Britpop and the English Music Tradition*. Surrey: Ashgate.

Bettelheim, B. (1976). *The Uses of Enchantment: The Meaning and Importance of Fairy Tales*. New York: Knopf.

Blackford, H. (2009). 'Recipe for Reciprocity and Repression: The Politics of Cooking and Consumption in Girls' Coming of Age Literature'. In *Critical Approaches to Food in Children's Literature*, eds K. K. Keeling and S. T. Pollard, pp. 41–57. Abingdon: Routledge.

Blyton, E. (2005) [1953]. *The Twins at St. Clare's*. London: Egmont.

Brent-Dyer, E. (1954). *The Chalet School and Barbara*. London: W. & R. Chambers.

Carpenter, K. (1983). *Penny Dreadfuls and Comics – English Periodicals for Children from Victorian Times to the Present Day*. London: Victoria and Albert Museum.

Cullen, L. M. (1989). *Eason & Son: a History*. Dublin: Eason & Son.

Devlin, K. (2008). 'Oliver Twist Did Not Need Any More Food', *Daily Telegraph*, 17 December, p. 6.

Dickens, C. (2012) [1843]. *A Christmas Carol: A Ghost Story of Christmas*. London: Sovereign.

Flanagan, M. (2011). '"Tales Told in the Turflight:" the Christian Brothers, *Our Boys* and the Representation of Gaelic Authenticity in the Popular Culture of the Free State'. In *Young Irelands: Studies in Children's Literature*, ed. M. S. Thompson, pp. 57–67. Dublin: Four Courts Press.

Gardiner, J. (1999). *From the Bomb to the Beatles: the Changing Face of Post-war Britain*. London: Collins and Brown.

Gifford, D. (1987). *Encyclopedia of Comic Characters*. London: Longman.

Giles, J. and T. Middleton (1995). *Writing Englishness 1900–1950: An Introductory Sourcebook on National Identity*. Abingdon: Routledge.

Keeling, K. K. and S. T. Pollard (eds) (2009). *Critical Approaches to Food in Children's Literature*. Abingdon: Routledge.

Lee, J. J. (1989). *Ireland 1912–1985: Politics and Society*. Cambridge: Cambridge University Press.

Knuth, R. (2012). *Children's Literature and British Identity: Imagining a People and a Nation*. Plymouth: Scarecrow Press.

McClelland, H. (1996) [1981]. *Behind the Chalet School*. London: Bettany Press.

Orwell, G. (1977) [1957]. 'Boys' Weeklies' in *Inside the Whale and Other Essays*. Harmondsworth: Penguin.

Sabin, R. (2001). *Comics, Comix and Graphic Novels*. London: Phaidon.

Sutton, J. (2012). 'Why the Famous Five Had the Perfect Austerity Diet', *The Guardian*, 18 April.

Webb, J. (2009). 'Voracious Appetites: the Construction of Fatness in the Boy Hero'. In *Critical Approaches to Food in Children's Literature*, eds K. K. Keeling and S. T. Pollard, pp. 105–125. Abingdon: Routledge.

Wullschlager, J. (1995). *Inventing Wonderland: The Lives and Fantasies of Lewis Carroll, Edward Lear, J. M. Barrie, Kenneth Grahame and A. A. Milne*. London: Methuen.

EAMON MAHER

The Rituals of Food and Drink in the Work of John McGahern[1]

John McGahern (1934–2006) was a writer with a keen sense of place. His novels and short stories are mainly set in the northwest midland counties of Leitrim and Roscommon and they bring to life a vast array of characters and situations that provide invaluable insights in relation to what it was like to live in traditional rural Ireland during the middle and later decades of the last century. Religion, the land, complex familial relations, emigration, the dancehall phenomenon, sexual abuse in the home, all these issues are courageously broached and realistically presented. McGahern's stark portrayals also attracted the unwanted attentions of the Censorship Board, which saw fit to ban his second novel, *The Dark*, in 1965, for containing material that was deemed injurious to public morality. The banning led to McGahern's dismissal from his position as a national school teacher in *Scoil Eoin Baiste* in Clontarf and to his temporary exile to England.

Given his insightful observation of Irish customs and practices, it is not surprising that food and drink feature to a significant degree in McGahern's work. The rituals associated with eating and drinking are memorably evoked in both his fiction and prose essays. This chapter will explore the role these rituals play in the work of someone who was described by no less an authority than Declan Kiberd as 'Ireland's foremost prose writer in English now in Ireland' (Kiberd 2002, p. 86). People's eating and drinking practices tell us much about their cultural *habitus*, religious beliefs and social standing; it is thus logical that they should attract the interest

---

[1]   The author would like to acknowledge the invaluable assistance of Dr Maire Doyle in pointing out many of the gastronomic examples in McGahern's work that are cited here.

of a writer such as McGahern, rightfully renowned for his accurate evocation of the cultural environment that moulded him and which he mined so exhaustively in his writing.

This chapter will not, of course, be claiming that McGahern was in any way unique in focusing to such a large extent on what his characters eat and drink. Literary texts abound with descriptions of meals, of aromatic odours emanating from kitchens, of the links between food and memory – one has only to think of Proust's *'petite madeleine'*, so memorably evoked in *A la recherche du temps perdu* –, or of the notorious food orgies witnessed in Rome during decadent times. Closer to home, we have the example of the splendid meal organised by the Morkan sisters in Joyce's short story, 'The Dead', which is described thus:

> A fat brown goose lay at one end of the table, and at the other end, on a bed of creased paper strewn with sprigs of parsley, lay a great ham, stripped of its outer skin and peppered over with crust crumbs, a neat paper frill round its shin, and beside this was a round of spiced beef. Between these rival ends ran parallel lines of side-dishes: two little minsters of jelly, red and yellow; a shallow dish of blocks of blancmange and red jam, a large green leaf-shaped dish with a stalk-shaped handle, on which lay bunches of purple raisins and peeled almonds, a companion dish on which lay a solid rectangle of Smyrna figs, a dish of custard topped with ground nutmeg, a small bowl full of chocolates and sweets wrapped in gold and silver papers and a glass vase in which stood some tall celery stalks.
>
> (Joyce 1996, p. 224)

The account goes on for a few more lines, but what is quoted underlines sufficiently the value attached to food by the foremost writer of the twentieth century. Such a vast array of victuals, the way in which they are presented and prepared, these tell us a lot about the social class to which the hostesses and their guests belong. This is a display of refinement and good taste: what else could account for the careful layout of the table, the at times exotic collection of meat, fruit and vegetables? Joyce probably understood better than most the truth of the adage: 'We are what we eat.' The Morkan sisters evidently belong to the Dublin middle class and they are at pains to ensure that their guests retain a positive memory of the food and drink they are served, the music and songs that they hear, the decor that they see.

The middle classes of Dublin at the turn of the twentieth century might appear to be at a remove from the preoccupations of John McGahern, a writer who was more concerned with those working the land and running small businesses in the West of Ireland. Nevertheless, the attention to detail, as we shall see, is very similar in both writers when it comes to recounting what people's gastronomic habits reveal about their personalities and levels of sophistication. This may well explain why so many memorable scenes in McGahern's novels and short stories revolve around the rituals that punctuate life in traditional rural Ireland: trips to pubs, attending wakes and weddings, special celebratory meals, religious ceremonies, and so on. The author's own predilections probably had a role to play in this. One of his prose essays from the *Love of the World* collection captures the enjoyment derived by himself and his wife from trips made to Blake's pub in Enniskillen during the postal strike in southern Ireland in the 1970s. There is a genuine appreciation of the strengths of this establishment contained in the following lines: 'The pint of Guinness you get in Blake's is as good as you can get anywhere. Michael draws a perfect shamrock in the cream of the stout with a flourish so neat and quick it cannot be followed. They have delicious sandwiches neatly cut into squares with generous measures of tea in old aluminium teapots' (McGahern 2009, p. 44). McGahern liked the ambience of Blake's, the tact and efficiency of the bar staff, the quality of their goods. One encounters many similar instances in his novels and short stories where characters enjoy a pint of Guinness in the local pub, or savour the fresh ham sandwiches served to them while working in the bog or saving the hay, or when the death of a friend or neighbour causes them to visit the deceased's house to partake of the copious amounts of food and drink provided by the family. In order to assess the pervasiveness of gastronomy in McGahern's writing, what follows is a brief survey of some of the most common tropes associated with this theme in his fiction.

McGahern's second novel, *The Dark*, charts the painful coming of age of Mahoney, the adolescent son of an abusive widower farmer in the West of Ireland. Mahoney's main objective, once he has decided that he is not really suited to the life of a priest that his dead mother had wanted for him, is to win a scholarship to university. When his Leaving Certificate results finally arrive during the summer and he discovers that his ambition has been realised, his father suggests that they celebrate in style, which for Mahoney Senior means a meal in The Royal Hotel. Much to the son's embarrassment, the father feels the need for everyone in the dining room of the hotel to be made aware of the success that has been achieved: "'Pick what you want. It's your day. It's not every day people get a University Scholarship", he said loudly enough for the room to hear' (D, p. 157). On discovering that the duck is dearer than the chicken, they order that and then have to negotiate what cutlery to use for the various courses. In the end, Mahoney is relieved to escape from the hotel and regain the anonymity of the outside world. His father pays the bill and is disgusted by the price: 'A disgrace, no wonder they're rotten rich. You pay for the silver and the "Sir", and the view of the river as if you never saw a river before. Think of all the loaves of bread you could buy for the price of them two meals' (D, p. 158).

For a man who lives a simple life and counts the pennies, such extravagance is unthinkable in the normal course of events. His dismissal of the service and the plush surrounds (he doesn't need to visit the hotel to see the river) reveals how he associates such luxury with the wealthy or the foolhardy. In a sense, this episode prepares us for young Mahoney's decision to leave University College Galway after a few weeks in order to take up a position in the Electricity Supply Board. Damaged by the claustrophobic and violent atmosphere in which he was brought up, he is unable to cope with change and freedom. His masturbatory fantasies of having passionate and sadistic sex with compliant women fail to materialise at university when he cannot even summon up the courage to attend the first student dance. The sophisticated world of education and opportunity are abandoned for the safe option of a dreary office job. One wonders if he ever managed to avail of the restaurants and dance halls of Dublin when he began working there – the novel does not cover his life after university – but it seems unlikely that he would do, given his background and personality.

With *The Leavetaking*, a strongly autobiographical novel mainly concerned with a young teacher's account of the death of his mother and his subsequent dismissal from his teaching position when it is discovered that he got married in a registry office in London to Isobel, an American divorcee. The novel also supplies abundant examples of the joys associated with gourmet food and fine wines. While in London, shortly after entering into a relationship with Isobel, they are invited to dinner in the house of the latter's stepmother. On arrival, Isobel hands over the bunch of irises and they are invited in:

> We entered an enormous room which was both a kitchen and dining-room, a high table in its centre, a big stove at the far end, with sinks and cupboards and a battery of copper pots and pans hanging from the walls. The floor was of light polished wood. A young girl was bent over lettuce leaves at one of the sinks.
>
> (*L*, p. 121)

There can be no doubting that the proprietor of this house is wealthy: everything from the dimensions of the rooms to the furniture and kitchen utensils suggests a lifestyle of ease and comfort. Coming as he does from a small village in the West of Ireland, this is a big step-up for the main protagonist: he is now engaging with the inhabitants of a Big House, an experience never enjoyed in Ireland. There is a maid preparing salad at the sink and later a governess enters with two young girls in nightdresses, the daughters of the hostess, to say goodnight to the guests. Then comes the food:

> The meal was elaborate and rich, beginning with a plain vegetable soup. Sole cooked in white wine with mussels and prawns and oysters, and some shallots and mush-rooms, followed and a bottle of chilled muscadet opened. I thought that was the meal but veal was to come accompanied with a green salad. A bottle of red Bordeaux was poured out. There were a number of cheeses. A bowl of fruit was passed around.
>
> (*L*, p. 122)

We are in a completely different culinary world from the duck ordered by the Mahoneys in *The Royal Hotel*. Sole and exotic shellfish, served with white wine, followed by veal, salad and Bordeaux, cheese and fruit for dessert, this is seriously high-class fare, especially for the period during which the novel is set, the 1950s or 1960s, when such culinary refinement would have been rare indeed. The antics of Isobel's abusive father, Evatt, during the meal are also significant. He has a gluttonous approach to his food: 'He seemed to look forward inordinately to each new dish, but once it came he wolfed it down, starting then to grow fidgety and despondent until the next course drew near' (*L*, p. 122). He resembles a drug addict awaiting the next fix. An annoying tendency he displays is to sample food from other people's plates, which is revealing of a predatory or parasitic nature. When he does this to Isobel, she reacts angrily and his wife tells him to desist: '"I like to pick", he smiled a disarming smile as if he'd made an unwelcome sexual pass at an attractive woman' (*L*, p. 123). The sexual innuendo is clear. Later in the novel, Evatt and the main protagonist go for a meal on their own. Having finished his main course, he starts picking at his companion's left-overs: 'he ordered several small dishes and a large steamed fish' (*L*, p. 132). Patrick, on the other hand, settles for just one course. A man of means, Evatt pines after the finer things in life and he feels entitled to taste everything that might tickle his demanding palate. When they are leaving their flat in London, Isobel and Patrick bring with them three cases of Bordeaux, six bottles of gin, ten bottles of very old Armagnac and a whole case of Glenlivet whisky, all of which belonged to her father. In *The Leavetaking*, therefore, much of which is set in Dublin and London, we have a real change in terms of the type of eating and drinking engaged in by the characters.

The Pornographer, much of which is again set in Dublin and London, could be described as a novel of appetites. The nameless protagonist makes a living from writing pornography and he carries out some of his fieldwork on women he encounters in the bars and dancehalls of Dublin. Aroused on one occasion after describing the sexual antics of his fictional characters, he looks forward to a night on the town: 'I am impatient for the jostle of the bar, the cigarette smoke, the shouted orders, the long, first dark cool swallow of stout, the cream against the lips, and afterwards the brushing of the drumbeat as I climbed the stained carpeted stairs to the dancehall' (*P*, p. 24).

Guinness could do worse than to employ these words in one of their advertising campaigns – it is a sensual and alluring evocation of their product. The drink is a prelude to the next stage, the dancehall, where young people rummage around for sexual gratification. He happens on an attractive bank official, Josephine, who is compared to 'a wonderful healthy animal' (*P*, p. 34). They return to his digs, where they 'feed' on each other's bodies. The pornographer is someone who callously uses women for sex without commitment. Josephine, who is in her thirties, seeks something more and conspires to get pregnant in the hope that her lover will marry her. However, that is not his plan at all and they end up estranged from one another. Not before they share some nice food and drink, though. On one occasion Josephine comes to his digs to cook him a meal: 'She unpacked the parcels from the basket: two steaks, a head of lettuce, mushrooms, three different types of cheese, four apples' (*P*, p. 78). The salad and cheese show a subtle continental influence, but it is the wine that is most revealing of more urbane habits. The pornographer has a lamp made from a Chianti bottle and the preference for red wine shows a developed palate – white wine would have been more popular in the initial stages of wine consumption in Ireland. When they go on a boat trip on the Shannon, the meal is washed down with two bottles of red wine: 'I was ravenous even before the meat started grilling, and as soon as I'd eaten, with the early morning on the river, all the raw air of the day, and the red wine, I began to yawn' (*P*, p. 90). His fatigue does not prevent the couple from making love, the sexual desire mirroring the gastronomic appetite once more.

Two trips to London, to visit the now pregnant Josephine, who decides to give birth and hold on to her baby, involve visits to restaurants. The first time he goes over, they end up in an Italian restaurant in Old Compton Street: 'It had glass-top tables, and a black and white blowup of the Bay of Naples along the whole length of one wall'. It is plush and exudes a certain refinement: 'The waiter brought the minestrone and a carafe of red wine. I finished a glass of red wine while she ate the minestrone. I wasn't hungry enough to begin with anything. I blamed it on the travelling. I asked the waiter to suggest something light, and he advised lamb cooked with rosemary' (*P*, p. 181).

The pornographer deliberately drinks too much, conscious of the ordeal that awaits him and determined to resist Josephine's attempts to get him to be a father to their child. On another occasion, the couple go to a French restaurant in Soho run by a fat Breton. She explains apologetically that it is a bit pricey, but that the food is delicious:

It could have been a hairdresser's window, except for the lobster pot and a piece of torn netting with rectangular cork floats and lead sinks ... The man [the proprietor] was very fat, in a chef's hat and apron, arms bared, and he was sweating profusely. I was still not hungry and ordered a steak tartare as an excuse to drink.

(*P*, p. 194)

The attention to detail is apparent – the decor reflecting the Breton origins of the proprietor, with the lobster pot and fishing nets showing a definite maritime influence. Once more the pornographer ends up inebriated and feasts on Josephine's body after the meal. *The Pornographer*, therefore, shows an increased tendency among McGahern's characters to eat in expensive restaurants and drink good wine. This is a reflection of the impact of increased prosperity and access to foreign travel among many Irish people during the 1960s and 1970s. The London and Parisian eating houses were no longer the sole preserve of the privileged classes, as more and more Irish travellers got to sample Italian and French cuisine both at home and abroad, but particularly abroad. Once sampled, they would not lightly relinquish such pleasurable gastronomic experiences. The winds of change were blowing through Irish society during the 1960s and 1970s and this is reflected in the middle phase of McGahern's oeuvre in particular.

Amongst Women brings us back to a farm, Great Meadow, in the West of Ireland. There is scant reference to fancy restaurants in this novel, which depicts an unchanging patriarchal world where simple food is *de rigueur*. Moran, a widower left with the care of five young children, one of whom, Luke, escapes from his clutches when he goes to work in London, often eats alone sitting opposite a mirror in the living room. This highlights his aloofness and revered role in the family. On Monaghan Day, the name given to a fair that took place in a nearby town during the month of February, McQuaid, Moran's second-in-command in a flying column during the War of Independence, came to visit Great Meadow. He would eat a hearty meal, drink whiskey, spend the night and depart next morning. For the daughters, the day was quite an ordeal. The lamb chops had to be bought at Kavanagh's – apparently he was the one butcher whose meat was up to scratch – and everything had to be laid out perfectly: 'They draped the starched white tablecloth over the big deal table. The room was wonderfully warm, the hotplate of the stove glowing a faint orange. They began to set the table, growing relaxed and easy, enjoying the formality of the room …' (*AW*, p. 9).

The sense of occasion is palpable, as the house is made ready for a special guest. McQuaid drives a Mercedes and has clearly become successful as a cattle dealer. Moran, his superior officer during the war, still seeks to exercise control over his subordinate. However, this proves more difficult over time as McQuaid reveals himself less willing to yield to his host's authority on every subject. On his last trip to the house, he flirts with the girls, praises their good looks and cooking prowess and then settles in to a hearty meal:

> The girls had the freshly cut bread, butter and milk on the table. The lamb chops sizzled as they were dropped into the big pan. The sausages, black pudding, bacon, halves of tomatoes were added soon after to the sides of the pan. The eggs were fried in a smaller pan. Mona scalded the large teapot and set it to brew.
>
> (*AW*, p. 12)

This is not the type of meal enjoyed by the Moran family on a regular basis: no expense is spared in ensuring that McQuaid is properly looked after. The painstaking way in which the meal is presented is striking: all the ingredients are named individually and the cooking methods described. One can almost smell and taste the food. McQuaid clears his plate and thanks the girls. He and Moran then start recounting episodes from their war experiences. Although appreciative of the hospitality shown to him, on this particular evening he baulks against the systematic authority of his former comrade in arms: 'Tonight a growing irritation at Moran's compulsion to dominate, to have everything on his own terms or not at all, had hardened into a sudden decision to overturn the years and quit the house at once' (*AW*, p. 21).

Aware that this brusque departure signals the end of a life-long friendship, Moran is nevertheless unwilling or unable to say the words that might heal the rift. Before he gets into his Mercedes, McQuaid utters under his breath in a voice loud enough to be heard: 'Some people just cannot bear to come in second' (*AW*, p. 22), a pointed reference to the changed social status of the two men. The way in which McQuaid breaks the etiquette of

hospitality is revealing of his rather uncouth manners – he treats his wife
in a very dismissive manner and is ruthless in his quest to become rich. It
is very unlikely that he, or Moran for that matter, would ever be found in
a French or Italian restaurant. They are the products of a time when plain
food was appreciated, usually supplied in plentiful quantities, but always
with an eye to the possibility of falling on hard times – the spectre of the
famine would still have loomed large in the minds of many inhabitants
of the West of Ireland. But occasions like Christmas had to be marked
appropriately. Hence the following account of the Christmas dinner in
Great Meadow:

> The room was already full of delicious smells. Two tables were put together out from
> the window and covered with a white cloth. The places were set. The huge browned
> turkey was placed in the centre of the table. The golden stuffing was spooned from
> its breast, white dry breadcrumbs spiced with onion and parsley and pepper. There
> were small roast potatoes and peas and afterwards the moist brandy-soaked plum
> pudding. Brown lemonade was squirted into the glasses from siphons with silver tops.
>
> (*AW*, p. 99)

Just as with his descriptions of certain religious rituals, there is something
almost sacred about the time-honoured conventions that are observed
in relation to this important family event. Things have been done in a
certain way for many years and these traditions must be preserved. One
has the impression that while outside of Great Meadow many customs
and practices are changing, here at least there is consistency, as though
the house were in some way a bastion of immutability. Hence there is
the white cloth, the special places at the table, the browned turkey with
stuffing in its breast, the roast potatoes and plum pudding – one might
add the Brussels sprouts and carrots, the trifle and cream and the other
ingredients of your typical Irish Christmas dinner. McGahern's objective
was to capture the atmosphere, smells and colour of a meal that reunites
the Moran family (with the exception of Luke) and highlights for them
the unique pull of home.

In the concluding part of this chapter, I will deal with McGahern's last
novel, *That They May Face the Rising Sun* and his classic short story, 'The
Country Funeral', in order to illustrate the writer's painstaking charting

of his characters' interaction with things gastronomic. 'The Country Funeral' describes the impact a trip to attend the last rites of their uncle Peter, a bachelor farmer, exerts on the brothers Fonsie, Philly and John Ryan. As children, their mother's precarious financial circumstances meant that the boys had to travel to Peter's farm during the summer holidays. The invalided Fonsie had particularly bad memories of these stays: 'The man [Peter] wasn't civilised. I always felt if he got a chance he'd have put me in a bag with a stone and thrown me in a big hole' (*CS*, pp. 381–382). Philly, who works on the oil rigs and squanders the good money he earns on trips home buying drinks in a Dublin pub, has a different perception of their uncle. What's more, during the few days he spends at the funeral, he comes to appreciate the tact and neighbourliness of the community where Peter lived. For example, on their arrival at Peter's house, the brothers notice that preparations have already begun for the wake: 'In the kitchen Fonsie and Philly drank whiskey. Mrs Cullen said it was no trouble at all to make John a cup of tea and there were platefuls of cut sandwiches on the table' (*CS*, p. 383). The Cullens had taken it on themselves to buy food and drink for the wake. Bill Cullen showed the brothers 'a bill for whiskey, beer, stout, bread, ham, tomatoes, cheese, sherry, tea, milk, sugar' (*CS*, p. 384). Nevertheless, they still need to travel to Henry's, the pub/ grocery in the local town, to get more provisions for the expected guests. Luke Henry, the proprietor, insists that they have a drink and discuss the passing of their uncle. He refuses the money they offer for the bottles of gin, whiskey, stout, beer, sherry and the food they get from him, saying that they can settle up after the funeral. Anything that is not consumed, he will take back.

The wake and funeral revolve around food and drink. It is noticeable that the mourners do not eat or drink to excess. It would appear that the food and drink are just an expression of welcome and gratitude on the part of the family for the solidarity shown by those friends and neighbours who come to pay their respects. Everything follows time-honoured traditions, expressions of sorrow being followed by anecdotes about the dead man's life, the qualities he encapsulated. Then there is the usual flurry of activity in the kitchen: 'Maggie Cullen made sandwiches with the ham and turkey and tomatoes and sliced loaves. Her daughter-in-law cut the sandwiches into small squares and passed them around on a large oval plate with blue flowers around the rim'. Those drinking beer often make use of the empty bottle as an ashtray: 'Some who smoked had a curious, studious habit of dropping their cigarette butts carefully down the narrow necks of the bottles ... By morning, butts could be seen floating in the bottoms of bottles like trapped wasps' (*CS*, p. 391). This is a studied portrayal of some typical rituals associated with the wake in Ireland where talk was interspersed with food and drink and where cigarettes were extinguished in empty beer bottles as described above. The reason why McGahern devoted so much time to immortalising such rituals was possibly because he realised how, in an age of globalisation, they were in danger of extinction. How long will the 'healthy' breakfast enjoyed by Philly on the morning of the funeral endure in the Ireland of the twenty-first century, I wonder: 'After managing to get through most of a big fry – sausages, black pudding, bacon, scrambled eggs and three pots of black coffee – he was beginning to feel much better when Fonsie and John came in for their breakfast' (*CS*, p. 397).

Throughout 'The Country Funeral' we encounter many such references to excessive eating and drinking. Once more, in keeping with tradition, the Ryans stop in various pubs on their journey back to Dublin after the funeral, something that would in all likelihood no longer happen with the stricter drink driving laws in Ireland. By the time they end up in Mulligan's of Poolbeg Street, one of Dublin's best-known hostelries, they are all inebriated and Philly has decided he will buy his uncle's farm from his mother and settle down there after he has finished working on the oil rigs. The time spent at Peter's funeral has convinced him that this would be a good place to live: neighbours look after each other, there is a timeless pattern to life there and he feels as though it is where his roots lie.

Published in 2002, *That They May Face the Rising Sun* contains elements of the pastoral, in that McGahern celebrates the disappearing culture of an aging local community living around a lake, a setting that has obvious resemblances to the writer's final residence in Foxfield Co. Leitrim. Jim and Kate Ruttledge, a childless middle-aged couple, come back from London to live in this secluded spot. They dabble in a bit of farming and their house becomes something of a magnet for the likes of their loveable neighbour, Jamesie, Ruttledge's uncle known as 'The Shah' and Bill Evans, a 'farm boy' who was committed to care at an early age and ended up working as a virtual slave on different farms around the country. On one occasion, the family for whom he worked locked him out of the house when they went away for a few days and he was forced to ask the Ruttledges for some food. When Jim explains rather apologetically that there is nothing, not even bread, in the house, Bill asks if there are any 'spuds'. We read: 'His eyes glittered on the pot as he waited, willing them to boil. Fourteen potatoes were put into the pot. He ate all of them, even the skins, with salt and butter, and emptied the large jug of milk' (*RS*, p. 10). It is interesting that the more urbane Jim Ruttledge would not have considered potatoes a proper meal, given the fact that they were the staple diet in Ireland for such a long time and are still extremely popular. Bill has no doubts about their nutritional value and is solely concerned with sating his hunger. Life in a religious-run institution, where food was scarce and unprovoked beatings commonplace, had taught him to appreciate the simple things in life.

When the Shah arrived to the Ruttledges' house for his dinner every Sunday, different proprieties were observed. Like Bill Evans, the Shah enjoys his food to the full: 'He ate in silence from a large white plate: sausage, rasher, grilled halves of tomato, mushrooms, onion, black pudding, a thin slice of liver, a grilled lamb chop. From another plate he drew and buttered slices of freshly baked soda bread'. And that wasn't the end of it: 'With an audible sign of satisfaction he reached for the slice of apple tart, the crust sprinkled with fine sugar. He poured cream from a small white jug. He drank from the mug of steaming tea' (*RS*, p. 87). There is a consistency between this meal and the one offered to McQuaid in *Amongst Women*. It conforms to what would generally have been referred to as a 'mixed grill' when I was growing up, a very popular choice in hotels and restaurants around the country. Ruttledge's uncle is most satisfied with his repast and thanks Kate for preparing it. It is likely that there is not much variety in what he wants and gets for his Sunday meal in the house beside the lake. Compare this to what happens when a friend of the Ruttledges comes to visit from London. In this instance, there is a dinner of steak, salad and wine:

The steaks were cooked over a fire of dried oak on an iron grill the Shah had made for the fireplace in the small front room. As they cooked, grease dripped from the raised grill and flared in the red embers. Robert Booth sat in silence with a whiskey, watching the fire and the lights from the fire play on the white walls. At the table he came to life.

(*RS*, p. 158)

Booth is a successful businessman and is keen to get Kate to come back to work with him in London. Originally from Northern Ireland, he settled in England and eventually assumed the accent and mannerisms of an English squire. During his stay with the Ruttledges, he sleeps long into the morning, reads the newspapers and springs into life when drinks are served and food is on the way.

Food for him has an aesthetic dimension and is not simply a means of satisfying a physical need. His hosts make a special effort to ensure that the meals served during his stay are varied and refined in order to meet his expectations. After he has left, they decide not to return to London, even though what he proposed was tempting. The couple have settled into the slow rhythm of life beside the lake and feel close to the inhabitants. They enjoy the feeling at the end of a hard day's work on the land as they settle into a meal with Jamesie and his wife:

Inside the house a reading lamp with a green shade was lit on the big table. On the red-and-white squares of the tablecloth stood a blue bowl filled with salad and large white plates of tongue and ham, a cheeseboard with different cheeses, including the Galtee Jamesie liked wrapped in its silver paper, a cut loaf, white wine, a bottle of Powers, lemonade. There was a jug of iced water in which slices of lemon floated.

(*RS*, pp. 113–114)

Jamesie is impressed, calling it a 'pure feast', and it is clear that all enjoy each other's company and sharing in the achievement of saving the hay through food and drink. Similarly, after a successful day at the local mart, there is another example of a celebratory meal: 'Mary made a hot whiskey for herself. Then she removed a damp cloth from a platter and a border of white and blue flowers on which small squares of ham and chicken sandwiches were sprinkled with sprigs of parsley' (*RS*, pp. 231–232). Whiskey and ham sandwiches seem to be constants at these gatherings, indicating that both these products appeal to the people involved. Simple, wholesome fare is what most people living in this rural setting appear to enjoy. At the wedding breakfast of the notorious womaniser John Quinn, the menu is more upmarket:

> The mushroom soup was home-made. Roast chicken was served with large bowls of floury potatoes and carrots and mashed turnips. There was plenty of crisp bread-crumb stuffing and a jug of brown gravy. Instead of the usual sherry trifle, a large slice of apple tart was served with fresh cream.
>
> (*RS*, p. 168)

Just as Guinness could profitably employ the sensual evocation of its product in *The Pornographer*, Bord Bia might equally use this description to extol the virtues of Irish food for an international audience. This is as close as one can get to ethnic Irish cooking and it whets the appetite for the cuisine that one finds on these shores.

There is no doubt that McGahern's appreciation of gastronomy informed his evocation of the rites associated with food and drink in his fictional and prose writings. The eating and drinking habits of his characters are revealing of their life experience and social standing and in addition they tell us much about how gastronomy evolved in Ireland over a period of time. In this, as in many other ways, John McGahern can be seen to be the bard of a particular period of Irish history, which saw great upheaval and change on a number of fronts. To read his fiction is to be given a gateway to understanding how exactly people behaved and what they ate and drank in the latter decades of the twentieth century. That is no mean achievement in itself.

Works cited

Joyce, J. (1996). *Dubliners*, London: Penguin Popular Classics.
Kiberd, D. (2002). 'John McGahern: Writer, Stylist, Seeker of a Lost World'. Interview with Eamon Maher, *Doctrine and Life* 51 (6) (July/August), pp. 346–355.

McGahern, J. (1965). *The Dark*, London: Faber & Faber. (Abbreviated as *D* in text).

McGahern, J. (1974). *The Leavetaking*, London: Faber & Faber. (Abbreviated as *L* in text).

McGahern, J. (1979). *The Pornographer*, London: Faber & Faber. (Abbreviated as *P* in text).

McGahern, J. (1990). *Amongst Women*, London: Faber & Faber. (Abbreviated as *AW* in text).

McGahern, J. (1992). *The Collected Stories*, London: Faber & Faber. (Abbreviated as *CS* in text).

McGahern, J. (2002). *That They May Face the Rising Sun*, London: Faber & Faber. (Abbreviated as *RS* in text).

McGahern, J. (2009). *Love of the World Essays: John McGahern*, S. Van der Ziel (ed.). London: Faber & Faber.

RHONA RICHMAN KENNEALLY

The Elusive Landscape of History: Food and Empowerment in Sebastian Barry's *Annie Dunne*[1]

Waiting for Godot has been described as a play in which nothing happens, twice. *Annie Dunne* is a novel in which nothing happens many times. The eponymous protagonist is an unmarried woman in her sixties who lives with her similarly solitary cousin Sarah in a Wicklow farmhouse. In the summer of 1959, they are asked to care for their grand-niece and grand-nephew whose parents are going to England to seek work.

Not much else happens. There are copious descriptions of the daily agricultural round, the introduction of a farm laborer, Billy Kerr, who has designs on Sarah, and some hints about possible child sexual abuse. These plotlines are abandoned unresolved, as if Barry couldn't be bothered to do anything more with them. What is most disappointing is that the writer's touch with prose seems to have deserted him. I very much hope his next book sees a return to form.

(Sweeney 2002)

Such is the conclusion of Eamonn Sweeney in his review of Sebastian Barry's 2002 novel, *Annie Dunne*, which appeared in *The Guardian* soon after the book's publication. While Sweeney's comments are comprehensively dismissive, their credibility is undermined in several ways. The second paragraph contradicts the first one by allowing that not much 'else' happens in the novel, which means that some things must indeed transpire – and

1   Research for this paper was funded by the Social Sciences and Humanities Research Council of Canada. An earlier version, dedicated to Professor Maureen Murphy in appreciation of her major contribution to Irish studies, appeared in Richman Kenneally (2011). I am grateful to Darina Allen for sharing her expertise regarding traditional methods of bread-baking, and to Pauline Kenneally and Margaret Ó hÓgartaigh for passing on primary sources to me.

this essay will demonstrate that there are a number of crucial potential and actual life-changing occurrences that befall the principal characters. Barry's 'writer's touch with prose' *is* in full evidence in this novel: Eagleton (2011) believes that, of all Barry's works, this one 'perhaps most superbly' demonstrates the author's 'tender feel for natural processes', and Kiberd (2002) argues that its strongest aspects are precisely 'those in which the rituals of country living are narrated with the sort of delicate, inquiring reverence which is the closest that fine writing can ever come to prayer'. And at least one plotline is profoundly resolved when Annie herself is assured, to her enormous relief, that she will not be banished from her home as a result of the marriage of her housemate, having had to overcome the same experience – a consequence of similar circumstances – two or so years earlier.

Sweeney's assessment is, however, an important reminder that the continuing narratives of everyday life tend to reverberate in more subtle rhythms than, for example, adventure tales about war. From a distant perspective, the 'copious descriptions of the daily agricultural round' might seem monotonous, or even boring. This is unfortunate for many reasons, not the least being the fact that, especially during the long 1950s (the timeframe of the novel), most Irish women, whether by choice or not, worked in the home, many on the farm, and their lives and toils and the domestic space occupied by this substantial and significant cohort well deserve abiding attention by writers and scholars. This is particularly the case since the Irish home has been mythologised in the hands of a variety of stakeholders, for example in a speech broadcast on national radio on St Patrick's Day, 1943, in which Irish Prime Minister Eamon de Valera referred to an idealised Ireland of 'cosy homesteads' and the 'romping of sturdy children … [and] the laughter of comely maidens; whose firesides would be forums for the wisdom of serene old age' (cited in Lee 1989, p. 334). The domestic responsibilities of the *bean an tí*, the woman of the house, are all the more synthesised (fused into a unified, simplified set of expectations) and hence vulnerable to stereotyping by virtue of Article 41.2.1 of the Constitution of Ireland, which states that: 'in particular, the State recognises that by her life within the home, woman gives to the State a support without which the common good cannot be achieved' (*Bunreacht na hÉireann* 1938). While this can arguably be interpreted as paying homage to women's work as giving care to her family, it leaves unspecified what 'her life within the home' would actually consist of, understood from her own point of view.

Another reason to devote care and attention to the performances of Irish domesticity has been the insufficient attention, until quite recently,[2] to Irish food and foodways – a ubiquitous preoccupation for the woman of the house especially during the period under review – and to relationships between food, identity, and empowerment. A number of critics have studied women's roles and agency with regard to food, especially as a means of redressing gender-based cultural imbalances. Carole A. Counihan (1998, p. 2), for example, works from the premise that '[m]en's and women's ability to produce, provide, distribute and consume food is a key measure of their power,' and 'the importance of their food work reveal[s] whether their self-concept is validating or denigrating'. In the case of Ireland, Hasia Diner (2001, p. 84) has argued that for most of its citizens: 'The Irish experience with food – recurrent famines and an almost universal reliance on the potato, a food imposed on them – had left too painful a mark on the Irish Catholic majority to be considered a source of communal expression and national joy.' Such circumstances '... alienated Irish women and men from using [food] as a way to structure a positive identity' (p. 85). However, my own research has suggested that food-related performances within the built environment of the home were indeed conceptualised by many as gratifying and empowering and, as we will see, that position is borne out in *Annie Dunne* (abbreviated to *AD* in references). Rather than working from the perspective of generalised assertions about Irish food, identity, and agency, it is the goal of this essay to gain some understanding of Irish food interactions at the grassroots level – focusing on an opportunity to explore one household – as socially and mentally enriching, supportive of individual empowerment and agency, and as forms of cultural or identity expression and creation, from the perspective of those who did the cooking and the eating.

---

2   See for example Cashman (2009), Mac Con Iomaire (2006; 2009; 2010), Mac Con Iomaire and Cashman (2011), Mac Con Iomaire and Cully (2007), and Mac Con Iomaire and Gallagher (2009; 2010).

The elusive landscape of history

Before delving into an analysis of *Annie Dunne*, however, it is necessary to acknowledge that this particular investigation is based on a novel, that is, a work of fiction, and it was written, not during the period in which it is set, but almost half a century later. Both these facts might conceivably undermine the reliability of the novel as accurately reflecting the circumstances of the time, were it not for two points. First, historians and other scholars acknowledge the need to investigate depictions of Irish society in fiction, alongside other primary sources including quantitative data, ethnographic research, text-based archival material, visual and material culture, and so on. Joe Lee (1989, p. 384), for example, argues that '[i]t is to the writers the historian must turn, as usual, for the larger truth' regarding the stories of modern Ireland.

This 'larger truth' is all the more important in the quest to gain insight about individuals who were not famous, rarely documented, and otherwise scant in the public record. Sean Ryder, in his introductory address on the occasion of Barry being conferred an honorary doctorate at the National University of Ireland, Galway, underscores the efficacy of its recipient's seeing history as '[...] a matter of those who lost the struggle or vanished from sight [...] of knowing how people feel and think as well as what they do; it is not a straight line but a tangled and complicated web, full of shadows as well as visible threads'. Writers such as Barry, he adds,

> [...] help us understand the conscious and unconscious factors that shape experience. The fact is that official histories cannot usually bear the full freight of human life, love, suffering and sympathy. Such is not the normal vocabulary of historians – it is the vocabulary of our creative writers, our chroniclers of the inner life, the ones who map our moral histories.
>
> (Ryder 2012)

The performers of what Sweeney calls the 'daily agricultural round,' precisely because their lives usually attract little attention beyond an immediate circle of family and acquaintances, are perfect examples of individuals who require the deftness of the skilled author to focus and amplify their often intense experiences of everyday life – as we will see in *Annie Dunne*.

The second point is that, in this particular novel, Sebastian Barry undertakes what might be considered a kind of auto-ethnographic study, inasmuch as he has revealed himself as the model for the young boy in the novel, having spent his summer, at the age of four, with his great-aunt on the farm in south Wicklow. Despite the fact that Kelsha was no more than a quiet place like so many others in Ireland, 'I wanted to spread the fame of this tiny town there throughout the globe' (Barry 2013). The farm and the adjacent area had a profound effect on the novelist: they 'seeped into me as a child, and showed themselves in all their aspects to me in what would amount now to visions, the ancient cinema of childhood' (Barry cited by Kurdi 2004, p. 45). The character of Annie is based directly on that 'beloved great-aunt who had a hunchback and didn't marry', trapped by her body because it was erroneously believed that any children she might bear could be similarly afflicted (Barry and Sanai 2011). In Barry's estimation, she deserved special acclaim. His inspiration for the book:

> [...] was a desire to draw her back in from the darks of history and time, so that this mirror or shadow of someone I as a child valued above all others might not be entirely lost. As a small child I loved the original Annie – I lived in her pocket, and in the pockets of her small cottage, so I felt at least I knew such a woman, like a spider perhaps 'knows' the human room it abides in. Furthermore, to some extent, a person very like Annie 'created' me in that I took my clue [cue?] from her and have tried to live by her lights.
>
> (Barry 2013)

Declaring that 'we are creatures in an elusive landscape of history' (Barry cited by Kurdi 2004, p. 42), Barry thereby throws open a window to reveal complex characters through rich narrative derived from biographical and historical precedent, or, more specifically, from the 'floating paintings and interior poems that they leave in their wake, the afterlife of facts and events in the human mind' (Barry 2013). In so doing *Annie Dunne*, the novel constitutes 'the sorting out of people from history, maybe, rather than in history' (Barry 2013). Given Barry's intimate understanding of his great-aunt and of her life in Kelsha – having experienced it as a child as well as in the retrospective stance of the author – he is able to carry forward to the reader opportunities for emotional, sensorial, and empathetic connection, to heighten an understanding of Annie's food-related actions and reasoning, and these prove of significant benefit in comprehending the often unquantifiable, and intangible, implications of the food culture of the time.

Food and empowerment in *Annie Dunne*

Annie Dunne, by virtue of being set during the late 1950s, is a compelling link to the legacy of food practices of that era. It devotes remarkable attention to growing, preparing, serving, eating, and even excreting food. Its principal character, despite owning no land, having to rely on the generosity of a relation for room and board, and feeling herself in precarious circumstances because of potential changes that might force her out of her current home, is nevertheless empowered, and her identity reinforced, by the role she has in giving nourishment and sustenance through growing and preparing food. Moreover, such self-esteem as she has, not to mention the esteem in which she is held by her cousin, Sarah Cullen (in whose house she is being sheltered), is predicated in large measure on Annie's accomplishments in this area.

Food permeates *Annie Dunne*. Similes and metaphors related to cooking, to specific ingredients, or to eating, punctuate the book. At a moment of repose, Annie feels 'relief like a luxury, like a strip of chocolate' (*AD*, p. 4). Annie has warm feelings about the pony that Sarah owns; she 'relish[es] the fatness of his girth, like a well-fed man' (*AD*, p. 34). And Sarah's laugh, at one point, 'is thick and chesty, like blackberries beginning to bubble in the big pot, when we are making preserves in the autumn' (*AD*, p. 32). The Dublin-raised children she is minding, her grand-niece and -nephew, set off a range of emotions for Annie, who feels:

buffeted, tormented even, again by this feeling I have for them. It is like the treacle in the pudding when it is first thrown down on the dough, and the spoon so slow and held back as the mixture is stirred, dragging on the muscles at the top of the working arm. And then the treacle begins to let itself be folded in, and surrenders, and imparts to the pudding that wild taste of sugar, foaming and cavorting in the mouth.

(*AD*, pp. 50–51)

Certainly, a pattern emerges early in the novel whereby major events are linked to food-related activities. Annie's very first gesture when the children arrive is to transition them slowly into country life, to 'herd the children like little calves through the lower leaf of the half-door and into the beautiful glooms of the kitchen,' where the 'big sandwiches lie on the scrubbed table, poised like buckled planks on blue and white plates' (*AD*, p. 1). A powerful passage about Annie taking care of a beloved crabapple tree is the preamble to two major events. In addition to talking to and caressing the tree, she fertilises it with the used tea leaves from the kitchen; indeed, '[w]hen I read the leaves in the cups for Sarah,' she admits, 'bringing into [Sarah's] head the dreams of soft futures, I am thinking quietly myself of the crab-apple tree, the nourishment it will get from the makings of such prophecies' (*AD*, p. 85). Annie's pleasure is interrupted by the arrival of Kerr, who, she will discover later, has begun a courtship with Sarah. He gives Annie a sweet called a Peggy's-leg as a treat for the children, and it is when Annie goes to pass along this 'true treasure,' she discovers the siblings in the midst of sexual activity – one that, itself, resembles eating (*AD*, pp. 86–87). Annie hears the boy describe his sister's genitalia as smelling 'of oranges ... like when Mummy peels oranges'; throughout the rest of the children's sojourn, Annie-the-narrator's allusions to oranges become a shortcut back to her disturbing memory (*AD*, pp. 88, 106, 107, 116, 119 and 201). Annie's immediate response to this event is to sweep the children out of the house to buy sweets at the local village, even as she finally denies them Kerr's Peggy's-leg and discards it instead. Other moments of crisis include Sarah being interrupted from making bread when the farm is threatened by vandals; Annie feeding hay to the pony when Kerr comes to threaten her; and Matt (her brother-in-law and the children's grandfather) injured when he chokes on the blackthorn inserted by Annie in the lump of her butter that she gave him as a gift, to help prevent it from going rancid.

More than just the driving force of the plot of the novel, Annie's food interventions give weight to her identity as a productive member of her household, and are the essence of her empowerment. This possibility of achieving self-worth through women's food interactions has particular significance given the timeframe of this novel. 1950s Ireland was by many accounts a period of hardship for a great proportion of its citizens, especially in rural areas. As Ferriter (2005, p. 462) noted, historians of the period have used words like '"doom," "drift," "stagnation," "crisis," and "malaise" to describe Ireland south of the border in the 1950s'. It was a trying time for women, especially those living in rural environments: '[t]he effects of post-Famine marriage patterns involving late and low rates of marriage, allied to high celibacy and female emigration rates, [the highest of any European country between 1945 and 1960] were still being felt in rural Ireland into the 1960s' (Kennedy 2001, p. 22). Caitríona Clear explains that at this time most women gainfully occupied by working on farms were employed by relatives; she concludes that 'oral and other evidence suggests that women who were working as assisting relatives up to the 1950s felt themselves to be unusually disadvantaged ...' (2004, p. 139).

To what extent, then, could women who had to tolerate such circumstances derive respect and/or satisfaction from putting meals on the table? In Barry's *Annie Dunne*, there are distinct manifestations of empowerment for both principal female characters, especially within, and derived from, the confines of their own household, and particularly, in the case of Annie, because she is accomplished as a food provider. Isolated by geographical distance from others of their village, they nevertheless share meals that both women deeply appreciate, take shelter on a farm that Sarah owns outright, and find comfort and solace in the sisterly love they have for each other. Sarah values Annie as more adroit than herself in dispensing, not only food, but also happiness, within their home. She highlights, in her admiration, two transformations by Annie of raw food material, one into nourishment for the children, and the other, milk, into butter: 'you, you have the knack,' Sarah tells Annie, 'you have the wrist for children, like for the butter, I could never make happy butter. I can make it, but not happy butter. I understand nothing of it, or of children' (*AD*, p. 77). Ironically, this 'happy' butter-making is at the heart of Annie's power over Matt (the person who had demanded that she leave his home and necessitated her moving in with Sarah) and, although it precipitates his injury, generates sentiments oddly satisfying to her: 'There is an unworthy feeling in me now,' she confesses, 'a kind of petty triumph. I could do him harm now. I could dispatch him from life in this weakened state. Of course I do not want to ... But and [sic], I could. That is the point' (*AD*, p. 192). What emerges from the pages of this novel, finally, is a portrait of two women who are, at least for the moment, in a fragile equilibrium vis-à-vis the challenges of their world. It is true that their farm, not atypically, during that period, without electricity or running water, enables only a bare-bones lifestyle in return for relentless work. But in this patriarchal culture – one in which sons normally inherit land – Sarah is the landowner and in sufficient control to be able to reject Billy, rescue Annie from his hostility toward her, and honour her for the role she plays in the household, as a giver of food.

Annie Dunne and the food culture of everyday rural life

It is impossible not to notice the abundance of detail elaborating on the food-related practices of the rural community in which the story is set. These details serve to illustrate that, entangled with the monumental events that transform history, lie the mundane but so meaningful practices and rituals that themselves profoundly activate and generate daily life. For example, Barry conveys the challenges of sharing a well, the only source of clean water, with a sloppy neighbour whose utensils might contaminate it. Mary Callan 'is a devil for disturbing the mud and the twigs at the bottom of any well. It is a penance to have to share a well with her, as we do' (*AD*, p. 26). Annie is concerned because she thinks that Mary has only one bucket in which to transport water, and also uses it to hold the tainted milk she obtains from her sick cow; Annie is therefore 'afraid of what [Mary] leaves in the well' and is thereby spurred to rise early in the morning to draw her daily water before Mary does (*AD*, p. 28). Such trepidations underscore the subsistence-level existence of so many in Ireland at this time, which just antedates a nation-wide project to bring piped water to rural homes (Ferriter 1995). There is also a fulsome account of butter-making, of Annie's efforts in keeping the dairy 'as clean as a prayer, with its limed upper walls and wooden counter,' against which 'I wield the scrubbing brush, mashing the stiff hair into the hard counter so that every hint of dust and grease is gone' (*AD*, p. 124). Beginning early one morning, Sarah is busy churning butter, 'turning and turning the metal handle, listening to the slosh of the cream inside, over and over, till the sweat sits along her arms and on her big, bare face'. Finally,

> [Sarah] gets the signal, a heavying up inside the barrel, a protest almost from the cream, as it gives up the ghost and becomes the different nature of the butter, only the whey washing about like a memory of cream. It is a delicious victory for Sarah. She gazes about with sumptuous pride, her own worst opinion disproved. This has happened a hundred times, and tomorrow she will be back to saying she has no knack for the butter, but no matter.
>
> (*AD*, pp. 124–125)

On another tack, the complex rituals of tea-making and tea-drinking are carefully drawn in one encounter between Sarah, Annie, and Kerr. When he makes his first visit to the farm during the course of the novel, looking for Sarah, Kerr enters the house and Annie narrates the silent interplay, thereby conveying her discomfort in his very presence:

> It suddenly strikes me that his eye is on the black kettle that rattles with heat over the turf. I concentrate my efforts on not glancing in the same direction, or I can be accused of rudeness later, down in the village where no doubt he laughs about my temperament.
>
> (*AD*, p. 20)

Sarah, who has been out feeding the chickens, enters the kitchen; she 'heads for the boiling kettle and relieves it of its turmoil by pushing it back on the crane, and she scours out the teapot with a splash of that water and then drops in four spoons of tea and wets it[3] as suddenly as she can with a deluge of water'. That gesture is sufficient for Annie to recognise that Kerr has been invited to join the cousins for a cup of tea, and she is distressed: 'The four spoons don't inspire. A spoonful for each drinker and one for the pot. The children are not interested in tea. So in the normal manner of things she would put in only three spoonfuls.' Kerr is quick to read the signal as well, and is 'emboldened by all this to step further in from the door ... [since] he can count as well as me' (*AD*, p. 23). Annie codifies her anxiety by refusing a cup to Sarah's surprise, silently admitting to herself that 'I cannot drink tea in this little muddiness of confusion' (p. 23). She goes out into the farmyard, but anxiously returns when she grasps that Kerr is now alone with Sarah. When she enters the kitchen, 'Neither is speaking. There is a sort of tea-drinking silence that country people have perfected over centuries. A lot can get said in those silences, they are dangerous elements' (*AD*, p. 27). Her instincts prove correct, as she learns later that Kerr and Sarah have been discussing whether they ought to marry.

More than just a parable on food-related performance as contributing to personal agency and identity, *Annie Dunne* broadens the lens to consider the role of food as a marker of Ireland's emerging identity as a modern nation. Within the pages of this novel the city – Dublin – stands as a domain of embedded modernity, versus the more tradition-laden (but nevertheless transforming) rural practices exemplified at Sarah's farm in Wicklow. Although conducive to fancy cooking, urban habits are represented as detrimentally supporting the infiltration of packaged, shop bought products, and hence contributing to a decline in culinary skills and a problematic de-personalisation of the task of making food. This transition to commercialised, standardised food production, and its increasing displacement from country to city, are sources of dissatisfaction to Annie, although it is true that she is also depicted as having missed Dublin life (and

---

3   This is an interesting point: my Irish mother-in-law, the woman of the house herself in 1950s Youghal, County Cork, recommended 'wetting' the tea (to coax the best taste from it) by first pouring over it only enough water to moisten it so it could bloom, then waiting a few moments before adding the remaining quantity of water as necessary.

food) during her first years in the country and, on one occasion, expresses nostalgia for the treacle pudding that was 'an item of my mother's in the old kitchen in Dublin Castle in our heyday, so the memory of the weak arm is my arm as a little girl helping her mother, in the eternal security of early years' (*AD*, p. 51). However, for the most part, Annie looks askance at food behaviour associated with the city and with modernity, and regrets what she perceives as a decline of culinary skill derived from the land itself and from time-honoured traditions. In recognition of the children's city-bred palate Annie is initially careful, in preparing sandwiches for them when they first arrive, not to include her unsalted butter since they are used to the taste of the more processed, salted variety they are fed in Dublin. She acknowledges that the children have to adapt to the conditions of their country holiday: 'adjust, and not just to the butter. Salted, unsalted, that is the difference, salted and unsalted life' (*AD*, p. 9). Annie is right to be cautious, since the boy admits, once his taste buds are eventually acclimatised, that he had been 'afraid of the sandwiches, ... [b]ecause of your butter' (*AD*, p. 5). On another vein, Annie attributes Matt's injury – resulting as it did from swallowing the thorn that Annie put in the butter – at least in part to the fact that she had not thought to warn him about the thorn, 'and him in truth a city man, and so not expecting such an item' (*AD*, p. 193).

But it is in the bread that the strongest evidence of the undesirable incursions of modernity can be read. At least one city person – the children's mother – cannot even slice, much less make, bread properly. Unlike Annie, she incorrectly squashes it down while stroking it with the knife, so reports the boy to Annie, having watched both women at this task (*AD*, p. 90). Sarah makes bread on two occasions in the novel. On the farm, this is a complicated affair, requiring manual labour[4] to 'bang and fold the dough ..., and plump it into loaves', and it is baked in a distinctly unmodern apparatus – a pot oven (*AD*, p. 152). This handmade product is

---

4   For a wider exploration of the performance of body-memory through acts of cooking, see Rhona Richman Kenneally, 'Memory as Food Performance: The Cookbooks of Maura Laverty,' to appear in a collection on memory and identity in Ireland and Quebec, co-edited by Margaret Kelleher and Michael Kenneally.

vastly superior, in Annie's eyes, to 'factory bread in its greaseproof wrappings'. 'Who would have thought it,' she wonders,

> years ago, that a woman would not wish to bake her own bread, that source of pride and difference, like the very waters of your own well, sweeter and better than all other wells of the parishes. Sweeter and better was your own bread ...
>
> (*AD*, p. 99)

But now, the bread is transported in from outside the village where she lives. Indeed, it is the van that 'brings the new bakery bread to Kiltegan, heaven help us', and that also transports Matt to the hospital after his injury (*AD*, p. 188). Factory bread, like the cars that have replaced the pony and traps, are signs of transformation even in Annie's world; sitting in her local shop, once 'newcomers to the shelves ... [they] seem old sights now ... here they reside, these trim, similar, thin-crusted loaves that everyone wants to buy' (*AD*, p. 99).

In critiquing shop-bought bread, Annie is in the company of a number of advocates lamenting the passing of traditional cooking practices. Darina Allen points out that by the early nineteen-sixties the routine of eating primarily home or locally-grown and -prepared foods in rural areas of the country,

> [...] a way of life, which we took so much for granted, was about to come to an abrupt end. [...] All over Ireland, within just a few years, people began to prize fancy shop-bought things. When the priest came to visit, for instance, he would always be offered white 'shop bread' in preference to homemade soda bread.
>
> (Allen 1995, p. 6)

It is transformations such as these that stimulated Allen to seek out and document heritage recipes culled from all over Ireland in order that they should not be lost.

Food experts writing during the long 1950s expressed similar views. Pronouncements advocating home-baking of bread can be found, for example, in the *Cookery Notes* of 1951 and 1952 (even if, in both cases,

advertisements for commercial bread also appeared in the booklets).[5]
These were government publications used as a form of textbook 'in Schools
and Classes for Girls, working under the Schemes of the Department of
Agriculture'. The 1951 version endorses homemade bread for four reasons:

(1) It is more economical.
(2) Where wheat is grown, whole meal bread, which is the best of
     all, can be had for the cost of growing and grinding.
(3) Home-made bread is sure to consist of pure ingredients; large shop
     loaves are often made of inferior flour, such as coarse American
     brands.
(4) Bread made with milk is more nourishing than bought bread.[6]

Another proponent was Maura Laverty, who produced five popular cookbooks during the late 1940s to early 1960s. In *Kind Cooking*, she privileges
Irish soda-bread as one component of the 'four-leaved shamrock [we have
given] to the world. One leaf is W. B. Yeats, another is boiled potatoes in
their jackets, another Barry Fitzgerald. The fourth is soda-bread. And the
greatest of these is soda-bread' (Laverty 1946, p. 67). She declares in *Full
and Plenty* that

> 'I believe in bread-making' [and this is] the first and most important article of my
> culinary Credo. I applaud every effort to revive this kindliest of domestic arts. ... I
> believe that the woman who bakes her family's bread brings this goodness into the
> kitchen.
>
>   (Laverty 1960, p. 1)

5   Department of Agriculture Ireland, *Cookery Notes: Originally Prepared for Use
     in Schools and Classes for Girls Working under the Schemes of the Department of
     Agriculture.* (Stationery Office, 1951 and 1952), pages 64 – a full page ad – and xiv
     – roughly a quarter-page – respectively.
6   Department of Agriculture Ireland, *Cookery Notes*, 1951, p. 42. Curiously, the third
     rationale was removed from the 1952 edition, but the others were unchanged.
     Department of Agriculture Ireland, *Cookery Notes*, 1952, p. 42.

A similar, if less effusive, sentiment also appears at least in the second edition of the very popular *All in the Cooking*, an Irish cookbook published by *Coláiste Mhuire* (Dublin College of Domestic Science): 'Unfortunately, little bread or cake-making is now done in the home; the shop product is so easily obtained, but it lacks the excellent flavour, purity of ingredients and high nutrient qualities of a well-made, properly baked home-made cake' (Marnell et al. 1946, p. 182). As we can see, then, *Annie Dunne* confirms that convenience foods such as shop-bought bread were not always seen as the entirely welcome consequences of 'progress' but, for some, signalled the passing of a long-standing tradition, whose replacement was, even though convenient, nevertheless inferior. What the novel also gives its readers, on top of such factual qualifications as these, are the sensorial and emotional underpinnings of such a turn to modernity, experienced by characters caught in its flux.

Two concluding thoughts

Annie Dunne the novel greatly repays scrutiny as a documentation of food and foodways in mid-twentieth-century Ireland, and as a (re-)imagined narrative of diverse food-related interaction. Honed out of the experiences of a child, told through the musings of a character based on a real person, by an author who witnessed events that would become its plot and setting, it exhibits layers of insight and complexity. Barry told Grene (2006, p. 255) that he himself found it hard to believe that he could remember as much of the experience of that summer as he did. It is true that certain ambiguities arise in this text concerning food activities that seem curious and therefore encourage triangulation with other sources. One example is an episode of bread-making on the farm, during which Sarah, Annie, and the children prepare six loaves of bread that 'we will make for the week', whereas traditional Irish practices tended to favour daily or almost-daily bread-making since there was a premium given to eating a fresh loaf. Moreover,

Annie carries three of these loaves of raw dough out to the farmyard to be baked presumably simultaneously in a pot oven set up there, although bread tended to be baked in the indoor hearth, and it is unclear how all three could fit in one pot oven[7] (*AD*, pp. 152–157). Notwithstanding these anomalies, the overarching reward of *Annie Dunne* is a unique and profound opportunity to revisit and experience vicariously, as Barry himself does, a site of dynamic food-related engagement that would otherwise be lost to succeeding generations. In so doing it complements the accounts of historians and other professionals, which is crucial because, as Barry (2013) says, both history and memory 'suffer from different modes of half fact, they acquire a battered truth, like old houses with the rot and insects teeming invisibly, assailed, but still standing'. Joe Lee made the point that authors writing about what he calls the 'fetid atmosphere' of the 1940s and 1950s added in significant measure to an understanding of that challenging period, by conveying 'the sense of pervasive, brooding hopelessness at home, the emptiness, the uncomprehending remorse, the heartbreak and heroism of many caught in the web of the "experience of abandonment" as families were sundered and communities withered' (Lee, p. 384). *Annie Dunne* can be seen as consistent with such works, but perhaps its greatest contribution is in adding essential and captivating nuance, thereby pulling the reader's attention close to the scale of one woman's remarkably courageous ability to draw surprisingly rich infusions of contentment and fulfillment out of an otherwise desolate existence. This ability, by the way, is, in its own right, a telling manifestation of Annie's power (and that of women like her). Moreover, utilising the lens of a foodways perspective to focus on constructions of agency and empowerment in this novel enables a vital amplification and means of reinforcing scholarship that has, as Linda Connolly (2003, p. 24) puts it, 'in various ways impressively challenged the pervasive theory that Irish women were unconditionally acquiescent

---

7   For specialized discussions and illustrations of Irish bread-making see, for example, Allen (1995, p. 221) (supplemented by a telephone conversation between her and the author of this essay on 5 December 2013); Danaher (1961, pp. 57–67); and Long (1993, pp. 2–8).

in the domestic context in the decades preceding sudden modernisation', that is, coming into the 1960s.

My second concluding point derives from Barry's use of language. Literary critics have observed that Annie Dunne's own words, as both narrator and participant, modulate in uncharacteristic ways. Grene (2006, p. 175) writes that '[t]he inner world of an Annie Dunne is rendered with a rich specificity she could never manage to voice herself'. He continues, '[a]t times the metaphors and similes used by Annie are ones that might well suggest themselves to a country person; but they are turned with a literary leap of the imagination, not according to the norms of orality where even the most vivid phrases tend to be traditional, inherited, employed generically' (pp. 176–177). In short, 'Barry enacts the feelings of Annie Dunne in language that is often obviously not her language' (p. 177). Especially thought-provoking, given this point, are several examples of proximate juxtapositions of two pieces of internal monologue by Annie, one in language that might be articulated by the author himself, and the other, implying that this woman's wisdom was not book-learned. For example, Annie signals her (and Sarah's) awareness that the children are vitalising forces in their lives, by communicating that '[a] glee suffuses us, like beaten egg whites folded into sugar', and two very short paragraphs later she allows that 'Sarah and *me* are the hags now' [my emphasis] (*AD*, p. 7). This duality seems a cue to reflect on the idea that Annie Dunne is a character that operates at two registers: as one individual living her own, unique existence, insecure but stabilised at least in part due to her abilities as a food provider, *and* as an everywoman, navigating and enduring, alongside others of her time and place, the challenges of quotidian existence, yet also reaping whatever pleasures and benefits as might be generated through culinary (and other) activity. Because if nothing else, *Annie Dunne* is a lesson about the complexity of everyday life, which can be terrifying or deeply satiating, sometimes concurrently, and which cannot be condensed or simplified into generalisations without sacrificing our understanding or indeed appreciation of what life might actually have been like in mid-twentieth-century Ireland. This realisation is powerfully supported toward the end of the novel, in Annie's extraordinary soliloquy as she contemplates her possible fate:

So let it be, as things are. I am a simple woman that shares a berth with Sarah Cullen. I work from dawn till dusk for my food and lodging. Soon I may again be homeless, hearthless, adrift. Perhaps I will be like an old woman of the roads, in the upshot, damp and wandering, with the real stars for a coverlet. Perhaps that will be my battle, what God ordains. I do not know. I am a solitary nothing, and on this morning of the world, by a ditch at the edge of Baltinglass, waiting for a friendly car, I am wonderfully happy.

(*AD*, p. 196)

Reassured, finally, that she will continue to be sheltered and treasured by Sarah, Annie even reconciles to the eternal forces that will inevitably take her life: 'We will survive in the … perpetual folding and unfolding of the blossom of my crab-apple tree, a thousand little scraps of crinoline fiercely crushed and fiercely released. Like the spider, although we will decay, something of us ever after will remain' (*AD*, p. 228). Her nurturing will be repaid: through nurturing, she will anchor her own achievement, and, thereby, her destiny.

Works cited

Allen, D. (1995). *Irish Traditional Cooking*. London: Kyle Cathie Ltd.
Barry, S. (2002). *Annie Dunne*. London: Faber and Faber.
Barry, S. (2013). Penguin.com (USA) Reading Guides: A Conversation with Sebastian Barry. <http://www.us.penguingroup.com/static/rguides/us/annie_dunne.html> [2 December 2013]
Barry, S. and G. Redwine (2013). Sebastian Barry Visits Ransom Center. <http://www.hrc.utexas.edu/ransomedition/2006/summer/barry/audio.html> [29 November 2013]
Barry, S. and L. Sanai (2011). 'Sebastian Barry: Troubles in the family', 31 July. <http://www.independent.co.uk/arts-entertainment/books/features/sebastian-barry-troubles-in-the-family-2328997.html>
Bunreacht na hÉireann (1938). Constitution of Ireland … Enacted by the people 1st July 1937 … In operation as from 29th December 1937. Dublin: Stationery Office, Cahill and Co.

Cashman, D. (2009). *An Exploratory Study of Irish Cookbooks* (unpublished Master's Thesis) completed in partial fulfilment of an MSc in Culinary Innovation and Food Product Development at the Dublin Institute of Technology.

Clear, C. (2000). *Women of the House: Women's Household Work in Ireland, 1926–1961: Discourses, Experiences, Memories*. Dublin: Irish Academic Press.

Clear, C. (2004). '"Too Fond of Going": Female Emigration and Change for Women in Ireland, 1946–61', in *The Lost Decade: Ireland in the 1950s*, eds D. Keogh, F. O'Shea and C. Quinlan, pp. 135–146. Cork: Mercier Press.

Connolly, L. (2003). *The Irish Women's Movement: From Revolution to Devolution*. Dublin: Lilliput Press.

Counihan, C. (1998). 'Food and Gender: Identity and Power', in *Food and Gender: Identity and Power*, eds C. Counihan and S. L. Kaplan. Amsterdam: Harwood Academic Publishers.

Cullen Owens, R. (2005). *A Social History of Women in Ireland 1870–1970*. Dublin: Gill and Macmillan Ltd.

Daly, M. E. (1995). 'Women in the Irish Free State, 1922–39: The Interaction Between Economics and Ideology', *Journal of Women's History* 7, no. 1: pp. 99–116.

Daly, M. E. (1997). *Women and Work in Ireland, Studies in Irish Economic and Social History no. 7*. Dublin: Economic and Social History Society of Ireland.

Danaher, K. (1961). 'Bread in Ireland', in *Food in Perspective*, eds A. Fenton and T. M. Owen, pp. 57–67. Dublin: Stationery Office IMC.

Diner, H. R. (2001). *Hungering for America: Italian, Irish, and Jewish Foodways in the Age of Migration*. Cambridge, Mass: Harvard University Press.

Eagleton, T. (2011) 'Overdoing the Synge-Song', *London Review of Books*, 22 September.

Ferriter, D. (1995). *Mothers, Maidens and Myths: A History of the Irish Countrywomen's Association*. Dublin: FÁS.

Ferriter, D. (2005). *The Transformation of Ireland*. Woodstock and New York: Overlook Press.

Grene, N. (2006). 'Out of History: From The Steward of Christendom to Annie Dunne', in *Out of History: Essays on the Writings of Sebastian Barry*, ed. C. Hunt Mahony, pp. 167–182. Dublin: Carysfort Press.

Kennedy, F. (2001). *Cottage to Crèche: Family Change in Ireland*. Dublin: Institute of Public Administration.

Kiberd, D. (2002). 'The Perils of Raj Revisionism; Annie Dunne', *The Irish Times*, 18 May. <http://www.highbeam.com/doc/1P2-24623367.html>

Kurdi, M. (2004). '"Really All Danger": An Interview with Sebastian Barry', *New Hibernia Review* 8, no. 1, pp. 41–54.

Laverty, M. (1946). *Kind Cooking*. Dublin: Electricity Supply Board.

Laverty, M. (1960). *Full and Plenty: A Complete Guide to Good Cooking*. Dublin: Irish Flour Millers Association.

Lee, J. J. (1989). *Ireland, 1912–1985: Politics and Society*. Cambridge: Cambridge University Press.

Long, L. M. (1993). 'Soda Bread in Northern Ireland', *Digest* 13, no. 1 & 2: pp. 2–8.

Mac Con Iomaire, M. (2006). 'The History of Seafood in Irish Cuisine and Culture', in *Wild Foods*, ed. R. Hosking, pp. 219–233. Devon, Prospect Books.

Mac Con Iomaire, M. (2009). *The Emergence, Development, and Influence of French Haute Cuisine on Public Dining in Dublin Restaurants 1900–2000: An Oral History* (Doctoral Thesis). School of Culinary Arts and Food Technology, Dublin Institute of Technology. <http://arrow.dit.ie/tourdoc/12>

Mac Con Iomaire, M. (2010). 'The Pig in Irish Cuisine and Culture', in *M/C Journal – the Journal of Media and Culture*, Vol. 13, no. 5.

Mac Con Iomaire, M. and D. Cashman (2011). 'Irish Culinary Manuscripts and Printed Books: A Discusssion', *Petits Propos Culinaires* 94, pp. 81–101.

Mac Con Iomaire, M. and A. Cully (2007). 'The History of Eggs in Irish Cuisine and Culture' in *Eggs in Cookery*, ed. R. Hosking, pp. 137–149. Prospect Books, Devon.

Mac Con Iomaire, M. and P. Óg Gallagher (2009). 'The Potato in Irish Cuisine and Culture' in *Journal of Culinary Science and Technology*, Vol. 7, Issues 2–3, pp. 1–16.

Mac Con Iomaire, M. and P. Óg Gallagher (2010). 'Irish Corned Beef: A Culinary History', in *Journal of Culinary Science and Technology*, Vol. 9, no. 1. pp. 27–43.

Marnell, J. B., Breathnach, N. A. and A. A. Martin (1946). *All in the Cooking Book 1: Coláiste Mhuire Book of Household Cookery* (second edition). Dublin: The Educational Company of Ireland, Limited.

Richman Kenneally, R. (2011). '"Blackberries Bubbling in the Big Pot": Food and Identity in Sebastian Barry's *Annie Dunne*', in *A Garland of Words: Festschrift for Professor Maureen Murphy*, eds M. Mutran and L. Izarra, pp. 201–217. Sao Paolo: Sao Paolo University Press.

Richman Kenneally, R. (2012). 'Cooking at the Hearth: The "Irish Cottage" and Women's Lived Experience', in *Memory Ireland: Volume 2*, ed. O. Frawley, pp. 224–241. Syracuse: Syracuse University Press.

Ryder, S. (2012). 'Introductory Address Delivered on the Occasion of the Conferring of the Degree of Doctor of Literature *Honoris Causa*, on Sebastian Barry' (National University of Ireland Galway, 29 June 2012).

Sweeney, E. (2002). 'Busted Flush?', *The Guardian*, 29 June. <http://www.theguardian.com/books/2002/jun/29/featuresreviews.guardianreview20>

Valiulis, M. G. (2012). 'Equality v. Difference: The Construction of Womanhood in Modern Irish Feminist Thought', in *Hilda Tweedy and the Irish Housewives Association: Links in the Chain*, ed. H. Tweedy, pp. 35–67. Dublin: Arlen House.

Culinary and Dining Traditions in Ireland

TONY KIELY

'We Managed':
Reflections on the Culinary Practices of
Dublin's Working Class Poor in the 1950s

The arrival of the 1960s brought about a major cultural shift in how Irish women viewed their roles, whereby as a result of, among other things, the modernisation of the kitchen environment, working women could be freed from what was, up to this, a daily grind to provide meals for their families. Furthermore, in appearing to have more time and money at their disposal, these women were increasingly encouraged by publications such as *The Irish Housewife* to engage in leisure pursuits such as art and travel. However, while the 1960s symbolised the 'shaking off' of the chains of drudgery, the previous decades were an altogether different proposition. Set in a time where there was little in the way of storage facilities or labour saving equipment, the economic challenges for those on low income were considerable. Additionally, high levels of unemployment, large families, wayward husbands, excessive control exerted by the Catholic Church, and poor housing conditions, further conspired to make the lot of the urban housewife or mother even more challenging.

During the 1950s, economically speaking, a three tiered society co-existed in Dublin. And while this decade has been described as 'the lost decade' (Keogh et al. 2004) and 'the decade of the vanishing Irish' (O'Brien 1953), recent research has shown that Dublin, on a per capita basis, could be considered the gastronomic capital of the British Isles for much of the 1950s. This argument is based particularly on two award winning 'world class' restaurants (Restaurant Jammet and the Russell Restaurant) across whose thresholds the poor never ventured (Mac Con Iomaire 2011a). Furthermore, the city also boasted an array of iconic hotel restaurants such as the Gresham, the Shelbourne, the Royal Hibernian, the Dolphin, the Moira and standalone restaurants such as the Metropole, the Red Bank, the Bailey and the Unicorn, each of which contributed to the city's burgeoning international reputation for *haute cuisine* and grandiose dining. Aligned with this conspicuous consumption, *The Irish Housewife*, a contemporaneous journal targeting the middle to upper social classes, articulated a sense of style and sophistication for its readers, through providing an informational conduit into cultural, historical and leisure pursuits, while simultaneously advertising the attractiveness of new food products, 'must have' labour-saving equipment, and richly endowed recipes. However, it should be pointed out that this journal also straddled the divide between rich and poor by articulating social concerns relating to family nutritional requirements, complicated by the ever increasing price of food during the early years of the 1950s, while simultaneously offering an *entrée* into a charmed lifestyle for the less well off.

Nevertheless, despite evidence of indulgent opulence and grandeur for the social elite and those who aspired to such a lifestyle, a different reality existed for many Dublin mothers. These women, charged with the responsibility of feeding those under their care on what was more often than not a meager income, were forced to perform a daily miracle in providing for the nutritional needs of their large and often under-nourished families. Furthermore, during this period, emigration was extraordinarily high, which fractured the support system and created a tense economic relationship between those at home and those employed abroad, who were depended upon to send money home on a regular basis (Ferriter 2005). So, while much of the extant literature on the lifestyles of the people of Dublin in the 1950s details a semi-sophisticated existence, wherein fine dining experiences were provided by highly trained chefs in internationally recognised restaurants (Mac Con Iomaire 2010; 2011a), and where much of the magazine advertising and cookbook content aimed at Irish women was conveyed in aspirational tones, illustrating an 'attainable' lifestyle, to mirror those residing in society's upper echelons (Clear 2000), there appears to be a relative dearth of literature illustrating the daily lives of Dublin's working class poor in the 1950s, who in straitened economic circumstances performed a minor miracle in providing meals for their families.

This chapter will endeavour to address this imbalance through re-animating their lives, by way of the recollections of women who lived through these challenging times. Utilising a qualitative methodology, which recorded the oral memoirs of a group of wonderful and indeed under-recognised Dublin women, this chapter recounts a tale of innovation and heroism in the face of a daily grind, viewed through the limiting, and often disempowering lenses of food availability, food affordability, social routines, and having to manage. However, it also records that the move to the more affluent 1960s, with the easier availability of what was promised in the previous decade, was in fact disempowering for many of these self-same women.

Dublin: a polarised culinary society

During the early years of the twentieth century, many women were stereo-typically classified either as homemakers, mothers, or housewives (Clear 2000). However, by the end of the 1940s, and the early years of the 1950s, the term 'housewife' became problematic for some, who openly advocated for the rights of women (Clear 2000). Sheehy Skeffington (1946), for example, lamented the use of this term, suggesting instead that the equivalent of the Irish *'bean a tighe'* (woman of the house), would be more appropriate, thereby suggesting that such a custodial representation, wherein women were portrayed as exercising control within their home environment, would more accurately signify their authority and importance.

As a consequence of this change of emphasis, organisations and magazine publications articulating the empowerment of women flourished in the 1950s. One such organisation, The Irish Housewives Association, founded in Dublin in 1942 by Hilda Tweedy, was consciously feminist in nature, and though catering and advocating for mainly middle class Protestant urban women, it also openly campaigned for social causes such as women's rights to receive a direct payment of children's allowance, the provision of school meals for children in National schools, equal pay for women workers, working class housing conditions, quality control in foodstuffs, food prices, and access to training and education (Clear 2000). However, though undoubtedly advocating a more ethical approach to the conditions in which many women and children were forced to live, such social campaigning put The Irish Housewives Association on a collision course with the Catholic Church. As a result, it failed to feature in the lives of the poorer Catholic families, due in the main to the power of the Catholic Church over its flock and, on a more pragmatic level, the high subscription cost for the magazine, which at the time represented approximately 10 per cent of a poorer family's weekly unemployment benefit, distanced poorer families from the advocacies of this organisation.

Furthermore, *The Irish Housewife* recipe corner illustrated recipes for 'family food', which were, economically speaking, way beyond the means and cognoscente of the average family in Dublin, or those living in the new sprawling local authority housing schemes. Examples of their menu starters referred to such delights as Avocados, Grapefruit Delight, Pearl Chutney, and Stuffed Tomatoes. Recipes for main dishes spoke of Spare Ribs in Barbecue Sauce, California Chilli Beans, Salmon Souffle, Top Rib, Spaghetti Meat Loaf, Creamed Salmon, and Halibut in Sour Cream, while desserts such as Angel Food Cake, Jelly Fluff, Spiced Apple Flan, Apple Snow, and Devil's Foodcake appeared to address an altogether different audience, who regularly dined out, and often procured the recipes from the restaurants, which they subsequently cooked at home from first principles.

Food purchasing and access to cooking skills

In terms of enabling universal access to cooking skills for the less well off
in society, there was no shortage of cookbooks offering skills and culinary advice. For example, Josephine Reddington's *Economic Cookery Book*
(1927), Roper and Duffin's *Bluebird Cookery Book for Working Women*
(1939), Josephine Marnell et al.'s *All in the Cooking: Coláiste Mhuire Book
of Household Cookery* (1943), Ann Hathaway's *Homecraft Book* (1944), The
Department of Agriculture's *Cookery Notes* (1944) and Maura Laverty's
Kind Cooking (1946) were universally used in secondary schools and
schools of domestic science, and detailed realistic recipes written within the
context of the time (Clear 2000). Furthermore, Laverty's *Flour Economy*
(1940) was a collection of recipes based on potatoes and oatmeal in a
drive to conserve the country's limited supply of wheat (Clear 2000).
But, again, these books were relatively expensive, costing from one shilling and sixpence to five shillings (up to 30 per cent of the weekly family
income at the time), thus making them prohibitively priced for women
struggling to put basic food on the table. In fact, a grim reality for many
Dublin women was the extent to which their daily lives counterpointed
the lives of those who could afford to participate or aspire to a more
sophisticated existence. This grim reality was brought into sharp focus
during the 1950s when there was a shortage of the basic necessities, namely
tea, margarine, butter, cooking fat and flour, along with a limitation on
the supply of the gas, which was required to cook the food (Tweedy
Archive 98/17/2/3/5, 1951). Allied to this, the cost of these basic food
items increased substantially in the final years of the 1940s and the early
years of the 1950s, due in the main to a deregulation on the part of the
Government of price control, and a post war shortage of some products
(Tweedy Archive 98/17/2/3/5, 1951). Illustrating the price rise for some
critical food staples highlights the stark challenges for Dublin mothers
between 1950 and 1951 (see Table 1).

Table 1: Price Rise of Staple Foods 1950–1951 (*The Irish Housewife*, 1951).
(Note: 1 shilling = twelve pence in the currency of the time, while £1 = twenty shillings.)

Ingredient	Price (1950)	Price (1951)	% Increase
Butter (per lb)	2 shillings	3 shillings	+50%
Bacon (per lb)	2 shillings 8 pence	4 shillings	+43%
Sugar (per lb)	5 pence	9 pence	+80%
Tea (per lb)	4 shillings	8 shillings	+100%
Eggs (per doz)	2 shillings 8 pence	7 shillings	+162%
Beef (per lb)	2 shillings 2 pence	2 shillings 9 pence	+30%
Potatoes (per stone)	1 shilling 10 pence	2 shillings	+9%
Milk (per pint)	2 pence	5 pence	+150%
Bread (per loaf)	6 pence	1 shilling	+66%
Rabbit (each)	1 shilling 6 pence	2 shillings 6 pence	+66%
Flour (per lb)	3 pence	4 pence	+33%
Corned Beef (per lb)	1 shilling 10 pence	2 shillings 5 pence	+30%
Liver (per lb)	2 shillings 8 pence	3 shillings	+6%
Lard (per lb)	1 shilling 2 pence	1 shilling 9 pence	+50%
Margarine (per lb)	1 shilling 11 pence	2 shillings 6 pence	+20%

To put this financial challenge into context, for those lucky enough to be in employment, the average weekly wage in Dublin in the 1950s was about £4 and 10 shillings (Central Statistics Office 2012), while unemployment benefit was only 16 shillings for an individual or £1 and 12 shillings for a couple, about one third of the average weekly wage figure (The Department of Social Protection 2012). Furthermore, this money was paid directly to the man of the house, who in many cases passed on but a fraction of it to the woman of the house. Indeed, while women were deemed to control the household spending, very few of them knew how much their husband earned (Humphreys 1966). The author further contends, while the tendency among labourers at the time was to give their wives control of the household finances, it is not clear whether these finances were what the man deemed 'necessary' for the family's subsistence.

Furthermore, due to the high levels of unemployment and emigration, a significant number of Dublin families found the economic situation particularly tight in the 1950s, wherein again the financial burden for providing for the family's basic needs (rent, food and fuel) fell on women. Many of these women had recently experienced the same financial strain, when their sons and husbands were precariously depended upon to send home a weekly sum of money from their soldiering activities in World War II. Ferriter (2005, pp. 465–466) evidences the scale of the dilemma created by the absent earner, when stating that 'between 1951 and 1961, 412,000 emigrated from Ireland' (approximately 10 per cent of the population), while between 1956 and 1957, 'Ireland was alone in Europe in being a country where the total volume of goods and services consumed fell'. Furthermore, within the period 1951–1959, 'employment fell by 38,000, approximating to 14% of the industrial labour force'. The financial straitjacket for the oppressed Dublin mother was further complicated in that where a shortage of money occurred, these women often resorted to the 'relieving officer', or charitable organisations such as the St Vincent de Paul and the Sick and Indigent Roomkeepers' Society. Other sources of relief, albeit at prohibitive interest rates, such as the large volume of moneylenders who operated in Dublin, became an option for those desperate for money to provide for costly events such as First Holy Communions and Christmas, or led to women forming a long term economic relationship with one of the city's many pawn shops for the normal day to day living (Kearns 1991; 1994).

Relationships between money, food choice and food storage

During the 1950s, a symbiotic relationship existed between the shortage of money, and the daily diet of many Dublin families. Consequently,
the nutritional value of their food was poor, not by choice, but due to
women having to provide for large families (ranging in size between six and
twenty-four), on a daily basis (Kearns 1994). Family diets were very basic,
consisting in the main of 'bread, tea, oatmeal, cocoa, potatoes, cabbage,
herrings and pairings of cheap meat pieces for stews and soups' (Kearns
1994, pp. 13–14). Sheep's heads, cow's heads, rabbits, pig's cheeks, pig's
feet (crubeens), sheep's hearts and oxtails were also popular where money
was even scarcer. Bread was both a staple, and a constant companion at all
meals, due to its bulking ability and its relatively low cost. Furthermore,
the social order determined that men and working sons often got the lion's
share of the available food (Kearns 1994). In addition, the daily dinner
menu in most households seldom varied:

> Sunday meals typically consisted of corned beef, cabbage and potatoes. On Mondays,
> Sunday's leftovers were reheated on the pan with some cabbage. Tuesdays and
> Thursdays saw vegetable stew, sometimes flavoured with marrowbones being brought
> to the table, whereas Wednesdays and Fridays were fish days (mackerel, cod or ray),
> and Saturdays were days for a rabbit and vegetable stew.
>
> (Cullen 2005, p. 120)

While all of the above meals delivered reasonable nourishment, the ingredients (being readily available and relatively inexpensive to buy for families in receipt of a weekly wage) also facilitated regularity and consistency
in the provision of the daily meal. In terms of stews (a constant in the
lives of poor families), leg of beef, stewing beef, beef heads, sheep heads
and kidneys, along with vegetables, were key elements in the making of a
meal to fill the family (Kearns 1994). Other cheap and nutritional meals
involved women buying cod's heads, boiling them and shaking the meat
off. This, with a large loaf of bread cut on the table with a scrape of butter
on it would make everybody happy (Kearns 1994). However, despite this
availability of cheap, bland, albeit nourishing food, a lot of illnesses were

born of the fact that people were not properly nourished. For many, who existed in the poorest of circumstances, their diet primarily consisted of bread, margarine and tea, which in many cases was hereditary, as these were the principle elements in the diet of their parents (Kearns 1994).

A further concern for families on low incomes in the 1950s was that of food storage. Fridges were unaffordable in many cases, resulting in innovative strategies being employed by many women to protect food from spoilage. Perishables, such as milk, margarine, butter and buttermilk, were placed in a basin of cold water. Tea, oatmeal, bread and sugar were sealed in biscuit tins to protect them from mice. As there were no such things for the poor as fridges or freezers, women would have to use their meat and other perishables on the day it was purchased. Indeed, many women bought from meal to meal. Exposed food was covered in gauze to protect it from disease carrying flies and bluebottles (Kearns 1994). During the 1950s, ancillary labour saving devices such as washing machines and fridges were prohibitively expensive. Indeed, at a time when the average weekly wage for those lucky enough to have a job was £4 (Central Statistics Office 2012), the cost of a washing machine in 1951 was £25, over a month's wages for a family (Clear 2000). Furthermore, while the cost of a fridge rose from 40 guineas[1] in 1951 to 98 guineas in 1958, the cost of a vacuum cleaner, if one aspired to such, was pitched at £21 (*The Irish Housewife*, 1951/1958), all of which conspired to condemn the ordinary Dublin mother, living in straitened circumstances, to the ongoing drudgery of work.

Methodology

This chapter seeks to record the views of a forgotten group of women who not only lived through 'the hungry 50s', but survived intact, with in many cases their stories lying buried within their own memories. Methodologically,

---

1   One guinea = £1 and one shilling in the currency of the time.

the author stands firmly within the interpretivist perspective (Burrell and Morgan 2000), wherein knowledge is seen as an emergent social process, and where understanding and explanation of the phenomenon of interest, comes through the language of the respondent. The specific methodological approach chosen by the author employed involved qualitative interviews, incorporating oral discourse. The use of oral history as a tool for culinary historians has long been advocated by key researchers, such as Mac Con Iomaire (2010; 2011b), who argues that one of the reasons for using oral history is the lack of available written material. To that end, eight women, all in their eighties agreed to be interviewed. Some of the interviews were on a one to one basis, while others were conducted in small groups. Themes were set by way of specific questions which sought their recollections on:

- How they made ends meet if there was a shortage of money;
- What food was cooked (the daily family menu);
- Food purchasing, food storage, and food waste;
- The psychological significance for the women of being able to cook and care for their families in the 1950s;
- Their perspectives on the arrival of the more affluent 1960s.

It should be noted that some interviews lasted much longer than originally planned, such was the clarity of recall and desire to speak on the part of some of the interviewees.

Findings

Although the sample size was small, most of the women interviewed also spoke of how their neighbours managed, thus conferring a more inclusive and generalised feel on the findings. For the purpose of this research, findings were grouped under a number of headings, namely:

(i)   The strategies employed by the interviewees to overcome the economic challenges of the time (making ends meet);

(ii)   Food choices (including remembrances associated with the day to day menu);

(iii) Food purchasing, food storage and food waste (if any), and

(iv)   The psychological significance of cooking and caring in the daily lives of these women, and whether this changed with the arrival of the 1960s.

(i) Making ends meet

Although throughout the interviews, the strong conviction emerged that money 'was in short supply', a sense emerged that women whose husbands had jobs in Guinness's, Jacobs, Patterson's Match Factory, or the Corporation 'were made up'. But these circumstances were spoken of as being the exception, rather than the norm, and, interestingly, with no tinge of begrudgery or jealousy. Rather, a view emerged that this minority of people were fortunate, and were to be admired. According to the interviewees, emigration was a reality for a sizeable portion of city dwellers, where many of the men had to 'emigrate to Birmingham or Bradford or London to work in the factories'. This caused a problem for women, who had to wait at home for a delivery of money. One interviewee poignantly painted a picture where, 'On a Saturday evening, most of the women in the street stood at their hall doors, waiting for the telegraph boy to come up from the GPO with the wired money. If you got it you went straight to the local shop, which stayed open until ten. But if you didn't get anything, you just closed the door'. For these women, the financial rescue provided by the pawn shop, or a loan from the local shopkeeper, where 'most families kept a book in the local corner shop', was more socially acceptable than becoming involved with charities like the St Vincent de Paul or the local priest. Comments on the latter options ranging from 'We just didn't like this sort of thing'; and, 'There was a kind of shame in it, and you know, you always wanted to keep the best side out', to 'We would rather sell what we had than do that', illustrated the dilemmas facing women at the time.

However, where a sense of shame seemed ingrained when contemplating a dependence on charity to fund meals, an altogether different sense of acceptable communal behaviour was articulated when it came to utilising the services of the pawnbroker. Here, ubiquitous comments such as 'sure everyone done it' and 'you met your neighbours outside the pawn at eight o clock on a Monday morning' were made with great mirth. Interestingly, one woman spoke of an innovative approach by one shop owner which gave some independence to local women when recalling:

> there was a woman called May who had a provisions shop at the top of the street, and if what you wanted, bread, milk and butter cost say four shillings, she would give you ten, and I liked that, because it gave you the freedom to say go to the butcher's with the six shillings cash in your hand. Yes, I liked that, even though you owed ten shillings instead of four.

But while the often fraught relationship with the pawnbroker was humorously illustrated through statements such as 'some stuff was never released', but 'if the interest was paid on your items every six months, they were then put back up on the shelf, and as long as it was not your husband's suit then you were safe', other women admitted to being forced to sell valuable possessions or family heirlooms to get money to buy food. One interviewee recalled: 'I took the curtains off the wall and sold them for food, and the next week, I sold two green lustres to an art dealer in Liffey Street, who paid me £9 without even seeing them.' Asked if she minded, selling these articles for less than they were worth, she replied: 'Sure what else could you do? You couldn't just look at the children hungry.' But while it was common for most women to have to manage as best they could, some were quite innovative when it came to raising money. This was evidenced when interviewees spoke of 'selling bananas that we picked up in the fruit-market or knitting that we had done at home from a breadboard on the street corner'. Another interviewee spoke of her neighbour 'washing out the floors of three shops in Mary Street for three shillings a shop', before adding kindly: 'you know, she had a big family, and her husband wasn't good to her'. Yet, another woman spoke of 'buying fish in the Fish Market in Chancery Street', and remembering, 'walking with my mother from the Four Courts to Chapelizod (a village three miles away) to sell to the people out there', humorously adding, 'sure we were entrepreneurs, before they even thought of it'.

(ii) Food choices and the daily meal menu

For most of the interviewees, there was a great consistency about what was served at mealtimes. Breakfast consisted of a cup of tea and a slice of toast or porridge before going to school or work, while dinner was served up to 'the sound of the factory sirens', giving a consistency and uniformity to the meal structure. Procedurally, dinner was served in the middle of the day. It consisted of a 'main course with bread, butter and tea', where in many cases, the men, or working sons, received a larger share. There were no starters, soups or desserts, except perhaps on Sundays, when occasionally 'jelly and ice cream' was served. In terms of the dinner, a majority of the interviewees spoke of their food choices being determined by both price and family custom and practice. A common thread here involved the choosing of 'cheap cuts of meat' such as heart, kidneys, oxtail, tongue, tripe, corned beef and brisket 'to stretch the money'. One woman spoke of 'barrels of salted corned beef standing outside butchers' shops in Capel Street' and of buying 'button end corned beef which was very tough and took longer to cook, but we bought it because it was cheap'. The weekly menu was fixed within families, and normally consisted of some form of roast with roast potatoes and vegetables on a Sunday. For women with large families, beef's heart was a cheaper alternative for Sundays, and gave 'full and plenty'. Potatoes were a significant constituent in every meal, with one interviewee commenting, 'once you had a pyramid of potatoes in the middle of the table, then everyone was happy'. Mondays were leftover days, where any surviving potatoes would either be 'fried up or made into potato cakes with a bit of flour and curly kale'. Tuesdays and Thursdays were stew days. Stews were 'your mother's stew', and being gleaned from family tradition, 'never changed'. Subtle practices such as 'adding in a bit of bisto', or 'leaving in or out the potatoes', or 'adding in flour dumplings to thicken it up', while sacrosanct to some families, were abhorrent to others. Indeed, this often caused familial problems after marriage, with one woman commenting 'He [her husband] spent the whole of his life longing for his mother's stew.'

But despite such differences in preparation, all were in agreement that a good stew was easy to make, was cheap and provided hot food for everyone at the table. Furthermore, some women felt that 'stew leftover to the next day tasted even nicer'. Interestingly, coddle, the quintessential Dublin dish, was not seen as a main meal choice, but rather as a breakfast option, 'particularly for men who had come in drunk the night before'. Wednesdays, except during Lent, were days on which 'boiling fowl' with potatoes and vegetables was quite common. Because of the church regulations on fast and abstinence, fish, particularly cod, mackerel or herrings, was the predominant choice on a Friday. But in terms of value for money, rabbit was the dish of choice, particularly on Saturdays, with one interviewee commenting, 'you could get a rabbit for one and six, and it made the best of a stew'. Another differentiated between rabbit and chicken, stating 'there were four legs on a rabbit, but only two on a chicken, and when you had hungry kids, there was no choice'. Interestingly, some of the interviewees lamented the fact that myxomatosis ended the use of rabbit as a dish, with two interviewees suggesting that 'this was deliberately introduced to make us buy dearer food'.

(iii) Food purchasing, food storage and food waste

How food was purchased was often determined both by the availability of money at particular times of the day and the amount of cooking utensils available in the kitchen. During the 1950s, women often shopped every day, or on more than one occasion during the day, to overcome the possibility of food 'going off', or being eaten up by unexpected visitors, hungry children or drunken husbands. Bread, whether made or bought, was a fixture at every meal, because it was filling. Indeed, more than one woman spoke of 'bringing a pillowslip to the local bread shop', or 'paying one and sixpence for a bag of fancy in Boland's Hole [the back door of Boland's bakery], in Meetinghouse Lane'. But due to the economic constraints, most food was bought in small portions, particularly tea (which was either rationed or very expensive) and butter. Local shops opened early (about 6.30 am), for breakfast purchases, and closed late (to cater for late money arrivals from the telegraph boy). For many, food was bought up to three times a day, with some women buying 'meal to meal'. One interviewee spoke of not being able to store things like tea or meat overnight because 'he might come in with a few drinks on him and leave nothing for the morning'.

Furthermore, kitchens were not well equipped in the 1950s, although most of the women interviewed were very aware of what was on offer, mainly through the reading of magazines and looking in shop windows (a pastime for many women at the time). Additionally, cooking utensils were limited, either through a lack of such items, or through being 'lent out to neighbours'. A breadknife, a large pot (for boiling potatoes and making stews) and a frying pan (for frying up the leftovers) were major constituents of every working woman's kitchen. In terms of cooking food, the gas cooker was the universal form of food preparation equipment. Electric cookers were seen as 'too dear' or 'not what my own mother used', and fridges or freezers were unavailable to keep perishable food fresh, due in the main to their prohibitive cost. However, examples of innovation and parsimony emerged during the interviews. In terms of food storage innovation, one woman commented that, 'the oven served as a fridge for keeping things cool, because it was insulated'. This interviewee also spoke of her mother 'picking up a meat safe in the Iveagh Market', where she 'safely stored food behind its wire mesh and locked steel door'. Moreover, for many Dublin women, heat-sensitive food items such as butter, margarine and lard were 'stored under a basin of water, particularly in the summer, to prevent them from running', while for others, food storage was less related to a lack of equipment, but rather that economic circumstances determined that food was purchased on a regular basis over the day, and it was by and large consumed at each meal. If there was leftover meat, it was 'covered in gauze', with most of the interviewees stating that they 'used flypaper that hung from the light-bulbs to kill flies in the kitchen'.

Throughout the interviews, there was a great sense that little or nothing was wasted. Indeed, attitudes to either the presence of waste, or what to do with it if it existed, were almost universal, in that there was normally none. Furthermore, a use could easily be found for leftover waste. References to the grease left over from cooking a roast being 'spread on bread the following day for the children going to school' were cited on more than one occasion. Even damaged, or as one woman gently characterised it 'bruised', fruit was peeled to provide some additional food for the family. These peelings and, for example, potato skins were either placed on the fire, or given to the local swine yard. One interviewee stated that 'even the food that we could not use was either fed to the neighbours' hens, or given to the pig man who came to the door for slops'.

(iv) The psychological significance of cooking and caring in the 1950s and 1960s

Despite the banality of much of the food, and the limited availability of labour-saving devices, each of the interviewees spoke at length of how they learned to cook, and what it meant to them. Here, perhaps, the most interesting of the findings emerged, in that cooking, in many ways, empowered these women, with one interviewee stating, 'You learned to cook, by just watching your mother.' Others spoke of 'learning to cook in the local convent', before adding that, 'you had to bring along a starched apron and hat, and the ingredients, which your mother had to pay for', and that 'you felt good when you brought something home'. One of the women spoke of going to Cathal Brugha Street (St Mary's College of Domestic Science) for two years, describing the college as 'trying to do something for the young girls of Dublin', and feeling very proud of learning skills like 'cooking, doing laundry, deportment and stitching'. Fundamentally, everyone knew how to cook from an early age, and being offered the opportunity of recollecting on their being 'busy' elicited fond memories for all but one of the interviewees. This lady spoke sadly of being isolated by her mother at meal preparation time, and as such feeling excluded from 'what women did' for much of her life thereafter. It is worth considering this lady's testimony, in that it encapsulates the social inclusiveness of what it meant to be able to cook and, indeed, the very opposite scenario, when one could not cook:

My mother had thirteen children, and I was the eldest. When my mother started a meal, she would ask me to take the children for a walk. When I came back, I would stand opposite my house with my back to the wall and my foot up like this, looking in through the window, and hoping for my mother to ask me in.

Asked how it impacted on her in later life, she continued:

When I got married, on the first night, I decided to cook a dinner for my husband when he came home from work. I put some cabbage into water but forgot to press it down, and it boiled away to nothing. My husband said that I could burn water, and as a result, he did the cooking for the rest of our married life.

When I suggested that this would be a blessing for today's women, she answered 'Oh no, no! I felt terrible for all those years', adding almost apologetically, 'but I could crochet'.

This, and previous comments, would suggest that despite recollections of financial hardship, lack of labour-saving equipment, large families, wayward husbands in some circumstances, and limited food choice, managing the home offered security and inclusion through being in charge the kitchen environment, which in many ways was where women did not have to be subservient, and where their opinions and food choices were, if not overtly so, respected within the wider family. And when enquiring as to how it felt for these women to move into the 1960s, the sense that there was a loss of power and control for them was evident. This decade, despite increased availability of kitchen equipment (fridges, hoovers, freezers, electric kettles etc.), televisions and record players (through hire-purchase agreements), the wider availability and lower costs of food (through greater mass production and food processing), the wider availability and acceptability of food takeaways, and the homogenisation of social classes through the wider availability of restaurant and leisure outlets, was not remembered so fondly. Asked why this was so, comments such as 'the children grew up and got jobs' and 'they went their own way' offered a sense that notwithstanding the perceived hardship of the 1950s, the 1960s took away the very things, namely being busy and valued, that made these women happiest.

Conclusion

This chapter has endeavoured to recollect the views of women who sought
to provide a basic food intake for their families in the 1950s in Dublin. The
research was carried out against a backdrop of what in some ways was both a
glorious period for Dublin fine dining restaurants (Mac Con Iomaire 2005,
2011a, 2011b), and an aspirational/image-forming period in the development of the roles and perceptions of post-war women. The findings would
suggest that for the ordinary women, the provision of the daily meal was
challenging due mainly to income constraints, food availability, how food
was purchased and stored, and the psychological importance of cooking for
and providing for their families. Of considerable significance also was the
fact that 'the swinging sixties', or as Tobin (1984) called it, 'the best of decades', were not remembered as fondly by these women as the hardship days
of the 1950s, as their pivotal role within the kitchen was gradually eroded by
increasing affluence. These were the days when the Beatles came to town,
and where the young children that they had cared for became independent
and found jobs. It was the era of show bands, fast food and fashion. They
were also the days where there was 'a virtual absence of the emigration that
had become a standard feature of Irish life since independence', and where
in 1961, *Raidió Teilifís Éireann* launched Ireland's first television service
(Ferriter 2005, p. 537). Moreover, these were the times when ordinary citizens realised that Continental package holidays had become an affordable
reality, thus fulfilling the aspirational predictions of *The Irish Housewife*
in the 1950s and, even more significantly, the availability of 'all mod con
kitchens', as promised in the previous decade, became a reality, freeing up
more time for these women, to do less. Indeed, the overwhelming compli-
ment to the women who endured the hard times of 1950s Dublin was that
they 'managed'. They learned to cook and to improvise in their cooking.
They were innovative in the face of economic shortages, large families, and,
in many cases, less than co-operative husbands, and there was little or no
waste from what they produced. We could indeed learn a lot from these
exceptional women, if we chose to listen.

Works cited

Burrell, G. and G. Morgan (2000). *Sociological Paradigms and Organisational Analysis,* Farnham, Surrey: Ashgate Publishing Limited.

Central Statistics Office. (2012). Personal correspondence with CSO official, 12 June 2012.

Clear, C. (2000). *Women of the House: Women's Household Work in Ireland 1922–1961.* Dublin: Irish Academic Press.

Cullen, B. (2005). *Golden Apples, 6 Simple Steps to Success.* London: Hodder and Stoughton.

Department of Social Protection. (2012). Personal correspondence with DSP official, 14 June 2012.

Ferriter, D. (2005). *The Transformation of Ireland: 1900–2000.* London: Profile Books Ltd.

Humphreys, A. J. (1966). *New Dubliners: Urbanisation and the Irish Family.* London: Routledge and Keegan Paul.

Kearns, K. C. (1991). *Dublin Street Life and Lore: An Oral History.* Dublin: Glendale.

Kearns, K. C. (1994). *Dublin Tenement Life: An Oral History.* Dublin: Gill and Macmillan Ltd.

Keogh, D., O'Shea F. and C. Quinlan (eds) (2004). *Ireland in the 1950s: The Lost Decade.* Cork. Mercier Press.

Mac Con Iomaire, M. (2005). 'Louis Jammet: A French Pioneer', *Hotel and Catering Review,* Vol. 38, No. 3, pp. 46–47.

Mac Con Iomaire, M. (2010). 'Hidden Voices from the Culinary Past: Oral History as a Tool for Culinary Historians', in *Food and Language,* ed. R. Hoskings, pp. 217–226. Totnes, Devon: Prospect Books.

Mac Con Iomaire, M. (2011a). 'The Changing Geography and Fortunes of Dublin's Haute Cuisine Restaurants, 1954–2008', *Food, Culture and Society: An International Journal of Multidisciplinary Research,* Vol. 14, Issue, 4, pp. 525–545.

Mac Con Iomaire, M. (2011b). 'Culinary Voices: Perspectives from Dublin Restaurants', *Oral History,* Spring 2011, pp. 65–78.

O'Brien, J. A. (ed.) (1953). *The Vanishing Irish and the Enigma of the Modern World.* New York: McGraw Hill.

Sheehy-Skeffington, H. (1946). 'Random Reflections on Housewives, Their Ways and Works', *The Irish Housewife,* Vol. 1, pp. 20–22.

Tobin, F. (1984). *The Best of Decades: Ireland in the 1960s.* Dublin: Gill & Macmillan.

Tweedy, H. (1950–1959). The Tweedy Archive 98/17/2/3/4–1 (1950–1959), National Archive, Dublin.

Tweedy, H. (1950–1951). The Tweedy Archive 98/17/2/3/5–1 (1950–1951), National Archive, Dublin.

MÁIRTÍN MAC CON IOMAIRE

'From Jammet's to Guilbaud's': The Influence of French *Haute Cuisine* on the Development of Dublin Restaurants

Gastronomy, fashion and philosophy are probably what most immediately capture the public imagination globally when one thinks of France. The most expensive and highly renowned restaurants in the western world are predominantly French whereas, historically, Ireland has not been associated with dining excellence. However, in 2011, the editor of *Le Guide du Routard*, Pierre Josse, noted that 'the Irish dining experience is now as good, if not better, than anywhere in the world'. Nonetheless, Josse reminds us that 'thirty years ago, when we first started the Irish edition, the food here was a disaster. It was very poor and there was no imagination' (Bramhill 2011). Thus it may well come as a surprise to many that Dublin had a previous golden age for *haute cuisine* in the decades after 1945, and that it centred on two world-class establishments, Restaurant Jammet and the Russell Restaurant. This chapter will outline the origins of French *haute cuisine* and will trace the story of its movement from private households to the public sphere in the form of restaurants. This brief history of Dublin's *haute cuisine* restaurants will outline the various stages of birth, prosperity, success, gradual decline, stagnation and then its subsequent resurgence in Dublin restaurants. It will also reflect on the public image of such cuisine and its purveyors over the years.

Since medieval times, Ireland had long been renowned for its hospitality. In the seventeenth and eighteenth centuries, employment of professional French chefs by an Anglo-Irish gentry class added a rich and varied cuisine to the Irish hospitality profile. These French chefs were a fashionable addition to the household. Keeping a male cook was considered the height of sophistication, but a French cook carried extra cachet. In Europe generally,

French *haute cuisine* developed in the large kitchens of the aristocracy during the seventeenth century, and the pattern spread to the kitchens of wealthy households, to restaurants and clubs. It is interesting that in most of Europe, up until the development of restaurants in the early nineteenth century, food served in public premises was less spectacular than the fare available in wealthy houses. This was also the pattern in Dublin where the appearance of restaurants was preceded by taverns, coffeehouses and clubs.

While Dublin's restaurant industry emerged in the latter half of the nineteenth century, it was from the dawn of the twentieth century that an international reputation for fine dining developed. Two leading French chefs, the brothers François and Michel Jammet, opened a restaurant in Dublin in 1901 and, up until its closure in 1967, it remained one of the best restaurants in the world. In 1949, another French chef, Pierre Rolland, arrived in Dublin as *chef de cuisine* of the Russell Hotel and the restaurant under his leadership also became world renowned. In the mid-1950s, both the Russell and Jammet's were presented with awards from the American magazine *Holiday* for being 'one of the outstanding restaurants in Europe' (*The Irish Times* 7/2/1956, p. 11). The high standard of food and service in these restaurants was confirmed in 1963 when the *Egon Ronay Guide* first covered Ireland. They awarded the Russell three stars, the highest possible award, and in the 1965 guide, Egon Ronay wrote: 'words fail us in describing the brilliance of the cuisine at this elegant and luxurious restaurant which must rank amongst the best in the world' (Ronay 1965, p. 464). However, by 1974, when the *Michelin Guide to Great Britain and Ireland* was first published, the only star awarded in Dublin to symbolise an exceptional restaurant was to the Russell Restaurant, which closed its doors that very year. It was not until 1989 that the *Michelin Guide* would again award a star to a Dublin restaurant, to Restaurant Patrick Guilbaud. However, by 2008, six Dublin restaurants shared seven stars (Guilbaud's has been awarded two stars since 1996), and three Dublin restaurants were awarded bib gourmands or Red 'M's, which symbolise excellent food and a reasonable price. The global recession and banking crisis made subsequent trading conditions extremely difficult, but Dublin's fine-dining restaurants, for the most part have withstood the recession and the 2014 *Michelin Guide* awarded stars to five establishments and four bib gourmands or Red 'M's. We are in the middle of a new 'golden age'.

Origins and spread of French *haute cuisine*

Haute cuisine has been influenced by various influential writers/chefs and has experienced a number of paradigm shifts over the centuries from La Varenne, Carême, Dubois, and Escoffier to Point, Bocuse, Guérard, Mosimann, Roux, Waters, Gagnaire, Adrià, Blumenthal and Redzepi. This chapter uses the term *haute cuisine* to cover the evolving styles of elite cuisine produced and served in restaurants by professional staff from the Escoffier orthodoxy of the early twentieth century through the '*nouvelle cuisine*' movement of the 1970s and 1980s, to the 'molecular gastronomy' or 'modernist' movement of the early twenty-first century.

French *haute cuisine* in the public sphere can be said to have originated in Paris with the appearance of restaurants during the latter half of the eighteenth century. This phenomenon was greatly boosted following the French Revolution when the number of restaurants increased dramatically (Spang 2000, pp. 130–133; Mennell 1996, pp. 141–142). Restaurants have been differentiated from a tavern, inn or a *table d'hôte* by a number of factors. Firstly, they provided private tables for customers; secondly, they offered a choice of individually priced dishes in the form of a *carte* or bill of fare; and thirdly, they offered food at times that suited the customer, not at one fixed time as in the case of the *table d'hôte* (Brillat-Savarin 1994, p. 267). The spread of restaurants to London or Dublin was slow, primarily due to the abundance of gentlemen's clubs which siphoned off much of the prospective clientele for restaurants in those cities. However, meals had been available to the public in Dublin's alehouses, taverns, inns and eating-houses for centuries. Indeed, Constantia Maxwell noted that Dublin was renowned for its taverns and ale-houses since Elizabethan times; such establishments mostly served good solid plain food such as steaks and chops, rather than the elite cuisine which was provided by French male cooks in the homes of the aristocracy (Maxwell 2010, p. 26).

Evidence of French *haute cuisine* in private Irish households

The eating habits of both the English upper classes, and subsequently the new Anglo-Irish upper classes, were influenced by their continental neighbours. Between 1603 and 1649, the first two Stuart kings, James I and Charles I, espoused Spanish, French and Italian fashions and ideas, including cooking (Spencer 2004, p. 134). Many of the Ascendancy families led hedonistic lifestyles (Robins 2001). The Anglo-Irish ascendancy adopted some of the extraordinary hospitality that had been part of the Gaelic tradition but, with the employment of a professional French chef having become the fashion, their conspicuous consumption was much more sophisticated; they thus emulated the eating patterns of London and Paris. Evidence exists in culinary manuscripts and in some printed cookbooks of the period that show how prevalent the influence of French *haute cuisine* was at this time among the Anglo-Irish aristocracy (Mac Con Iomaire and Cashman 2011, pp. 81–101).

The emergence of restaurants in Dublin

Establishments using the term restaurant became common in the latter half of the nineteenth century. More than twenty-six different Dublin-based restaurants advertised in *The Irish Times* from 1865 to 1900, and the notices included an advertisement announcing the opening of a 'High-Class Vegetarian Restaurant' at 3 and 4 College Street (22/6/1899, p. 1). The first specific evidence of a French restaurant serving *haute cuisine* in

Dublin is an advertisement in *The Irish Times* for the Café de Paris in 1861. The advertisement is clearly aimed at an upmarket clientele as it directs the attention of the nobility and gentry to their establishment where 'Breakfasts, Luncheons and Dinners &c. are supplied in the best French style' (14/2/1861, p. 1). This restaurant was linked with a Turkish Baths in Lincoln Place and was run by Messrs Muret and Olin. The Café de Paris was enlarged in 1865 for the International Exhibition with the addition of three private dining rooms. They also advertised both 'dinners à la Carte and Table d'Hôte; choicest Wines and Liqueurs of all kinds, Ices, &c. &c.' (25/9/1865, p. 1). In February 1870, the lease of the Café de Paris was offered for sale, and by November of 1870, an advertisement appeared for the Café de Paris with a T. Woycke as proprietor, heralding a 'Restaurant Français A la Carte' with a ladies' coffee room and dining rooms for small parties provided for' (26/11/1870, p. 4).

The opening of a second 'French' restaurant at Maloz Hotel, 20 and 21 South Anne Street, was advertised in *The Irish Times* in December 1870. The proprietor was a Mr G. Beats, late of the Provence Hotel, Leicester Square, London. He advertised dinners at two shillings at all times, and noted that 'Every thing served in the Parisian style. French Men-cooks kept. A speciality for soups' (9/12/1870, p. 1). It is unclear how long the restaurant prospered, since in November of the following year, advertisements appeared for Walshe's Hotel at the same address. An advertisement in 1876 for the Corn Exchange Hotel and Restaurant on Burgh Quay boasts that no expense will be spared 'to make the Cuisine under a French Chef, the most attractive in the city'. In November 1884, Thomas Corless advertised in *The Irish Times* the presence of a 'First-class French Cook' in the Burlington Restaurant and Dining Rooms, Andrew Street and Church Lane (1/11/1884, p. 4). However, the next specific mention of a French restaurant, rather than a restaurant with a French cook, is not until an advertisement in *The Irish Times* in August 1890 for a French restaurant attached to the Bodega on Dame Street (28/8/1890, p. 4).

Influence of foreign chefs/restaurateurs

Analysis of the 1911 Census shows that the leading chefs, waiters and restaurateurs during the first decades of the twentieth century were predominantly foreign-born, and had trained in the leading restaurants, hotels and clubs of Europe (Mac Con Iomaire 2008, pp. 92–126). *Haute cuisine* was advertised as available in the dining rooms of the best hotels in Dublin (Gresham, Shelbourne, Metropole, Royal Hibernian) in the first half of the twentieth century and these were the workplaces of those immigrant chefs. Along with the Jammet brothers, other European families such as the Geldofs, Oppermanns, Gygaxs and Bessons were also influential in developing the restaurant business in Dublin. Paul Besson came to Dublin from London in 1905 as manager of the Royal Hibernian Hotel on Dawson Street. Over the decades, Paul Besson, along with his son Kenneth and other members of his family, took control of the Royal Hibernian, the Russell Hotel and the Bailey Restaurant on Duke Street.

Arguably, the most notable amongst those chefs were the Jammets. Michel (1858–1931) and François (1853–1940) Jammet were born in St Julia de Bec, near Quillan, in the French Pyrenees. Michel first came to Dublin in 1887 as chef to Henry Roe, the distiller. Following four years working in London for Lord Cadogan, he returned to Dublin in 1895, becoming head chef at the Vice Regal Lodge when Lord Cadogan became Lord Lieutenant of Ireland. In 1888, François became head chef of the Café de Deux Mondes, rue de La Paix, Paris, and he then moved to the Boeuf à la Mode, Rue de Valois, Palais Royal, where he married the owner's daughter, Eugenie. In 1900, Michel and François Jammet bought the Burlington Restaurant and Oyster Saloons at 27 St Andrew Street, Dublin from Tom Corless. They refitted, and renamed it The Jammet Hotel and Restaurant in 1901, and it became preeminent among the restaurants of Dublin. Its clientele included leading politicians, nobility, actors, writers and artists such as William Orpen and Harry Kernoff, whose painting of the restaurant now hangs in Dublin's Restaurant Patrick Guilbaud (see Figure 1). In 1908, François Jammet returned to the Boeuf à la Mode in Paris. There, his

Figure 1: The Jammet Hotel and Restaurant (Andrew Street) by Harry Kernoff.
Source: Restaurant Patrick Guilbaud – The Merrion Hotel, Dublin.

two children, Hippolyte and Jeanne, both followed him into the catering trade. They acquired the Hotel Bristol in 1925 which remained in the family until 1978 (Mac Con Iomaire 2009, pp. 956–958).

Jammet's Hotel and Restaurant traded at 26–27 Andrew Street and 6 Church Lane until the lease reverted to the Hibernian Bank in 1926. Michel Jammet acquired Kidd's Empire Restaurant and Tea Rooms at 45–46 Nassau Street at this time and brought some of the fittings from the original premises. When he retired in 1927, his son Louis took over the running of the business while Michel returned to Paris where he was a director and the principal shareholder of the Hotel Bristol until his death in 1931.

The new Restaurant Jammet in Nassau Street traded successfully from 1927 until its closure in 1967. It became *the* haunt for artists and the literary set, and the Jammets took pride in the fact that it was Dublin's only French restaurant. The new restaurant had, as a centrepiece, four murals depicting the Four Seasons – they had been painted by the artist Bossini in order to discharge his bill in the old Burlington Restaurant. The new premises was described by John Ryan, a regular customer, as: 'the main dining room was pure French Second Empire, with a lovely faded patina to the furniture, snow white linen, well cut crystal, monogrammed porcelain, gourmet sized silver-plated cutlery and gleaming decanters' (1987, p. 3). There were two entrances: the 'posh' one was in Nassau Street, the ordinary one was in an alley off Grafton Street at Adam's Court. The premises boasted a smoking room and an Oyster Bar where lunch could be taken at a wide marble counter from a high stool. The literati, like Liam O' Flaherty and Seán O' Sullivan, drank here. Louis's wife Yvonne had a reputation in her own right as an excellent painter and sculptor and as a member of the *avant garde* painters' group, 'The White Stag'. She also worked on stage and in costume design for the Gate Theatre. W. B. Yeats had his own table in Jammet's. On 6 March 1933, he dined in the 'Blue Room' with fellow writers A. E., Brinsley Macnamara, James Stephens, Lennox Robinson, F. R. Higgins, Seamus O' Sullivan, Peadar O' Donnell, Francis Stuart, Frank O' Connor, Miss Somerville, J. M. Hone and Walter Starkie. When Josef Reukli, the Swiss maitre d'hôtel, was asked to describe the clientele, he replied '*La crème de la crème*'. In 1944, the new Grill Room was opened upstairs. It was designed by the architect Noel Moffet in a futurist style (Mac Con Iomaire 2009, p. 957).

Over many years, Restaurant Jammet maintained its position as the finest restaurant producing *haute cuisine* in Dublin. Until the appointment of Pierre Rolland as head chef of the Russell in 1949, Jammet's was also 'the only restaurant in Dublin with an international reputation for its cuisine' (Graves 1949). Indeed, according to Lacoste, Jammet's was the only place in the British Isles where one could eat well in the grand French tradition: '*À Dublin, ... on trouve une cuisine digne de la grande tradition française*' (Lacoste 1947).

A golden age of *haute cuisine* in Dublin

The 1947–1974 period can be viewed as a 'golden age' of *haute cuisine* in Dublin, since more award-winning world-class restaurants traded in Dublin during this period than at any other time in history. In the late 1940s, the Red Bank Restaurant re-opened as a fine dining restaurant with a French head chef producing *haute cuisine*. Newspaper reports of gastronomic dinners held by the Irish branch of André L. Simon's Food and Wine Society provide evidence of the growing interest in *haute cuisine* during this time. Both the Russell Restaurant and Restaurant Jammet received awards from the American magazine *Holiday* in the 1950s for being 'outstanding restaurants in Europe' (*The Irish Times*, 7/2/1956, p. 11). Further evidence of Dublin restaurants' status as culinary leaders became evident when the *Egon Ronay Guide* first covered Ireland in 1963. By 1965, Ronay suggested that the Russell Restaurant 'must rank amongst the best in the world' (Ronay 1965, p. 464). The majority of the award-winning Dublin restaurants produced a form of *haute cuisine* that had been codified by Escoffier; it was labour-intensive and it was silver-served by large teams of waiters in elegant dining rooms.

The beginnings of expertise transfer occurred in the early 1950s when an agreement between Ken Besson and the Irish Transport and General Workers Union (IT&GWU) allowed foreign-born chefs and waiters to work in Ireland in return for Irish apprentices being indentured in the Besson-owned Russell and Royal Hibernian Hotels under the guidance of chefs Pierre Rolland and Roger Noblet. *The Irish Hotelier* described Rolland as 'numbered among the ten most distinguished culinary experts in France' (Anon 1954, p. 13). Under his leadership, the Russell Hotel kitchen became a training ground for generations of Irish chefs. By the late 1950s and early 1960s there were fewer foreign chefs or waiters working in Dublin. They had been replaced by foreign-trained Irish chefs and waiters. During this period, the catering branch of the IT&GWU strongly opposed the employment of foreign staff. Oral evidence suggests that some Irish chefs and waiters were pressurised to take senior positions, in order to exclude suitable foreign-born candidates (McGee 2004; Sands 2003). Two Irish chefs, Vincent Dowling in Restaurant Jammet, and Joe Collins in Jury's Hotel, Dame Street, were sent abroad for training – to Paris and Switzerland – before returning to become *chef de cuisine* in their respective restaurants. The move from French to Irish head chefs, combined with a new Irish culinary aesthetic inspired by *An Tóstal*, may have influenced the change in listings of certain Dublin restaurants in the 1965 *Egon Ronay Guide*. In that year, the classification of Shelbourne Hotel Restaurant, Red Bank Restaurant, Haddington House Hotel Restaurant, Metropole Georgian Room, Intercontinental Embassy Restaurant and Gresham Hotel Grill room was changed from 'French' cuisine to 'Franco-Irish' cuisine. Restaurant Jammet and the Royal Hibernian's Lafayette Restaurant remained listed as 'French', whereas the Russell was listed as '*Haute Cuisine*'. However, restaurants such as the Old Ground Hotel in Ennis and the Pontoon Bridge Hotel in Mayo were listed as 'Plain Cooking' (Ronay 1965).

In the 1950s and 1960s, French classical cuisine was dominant in the Shelbourne, Gresham and Moira Hotels, although analysis of the *Egon Ronay Guide* indicates a drop in the standard of food in some Dublin hotels by the mid-1960s. The arrival of the Swiss master chef, Willy Widmer, helped to improve the standard of food in Jury's Hotel, Dame Street, during the 1960s; the opening of the Intercontinental Hotel in Ballsbridge in 1963 brought several more foreign-born chefs to Dublin. Both hotels became nurseries for future native culinary talent. However, oral evidence from one of the Intercontinental's Irish chefs, Jim Bowe, suggests that standards dropped again when the foreign chefs left, and as the owners began to focus more on making a profit than on maintaining standards. This was also reflected in the *Egon Ronay Guides*, with the Intercontinental Hotel's Embassy Restaurant which was awarded one star from 1964–1966, failing to repeat that success in 1967 or in subsequent years.

Decline of *haute cuisine* (1967–1974)

A new phenomenon appeared towards the end of the 1960s when enthusiastic amateurs opened restaurants such as Snaffles on Leeson Street
(Nicholas Tinne) and The Soup Bowl in Molesworth Lane (Peter Powrie).
This reflected a similar trend that had occurred slightly earlier in England
(Driver 1983; Houston-Bowden 1975, p. 127). A number of factors led to
the demise of the traditional Escoffier style *haute cuisine* in Dublin restaurants by the early 1970s. Political and economic factors such as the Dublin
bombings, the OPEC oil crisis, and banking strikes, all played some part
in the demise. It has also been suggested that another factor, the revival of
'wealth tax' by the Fine Gael political party in their 1973 election mani-
festo, resulted in a mass exodus of landed gentry from Ireland. O'Sullivan
and O'Neill (1999, p. 161) claim that the Shelbourne Hotel witnessed an
instant 20 per cent drop in business in 1973, and that the Russell Hotel
was also affected. The latter closed in 1974.

It must also be taken into account that the growing trend towards
suburban living and the rising importance of car parking were two relevant
factors: they were reasons given for the closure of Restaurant Jammet in
1967 (Hood 2006). Dublin's golden age of *haute cuisine* ended with that
closure, and the subsequent closures of the Red Bank Restaurant in 1969
and the Russell Hotel in 1974. The Royal Hibernian Hotel then assumed
the mantle of Dublin's last bastion of 'Escoffier style' *haute cuisine* until it
too closed its doors in 1982.[1]

---

1   The building was subsequently redeveloped into offices and a shopping arcade, the
     Royal Hibernian Way.

Haute cuisine (1974–1986)

The appearance of a growing number of suburban restaurants such as The Mirabeau, Goat Grill, Shangri la, Guinea Pig, Sutton House and The King Sitric during the 1970s reflects this trend towards the suburban, while centre-city restaurants such as Snaffles and The Soup Bowl, opened by enthusiastic amateurs, became the new venues for Dublin gourmands. Country house hotels such as Ashford Castle and Arbutus Lodge, with Russell-trained chefs in their kitchens, then emerged at the centre of *haute cuisine* in Ireland in the 1970s and early 1980s. Declan Ryan of Arbutus Lodge credits discerning French tourists with being the arbiters of taste at his Cork city restaurant and their arrival was facilitated by the new direct Rosslare-Le Havre ferry link in 1973.

Fine dining restaurants in Dublin did not totally disappear during the 1970s and 1980s, but there was a distinct decline in restaurants with an international reputation. Restaurants such as The Lord Edward (run by ex-Red Bank chefs and waiters) and The Celtic Mews, run by Joe Gray (ex-Jury's Dame Street) provided consistent '*cuisine bourgeoise*'. The real growth area in good dining at this time, both in Dublin and elsewhere in Europe, was the emergence of restaurants run by chef/proprietors.

Nouvelle cuisine and the rise of the chef/proprietor

The *nouvelle cuisine* movement was rooted in the '*cuisine de marché*' which originated as a rebellion against the Escoffier orthodoxy, particularly as it had become stultified in international hotel cuisine. A synopsis of Henri Gault's 'ten commandments' of *nouvelle cuisine* includes: reduced cooking time for fish, game, vegetables and pasta; smaller menus based on market fresh ingredients; invention of new dishes; embracing advanced technology; the aesthetics of simplicity; and a knowledge of dietetics (Gault 1996, pp. 123–127). Stephen Mennell has pointed out that Gault and Millau forgot to include one characteristic common to most of the *nouveaux cuisiniers*, that they were mostly chef-proprietors of their own restaurants (Mennell 1996, p. 164).

One of the first Dublin restaurants to be opened by a chef/proprietor was The King Sitric (Aidan McManus) in Howth (1971–present). This was followed by The Mirabeau (Sean Kinsella) in Sandycove (1972–1984), Johnny's (Johnny Opperman) in Malahide (1974–1989), Le Coq Hardi (John Howard) in Ballsbridge (1977–2001), The Guinea Pig (Mervyn Stewart) in Dalkey (1977–present), and Rolland (Henri Rolland) in Killiney (1974–c.1986).[2] The most famous of these early chef/proprietor restaurants were The Mirabeau and Le Coq Hardi. Some of the restaurants listed above shared many characteristics covered in Gault's 'ten commandments' of *nouvelle cuisine*, most particularly the use of fresh seasonal local produce. However, the lack of a codified repertoire makes it difficult to pinpoint who was serving *nouvelle cuisine* in Dublin, chiefly since trends were changing quite rapidly, particularly in the 1980s with influences coming from various ethnic and fusion cuisines.

Three restaurants, all of which opened in the 1980s, can be said to best represent the *nouvelle cuisine* movement in Dublin. They are Restaurant Patrick Guilbaud, The Park and White's on the Green. Patrick Guilbaud, a French-born chef, had trained in the leading restaurants in Paris before moving to Manchester to learn English and eventually opening his own restaurant in Cheshire where one of his customers, Barton Kilcoyne, invited him to visit Dublin. He soon moved to Dublin and opened a purpose-built restaurant that set new standards in dining, ones that had been missing since the Jammet era. A description of Restaurant Patrick Guilbaud in *The Irish Times* is brief: 'the restaurant is bright and elegant with French staff serving French food' (2/6/1982, p. 7). The restaurant did not enjoy immediate commercial success; it took a while for the Irish clientele to become accustomed to the small portions and *la nouvelle cuisine d'Irlande* served by Guilbaud. The restaurant, however, did receive critical acclaim, being

---

2   Henri Rolland was the son of the famous Pierre Rolland from the Russell Hotel and was awarded a Red 'M' from the Michelin Guide from 1978–1981 (see Table 1).

awarded an Egon Ronay star in 1983, and also earning a recommenda-
tion from *The Good Food Guide* in 1983, and a Bord Fáilte award in 1984.
From the opening of the restaurant, Patrick Guilbaud remained in charge
of the front of house and promoted Guillaume Lebrun as his head chef.
Aidan McManus dined in Restaurant Patrick Guilbaud within weeks of
its opening and records his shock that the bar 'had been raised so high'
(McManus 2008).

The early 1980s proved to be a difficult time for Irish restaurateurs
due to a combination of general economic conditions and particular fiscal
changes made by the government. Many young Irish chefs and waiters
emigrated during this period although some would return during the late
1980s and early 1990s with experience of *nouvelle cuisine* and fusion cuisine gained in the leading restaurants of London, Paris, New York and
California. Restaurant Patrick Guilbaud ran into financial difficulties in
the mid-1980s, but an investment by two wealthy clients cleared the restaurant's debts. Their trust was rewarded when the restaurant won its first
Michelin star in 1989, the first Dublin Michelin star since the closure of
the Russell Hotel in 1974. The restaurant was awarded two Michelin stars
in 1996 and it moved premises in 1997 with the opening of the five-star
Merrion Hotel where it is now located.

For the last two decades of the twentieth century, Restaurant Patrick
Guilbaud set the standard of *haute cuisine* that other restaurants emulated.
Its kitchen and dining room also acted as nurseries for young talent, both
Irish and foreign-born. Some restaurants even advertised that their chef was
'ex-Patrick Guilbaud's' as a marker of the high standard of food they served.
Ex-Guilbaud staff have been involved in most successful Dublin restaurants
during the last twenty years, including Sebastian Masi (Commons, Pearl
Brasserie, Locks), Stefan Couzy (Morels, Duzy's), Bruno Bertha (Brunos)
and Penny Plunkett (Venu, Mercantile).

Other acclaimed *nouvelle cuisine* restaurants in Dublin in the mid-
1980s were Colin O'Daly's The Park in the south city suburb of Blackrock
and White's on the Green in the city centre. O'Daly had trained under
Russell Hotel chefs in Dublin Airport and in Ashford Castle. The chef
in White's was Michael Clifford, who had trained in Arbutus Lodge in
Cork and had won a Michelin star with the Ryan family in Cashel Palace,

Co. Tipperary, in 1982 and 1983. Clifford had spent twelve years working outside Ireland in restaurants such as Le Gavroche and the Waterside Inn in England, run by the Roux brothers. He had also worked at the two-star Michelin Parisian restaurant Michel Rostang (O'Byrne 1988, p. 23). His food and its presentation were influenced by the *nouvelle cuisine* that he had experienced abroad. In 1988, however, Clifford left to open his own restaurant in Cork. Giles O'Reilly, who worked as chef in both The Park and White's on the Green notes that the late 1980s was a difficult time for fine dining restaurants in Dublin. He points out that apart from Restaurant Patrick Guilbaud and The Park, the new interesting restaurant at that time was Shay Beano's, where Eamon Ó Catháin, an enthusiastic amateur in the style of Powrie and Tinne, cooked French provincial food (O'Reilly 2008). The late-1980s and early-1990s saw the opening of exciting new restaurants such as The Wine Epergne (Kevin Thornton) and Clarets (Alan O'Reilly), both of which produced fine dining despite difficult economic conditions.

Rebirth of *haute cuisine* (1994–2008)

Some Irish chefs such as Johnny Cooke (Polo One, Cooke's Café) had worked in America and returned in the late 1980s with the latest Californian food ideas, influenced by Alice Waters and Jeremiah Towers. Other Irish chefs such as Kevin Thornton (The Wine Epergne, Thorntons), Michael Martin (La Stampa, The Tea Rooms), Shay Kirwan (The Commons), Paul Cartwright (Roly's Bistro), Paul Flynn (La Stampa, The Tannery), James Carberry (ESB, DIT), John Dunne (Les Frères Jacques, The Park, Duzy's), and Conrad Gallagher (Morels, Peacock Alley, Christopher's, Mango Toast) returned to Dublin having worked in the kitchens of Michelin-starred chefs in England and France. In turn, these returning Irish chefs trained the current generation of Irish chefs in the latest techniques of *haute cuisine* which remained firmly rooted in the French culinary canon. Thus the 1990s was an exciting time for Dublin restaurants, particularly in the latter half of the decade. *The Irish Times* reported that Ireland had the most dynamic cuisine in any European country, a place where in the last decade 'a vibrant almost unlikely style of cooking has emerged' (McKenna 1996, p. 44). Yet, the real growth in *haute cuisine* did not become apparent until 1994 when The Commons on Stephen's Green was awarded a Michelin star and both Ernie's (Ernie Evans) in Donnybrook and Clarets (Alan O'Reilly) in Blackrock were awarded Red 'M's.

Table 1: Dublin Restaurants awarded Michelin Stars or Red 'M's 1989–2001.
Note: From 1974 to 1989 only two awards in Dublin (1974 one star Russell Hotel; 1978–1981 Red 'M' Restaurant Rolland).

Name of Restaurant	1989	1990	1991	1992	1993	1994	1995	1996	1997	1998	1999	2000	2001
Restaurant Patrick Guilbaud	*	*	*	*	*	*	*	**	**	**	**	**	**
The Commons						*	*	*	*				
Thornton's, Portobello								*	*	*	*	*	**
L'Ecrivain, Baggot St.								M	M	M	M		
Peacock Alley										*	*	*	*
Chapter One								M	M	M	M	M	M
Ernie's, Donnybrook						M	M	M	M	M	M	M	M
The Park, Blackrock		M	M	M									
Clarets, Blackrock						M	M						
Blueberry's, Blackrock												M	M
Jacobs Ladder, Nassau St.											M	M	M
Lloyd's Brasserie											M	M	
Mermaid Café, Dame St.											M	M	M
Morel's at Stephens Hall											M	M	M
Roly's Bistro, Dublin 4							M	M	M				
Morels (Duzy's Café in 2001), Glasthule									M	M	M	M	M

Table 2: Dublin Restaurants awarded Michelin Stars or Red 'M's 2002–2014.

Name of Restaurant	2002	2003	2004	2005	2006	2007	2008	2009	2010	2011	2012	2013	2014
Restaurant Patrick Guilbaud	* *	* *	* *	* *	* *	* *	* *	* *	* *	* *	* *	* *	* *
The Commons	*												
Thornton's Resaturant, Fitzwilliam Hotel	* *	* *	* *	* *	*	*	*	*	*	*	*	*	*
L'Ecrivain, Baggot St.		*	*	*	*	*	*	*	*	*	*	*	*
Peacock Alley	*												
Chapter One, Parnell Sq.							*	*	*	*	*	*	*
Bon Appétit, Malahide							*	*	*	*	*	*	*
Mint, Ranelagh							*	*					
Locks Brasserie												*	
Jacobs Ladder Nassau St. (The Pigs Ear in 2010)	M	M	M	M	M				M	M	M	M	M
Mermaid Café, Dame St.	M												
Duzy's Café, Glasthule	M	M											
La Maison de Gourmet		M	M	M	M	M	M	M	M	M			
Bang Café, Merrion Row		M	M	M	M	M	M	M					
The Winding Stair							M	M					
Pichet, Andrew St.									M	M	M	M	M
Box Tree, Stepaside											M	M	
Downstairs at Gilbert & Wright, Clontarf												M	M
Brasserie at Bon Appétit													M

Factors influencing this new dynamism included the rising wealth of
Irish citizens which made dining in restaurants a regular pastime rather
than an occasional treat, and also the changing tastes of the Irish public
who were more widely-travelled than any previous Irish generation. In
1996, the year Michelin awarded two stars to Restaurant Patrick Guilbaud,
Thornton's Restaurant in Portobello received its first star. In 1998, another
Michelin star was awarded to Conrad Gallagher's Peacock Alley in South
Anne Street. Peacock Alley moved to the Fitzwilliam Hotel on Stephen's
Green the following year. By 1999, the chief executive of the Restaurant
Association of Ireland (RAI) declared 'we have a dining culture now, which
we never did before' (Holmquist 1999, p. 43). In 2000, Dublin restaurants
were awarded four Michelin stars and eight Michelin red 'M' symbols; in
contrast, only two Michelin stars were awarded in the Republic of Ireland
outside Dublin, and a further two stars were given in Northern Ireland.
Dublin, once again, had become the centre of *haute cuisine* in Ireland and
a second 'golden age' was emerging (see Tables 1 & 2). A full breakdown
of Michelin stars and Egon Ronay stars for the island of Ireland can be
accessed in Mac Con Iomaire (2015 forthcoming).

In 2001, Kevin Thornton became the first native Irish chef to be
awarded two Michelin stars. In the first years of the new millennium,
Michelin stars were awarded to L'Écrivain (Derry Clarke) on Baggot Street,
and to Chapter One (Ross Lewis) in Parnell Square which had held Red
'M's from the mid-1990s. Lorcan Cribben returned from working in the Ivy
in London to win a Michelin Red 'M' in three different Dublin restaurants
in the last decade: Lloyd's Brasserie, Morel's at Stephen's Hall and Bang
Café. Two further Michelin stars were awarded in 2008 to Bon Appetit
(Oliver Dunne) in Malahide, and to Mint (Dylan McGrath) in Ranelagh.
Both Dunne and McGrath trained in Dublin's best restaurants, such as
The Commons, then in London with Gordon Ramsay, Tom Aikens and
John Burton Race before returning home. They both remain key players in
Dublin's fine-dining industry and their kitchens have become the training
ground for the next generation of Irish chefs.

In January 2011, *Le Guide du Routard*, the travel bible for the French-
speaking world, praised Ireland's restaurants for being unmatched the world
over for the combination of quality of food, value and service (Bramhill

2011). This second 'golden age' has been maintained despite the difficult economic conditions of the recession. The 2014 Michelin Guide not only awarded stars to five Dublin restaurants, but also awarded stars to four other Irish restaurants outside Dublin – the highest number of starred restaurants in Ireland since the Guide was first published in 1974. The projection and presentation of Irish cuisine, both foreign-influenced and home-inspired, have given it a notable public profile. Its beginnings were in the origins of French *haute cuisine*; its further progress came in the development of restaurants, especially in the early golden age of Dublin restaurants, the ones so strongly influenced by French families such as the Jammets, Bessons and Rollands, all of whom adopted Ireland as home. The latest important French influence is prospering: Patrick Guilbaud was advised that if his restaurant was half as successful as Jammet's had been, he would be doing extremely well. Restaurant Patrick Guilbaud, now over thirty years in business, has already outlasted the Russell Restaurant in longevity but has still has over another thirty years to go to equal Jammet's as the most influential and successful French restaurant Ireland has had (Ryan 2011, p. 3). There is a neat symbolism involved in Patrick Guilbaud's purchase of the Harry Kernoff painting of Jammet's: it signifies both continuity and tradition, it ties *haute cuisine* to Irish imagery, and it reflects the degree to which French influence has dominated Irish public imagination in that most important area over at least two centuries.

Works cited

Anon. (1954). 'The Russell Hotel'. *The Irish Hotelier*. (Feb 1954). p. 13.

Bowe, J. (2008). Unpublished interview with Mac Con Iomaire in Blackrock (30 April 2008).

Bramhill, N. (2011). 'Irish chefs best in World', *Sunday Independent*, 9 January. <http://www.independent.ie/irish-news/irish-chefs-best-in-world-26612329.html> [accessed 7 January 2014]

Brillat-Savarin, J. A. (1994). *The Physiology of Taste*. Translated by A. Drayton. London: Penguin Classics.

Driver, C. (1983). *The British at Table 1940–1980*. London: Chatto & Windus – The Hogarth Press.

Gault, H. (1996). 'Nouvelle Cuisine'. In *Cooks and Other People: Proceedings of the Oxford Symposium on Food and Cookery 1995*, ed. H. Walker, pp. 123–127. Totnes, Devon: Prospect Books.

Graves, C. (1949). *Ireland Revisited*. London, New York: Hutchinson.

Holmquist, K. (1999). 'Take a top chef, place in a swanky location and stir well for a winning restaurant'. *The Irish Times*, 20 October, p. 43.

Hood, R. (2006). Unpublished interview with Mac Con Iomaire in Enniskerry (18 January 2006).

Houston-Bowden, G. (1975). *British Gastronomy: The Rise of Great Restaurants*. London: Chatto & Windus.

Lacoste, R. (1947). 'Les Cuisiniers Francais Partis: Les Anglais ne mangent plus que des conserves et des soupes en poudre'. *Journal l'Epoque*, 22 June 1947.

Mac Con Iomaire, M. (2004). 'Pierre Rolland – Ireland's First Michelin Star Chef'. *Hotel & Catering Review* Vol. 37, no. 12. p. 45.

Mac Con Iomaire, M. (2005). 'Louis Jammet: A French Pioneer'. *Hotel & Catering Review* Vol. 38 no. 3, pp. 46–47.

Mac Con Iomaire, M. (2006). 'Louis Jammet'. In *Culinary Biographies*, ed. A. Arndt, pp. 218–219. Houston, Texas: Yes Press Inc.

Mac Con Iomaire, M. (2008). 'Searching for Chefs, Waiters and Restaurateurs in Edwardian Dublin: A Culinary Historian's Experience of the 1911 Dublin Census Online'. *Petits Propos Culinaires* Vol 86. pp. 92–126.

Mac Con Iomaire, M. (2009). 'Louis Jammet'. In *Dictionary of Irish Biography*, Vol. 4, ed. J. McGuire, pp. 956–958. Cambridge: Cambridge University Press.

Mac Con Iomaire, M. (2011). 'The Changing Geography and Fortunes of Dublin's Haute Cuisine Restaurants 1958–2008'. *Food, Culture & Society*, vol. 14. no. 4. pp. 525–545.

Mac Con Iomaire, M. (2013). 'Public Dining in Dublin: The History and Evolution of Gastronomy and Commercial Dining 1700–1900'. *International Journal of Contemporary Hospitality Management*. vol. 25 no. 2. pp. 227–246.

Mac Con Iomaire, M. (2015 forthcoming). 'The Development of Haute Cuisine Restaurants in Ireland'. *Proceedings of the Royal Irish Academy (Section C)*. Special issue: Food and Drink in Ireland. Thematic volume 115C.

Mac Con Iomaire, M. and D. Cashman. (2011). 'Irish Culinary Manuscripts and Printed Cookbooks: A Discussion'. *Petit Propos Culinaires*. vol. 94. pp. 81–101.

Maxwell, C. (1979). *Dublin under the Georges 1714–1830*. Dublin: Gill & Macmillan.

McGee, A. (2004). Unpublished interview with Mac Con Iomaire in Monkstown (6 January 2004).

McKenna, J. (1996). 'Euro Nosh'. *The Irish Times*, 26 June, p. 44.

Mennell, S. (1996). *All Manners of Food (Second Edition)*. Chicago: University of Illinois Press.

Michelin Guide. (1974). *Michelin Red Guide 1974 Great Britain and Ireland*. London: Michelin Tyre Public Limited Company.

O' Sullivan, M. and B. O' Neill (1999). *The Shelbourne and its people*. Dublin: Blackwater Press.

O'Byrne, S. (1988). 'Cooking Come Home: Is it time for Irish cuisine to come of age?' *The Irish Times*. 3 December 1988. p. 23.

O'Reilly, G. (2008). Unpublished interview with Mac Con Iomaire in Rialto (19 May 2008).

Robins, J. (2001). *Champagne & Silver Buckles: The Viceregal Court at Dublin Castle 1700–1922*. Dublin: The Lilliput Press.

Ronay, E. (1965). *Egon Ronay's 1965 Guide to Hotels and Restaurants in Great Britain and Ireland with 32 Motoring Maps*. London: Gastronomes Limited.

Ryan, J. (1987). 'There'll never be another Jammet's'. *The Irish Times*, Weekend, 11 April, p. 3.

Ryan, S. (2011). *Restaurant Patrick Guilbaud: The First Thirty Years*. Dublin: Guilbaud Books.

Sands, C. (2003). Unpublished interview with Mac Con Iomaire in DIT Cathal Brugha Street (5 June 2003).

Spang, R. L. (2000). *The Invention of the Restaurant: Paris and Modern Gastronomic Culture*. Cambridge: Harvard University Press.

Spencer, C. (2004). *British Food: An Extraordinary Thousand Years of History*. London: Grub Street.

MARJORIE DELEUZE

A New Craze for Food:
Why is Ireland Turning into a Foodie Nation?

As one observes the Irish culinary scene today, an impression of abundance, hedonism and hyperconsumption pervading all food-related areas emerges. Ireland has gone mad about food: there has been a profusion of cookbooks and TV cookery programmes, starring celebrity chefs as well as completely unknown figures. In addition, there are numerous food festivals, farmers' markets, food blogs, food exhibitions and eclectic restaurants to cater for gourmet cosmopolitan tastes; and the explosion of food-oriented businesses has changed the face of modern Ireland. The Republic is writing a new page in its culinary history and this new phenomenon cannot go unnoticed. How can these changes be interpreted? Should this be regarded as a mere fashion fad within a wider global context, or as a real cultural, artistic and sociological revolution reflecting Ireland's current aspirations?

Interest in food in Ireland is not new, but it seems to have reached a peak in recent years. One could say that Ireland is turning into a 'foodie nation'. First coined in 1980 by Gael Greene, a food critic writing at the time for the *New York Magazine*, the word 'foodies' (Greene 1980, p. 33) was used to depict the devotees of a renowned French chef, *aficionados* enraptured by her refined cuisine. In 1984, Ann Barr and Paul Levy popularised its usage in *The Official Foodie Handbook*. They define 'foodies' as 'children of the consumer boom [who] consider food to be an art, on a level with painting or drama. [...] Foodism crosses all boundaries and is understood in all languages' (Barr and Levy 1984, p. 6). As the book is intended as a satire of its time, the word pejoratively connotes people who demonstrate a rather snobbish and demanding attitude towards what they eat, as well as food-fetishism. The term has progressively lost its negative meaning. It has evolved into a generally accepted term, though one which sometimes retains a 'mocking edge' (Goldstein 2011, pp. iii–iv). According to the *Oxford Dictionary*, a foodie is 'a person with a particular interest in food or a gourmet', or for the *Collins Dictionary*, 'a person having an enthusiastic interest in the preparation and the consumption of good food'. In short, since everyone has their own definition of what 'good food' is, anyone can be a 'foodie' today; it is no longer the exclusive preserve of the well-off.

In many ways, Ireland seems to follow the social trends of globalised societies. The Celtic Tiger launched Ireland onto the international scene. It is now commonly acknowledged that Ireland is a serious competitor in many sectors (notably in the IT and pharmaceutical industries) and that, in recent decades, Irish society, as is true of the Western world more generally, has undergone a process of homogenisation, especially in terms of consumerism. With the economic boom, Ireland entered the age of 'hyperconsumption'. As Lipovetsky (2005, p. 32) explains: 'In every domain there is a certain excessiveness, one that oversteps all limits. [...] The frenzied escalation of "more, always more" has now infiltrated every sphere of collective life'. As the philosopher asserts, hypermodern societies prioritise private over collective pleasures, they are societies of fashion, worshipping the 'here-and-now' (Lipovetsky 2005, p. 57). Technologies of ephemerality, of permanent seduction and of novelty such as television or the internet are predominant in our lives and entice populations to consume ceaselessly. Leisure and self-fulfillment have been set up as a complete philosophy. Moreover, it is imperative, in such societies, to differentiate oneself from others. Competition is fierce. Thus, social recognition and personal merit have been put on a pedestal. Individuals wish to participate in building history in their own way: the impressive number of cooking programmes, cookbooks, and other food blogs perfectly illustrates both the idea that everything converges towards the individual, and that leisure is ardently pursued. This society of 'hyperchoice' is perfectly suited to the emergence of foodies, since, in a sense, food can be regarded as the ultimate expression of individuality. How is this conveyed in twenty-first-century Ireland? Given the context elaborated above, to what extent has Ireland been transformed in the culinary domain?

Back in the 1950s, when Bord Fáilte – the Irish Tourist Board – was created, and for several decades thereafter, Irish cuisine had a very poor reputation. The role played by the Tourist Board in promoting Irish food over the years has been huge, notably through brochures. One particular brochure aimed at the French in 1974 states: 'Ireland is certainly not the country of gastronomy. But there's no need to denigrate Irish cuisine as a whole ... With modesty, we let those who know, make complicated culinary preparations. What we serve is first and foremost simple' (Bord Fáilte 1974, p. 12). In 1987, however, a more positive and self-confident image can be seen: 'It is obvious now, that over the last few years, Irish cuisine is getting better. Good restaurants are opening everywhere and for all pockets. Obviously, people are not coming for Irish cooking alone, but you never know ...' (Bord Fáilte 1987, p. ix).

Twenty-five years later, Fáilte Ireland (current name of rebranded Irish Tourist Board) is implementing measures to attract tourists to Ireland for an 'authentic and local' food experience. On its website, it offers advice to food tourism businesses with menu suggestions, but also recipes showcasing the best of Irish produce: Mussels with Cream, Dill and Lemon; Braised Shin of Beef with Champ; or Honey and Whiskey Crème Brûlée. These recipes clearly epitomise a new Irish cuisine, subtly intertwining traditional and more exotic ingredients with both modern and rustic cooking techniques. Admittedly, the tenet of 'authenticity' is questionable. These recipes offer a re-imagined 'authenticity' destined for tourists. They evince a cuisine that is both rooted in the past and reinvigorated by new techniques. This is hardly surprising, given that at the heart of tourism are found dream and escape, not daily routine and mundane reality.

In terms of production and consumption, the globalisation of markets has facilitated great change. Eating tomatoes or strawberries in December, for example, is now unremarkable. However, the policies implemented by Fáilte Ireland visibly express a wish for food tourism businesses to show a more sustainable approach to food. A seasonal food calendar is thus accessible on their website to remind (or perhaps educate) tourism businesses of the cyclical nature of food production in Ireland. It is also worth noting that Fáilte Ireland identifies thirteen food trends, each providing an insight into what should be emphasised in terms of marketing strategy. They are listed as follows: local and regional provenance of food, in-house and homemade, new flavours, telling the story, nose-to-tail, comfort food

reinvented, casual dining, healthy options, children's menus, locally produced beer, pop-up restaurants, artisan cocktails, and finally, food trucks
and street food (Fáilte Ireland 2013). Proximity, minimum waste, a focus
on the well-being of the family, these trends – expressions of the tourists'
expectations – reflect both the same values as the Slow Food movement
based on a eco-friendly philosophy, which insists on the quality of ingredients as well as on trading ethically with producers, and a desire to construct
one's own sense of Irishness, to reinvent oneself through food and the
story behind it. From a sociological perspective, as Claude Fischler (2001,
p. 68) explains, through the principle of incorporation, nutritive qualities
are transferred to the eater, but also symbolic qualities sometimes associated with the place and the people who produced and cooked the food.

Perhaps more than anything else, the development of catering, and
particularly of restaurants, owes a lot to the Tourist Board. In the late fif-
ties, those who wished to dine out as well as visitors from abroad had to
go to restaurants in large hotels. Very few individual restaurants existed at
the time. As Josephine Mac Sorley (1955, p. 17) pointed out, 'the country
is small and, except in the cities, the eating-out population is limited by
the fact that everyone is within walking distance of his own home'. For
obvious economic reasons, eating out had not yet become fashionable; it
was reserved for special occasions.

The seventies paved the way for gastronomic changes. Not only did
the Tourist Board play a role in advertising Irish food assets, but it also
contributed to changing people's opinions on the subject. In 1972, Bord
Fáilte published its first *Guide to Good Eating*. The *Bord Fáilte Review of
1978* notes that:

> a major survey of dining-out requirements was undertaken to find out what tourists
> and home holiday makers look for in food and eating out facilities. The results were
> published in a booklet, *Thought for Food*. Bord Fáilte and the Regional Tourism
> Organisations published a national guide, *Dining in Ireland*, covering 600 restau-
> rants. A *Dining in Dublin* guide was also produced.
>
> (Bord Fáilte 1978, p. 19)

The publication of guides soon had a major impact on the industry. Firstly,
it was a reassuring guarantee of quality at the time. The popularity of guides

such as those of Bridgestone or Georgina Campbell, proves this is still the case today. Secondly, emulation and a competitive desire to feature in the guides not only encouraged restaurant owners to give their best, but also motivated chefs and all other actors in the sector. In addition to the various guides, the Awards of Excellence scheme for restaurants was introduced in 1979 and sponsorship began in 1987 with Ballygowan Spring Water Company sponsoring the Dining in Ireland Awards of Excellence. The creation of Bord Bia – the Irish Food Board – in 1994, and its partnership with Bord Fáilte, reinforced sponsoring throughout the country.

The most important change took place in 1988 when the Intoxicating Liquor Act was implemented. As the Minister of State at the Department of Tourism and Transport, Mr. Lyons, stated: '[it] sets out, for the first time in the history of the State, a procedure for the full licensing of restaurants' (Seanad Éireann 1998). Designated as the only inspecting authority, Bord Fáilte was, from that point on, charged with the registration and grading of hotels, guesthouses and other forms of tourist accommodation. Predictably, as the Celtic Tiger cub was gaining strength, the number and the variety of restaurants soared – to more than 4,000 in 2012 with over a quarter of these restaurants in Dublin.

Furthermore, Bord Fáilte's role in training and employment in the food sector, in partnership with the Institutes of Technology, greatly transformed the Irish culinary scene. In 2009, according to the website of the Restaurants Association of Ireland, restaurants employed about 64,000 people and the food-related industry as a whole generated €2 billion for the Irish economy. The negative reviews Irish gastronomy used to receive seem to be a thing of the past. Ireland now has highly-qualified chefs and cooks thanks to continuous and significant efforts in training and education since the 1950s. The Council for Education, Recruitment and Training (CERT), was set up in 1963. Its mission was to 'establish formal training for hotel and catering staff through specialised training centres' (Corr 2006, p. 42). It was to work in partnership with Bord Fáilte for several decades before merging in 2003 to become Fáilte Ireland, the National Tourism Development Authority (Mehta 2007, p. 41). When, in 2011, and in response to the economic turmoil, Fáilte Ireland drew up a new plan for food tourism businesses, food was identified as a key attraction for tourists:

'Ireland will be recognised by visitors for the availability, quality and value of our local and regional food experiences evoking a unique sense of place, culture and hospitality' (Fáilte Ireland 2011). The implementation of the 'place on a plate' concept has proven to be very successful. Culinary tourism attracts more and more curious taste buds eager to experiment with new flavours.[1]

'Culinary tourists' are not just drawn from abroad. A recent survey (Fáilte Ireland 2007, pp. 16–17) identifies three categories of home holiday-makers. The first category, 'the Food and Luxury Seekers' (20 per cent of the domestic tourism demand), essentially comprises urban-based couples aged 25–50, looking for rest and relaxation, weekends away with good food and value for money. The second category, the 'Nightlifers' (25 per cent of the domestic tourism demand), is mainly made up of single people aged 18–35, looking for fun, good food, drink and entertainment, and weekend breaks. The last category, the 'Country Ramblers' (20 per cent of domestic tourism demand), mainly comprises people over 50 looking for good deals, comfort and good food. According to the survey, therefore, 65 per cent of Irish tourists want 'good food'. These figures are significant, and help explain the marked increase in the popularity of culinary tourism and gastronomy. Many initiatives have flourished throughout the country. Projects for culinary visitor centres have been set up (Deegan 2011). Another example is the start-up Irish Food Tours which, seizing the opportunity to satisfy actual demand, provides guided food tour holidays by coach around the thirty-two counties in order to introduce visitors (both domestic and foreign holidaymakers) to the vast array of artisan food producers (Walsh 2013).

As *Masterchef Ireland* 2011 winner Mary Carney told *The Irish Times*: 'Food needs to do more than taste good, it also needs to tell a story. People want to connect to the food' (Hunt 2011). Another way Irish people like to connect to the food is by attending food and drink festivals. Taste of

---

[1]   'Culinary or food tourism' is defined by the World Food Travel Association, former International Culinary Tourism Association, as: 'the pursuit and enjoyment of unique and memorable food and drink experiences, both far and near'. <http://www.world-foodtravel.org/our-story/what-is-food-tourism> [28 May 2013]

Dublin 'the must-do foodie social event of the summer'[2] first held in June 2006, welcomed 30,000 visitors in 2012.[3] Most of these festivals were established quite recently, with the notable exception of the Galway International Oyster and Seafood Festival, which has been running since 1954. This festival, which began with thirty-four guests, welcomed around 22,000 in 2012.[4] Overall, Fáilte Ireland listed forty-seven food and drink festivals for 2012 alone. In addition, food trails offer tourists and local food enthusiasts an alternative way to visit Irish cities. But the most popular venue among the foodies is undoubtedly the farmers' market. As stated on Bord Bia's website:

> Farmers' Markets in Ireland have experienced considerable growth in recent years with fewer than 100 markets in 2006 and almost 150 currently in existence throughout Ireland. With unemployment on the increase, consumers are certainly keen to support local jobs and with producers usually manning stalls themselves, a farmers' market is perhaps the most tangible way for them to do this.[5]

Farmers' markets and country markets have a special appeal to consumers because they find themselves in direct contact with local producers: they thus provide a more personal approach to shopping, in that they enable dialogue and it is probably more reassuring to associate a face with a product. It is a highly-valued guarantee of quality in these times of food scandals resulting from a lack of traceability in food processing.

Among other experiences available to the foodie, classes in cookery schools enable anyone to become a chef for a day, or even to obtain a certificate within a few weeks if they wish to pursue it as a profession. While the Institutes of Technology provide professional training for those who wish to opt for one of the various culinary professions, courses are also available

---

2   <http://atasteof-ireland.com/2012/04/20/food-festivals-ireland-2012> [20 April 2012]

3   <http://www.tasteofdublin.ie/exhibitors/why-choose-taste-2> [22 May 2013]

4   <http://www.galwayoysterfest.com/en/aboutthefestival-Irish-oysters/about-the-festival.html> [27 May 2013]

5   <http://www.bordbia.ie/aboutfood/farmersmarkets/pages/goodpracticeforfarmersmarkets.aspx> [20 April 2012]

in some of the most renowned cookery schools such as the Ballymaloe
Cookery School. As specified on the Tannery website, a course in a cookery school is 'an ideal getaway for a foodie'. Foodism in Ireland takes many
other forms: *Food and Wine Magazine* has a readership of almost 67,000;
Easy Food has recorded a staggering 15 per cent increase in sales year on year
and its readership currently stands at more than 110,000.[6] It goes without
saying that British magazines (*BBC Good Food, Jamie Magazine*) cover a
fair share of the market as well. One could also mention the food blogs,
which represent an important new way for foodies to express their passion.
According to TV presenter Donal Skehan, who became famous thanks to
his food blog, there were fifteen members in the Irish food blogging community in 2007 (Digby 2012) and there are now more than 500. The Irish
Food Bloggers Association was set up in 2010 in order to respond to the
need to create a community of foodies via an exchange platform.[7] Another
way for food fans to share their passion and exchange their views is to attend
events such as the cookbook club meetings. This Dublin-based association
meets monthly at the Radisson Blu Hotel where the kitchen team recreates
recipes from a famous chef's cookbook. So far, chefs like Derry Clarke,
Clodagh McKenna or Kevin Dundon have been invited to present their
books. Mention has already been made of the food and drink festivals as
the ultimate foodie event, but more scientific or academic gatherings seem
to attract many members of the general public as well. In February 2012,
the Science Gallery at Trinity College Dublin launched *Edible: The Taste
of Things to Come*, the first exhibition of its kind in Ireland. With a giant
inflatable stomach on display, with quirky dining experiences and lectures
available, the aim was to 'focus on actual eating and the role of the eater'
(Mullally 2012), as well as making people reflect upon the ecological consequences of their food habits: this exhibition attracted no less than 38,000
visitors. In September 2011, both the Alliance Française and the Dublin
Institute of Technology invited the French scientist Hervé This, co-founder
of 'molecular gastronomy', to give lectures on his research. In April 2011, the

6   <http://www.magazinesireland.ie> [20 April 2012]
7   <http://www.irishfoodbloggers.com/about> [21 April 2012]

Institute of Technology Tallaght organised their first Gastronomy Research Day. The effervescence surrounding the Inaugural Dublin Gastronomy Symposium, hosted by the Dublin Institute of Technology in June 2012, proved once again that food could bring together many enthusiasts from very different backgrounds.

Clearly, the possibilities for a foodie to satisfy his or her voracious appetite for knowledge in the company of other foodies are endless. Nonetheless, the most popular method is undeniably a quite solitary one: through cookbooks and TV cooking programmes. In fact, Raidió Teilifís Éireann (RTÉ) – the state broadcaster – had its own 'celebrity chef', Monica Sheridan, from 1963, and the broadcasting of culinary shows has continued unabated to the present day, with a host of Irish and British chefs regularly appearing on our screens for on average ten hours per week. Such programmes include: *Masterchef Ireland*; *The Restaurant*; *Catherine's Italian Kitchen*; *Paul Flynn: Irish Food*; *Fresh from the Sea*; *Kitchen Hero*; *Come Dine with Me*; *Martin's Mad about Fish*; *Aingeal sa Chistin*; *Bean an Tí sa Chistin*; *Bia Dúchais*. In addition, most people equally have access to all the programmes available on British channels. In 2011, *The Restaurant* recorded the highest audience figures for a culinary programme with 329,000 viewers; it was followed by *Neven Maguire: Home Chef* with 315,000 viewers and *Kitchen Hero* with 289,000 viewers (Gittens 2011). Given the choice available to them, we might assume that some foodies probably spend more time on their sofas than experimenting in the kitchen. Yet, a recent survey has shown that: 'perhaps inspired by such shows [*Masterchef*], [...] 1.9 million Irish consumers really enjoy cooking. This figure has risen dramatically by 24% in the last five years, indicating more consumers are enjoying being in the kitchen.'[8] This food-entertainment revolution has primarily made people dream of a different lifestyle, helping them escape from their daily routine. Secondly, it has raised awareness of environmental issues.

As regards cookbooks, a simple stroll through any bookshop will tell you that it is a hugely profitable and dynamic market in Ireland today. They

---

8 'Insight of the Week: a Nation of Foodies'. <http://www.adworld.ie/news/read/?id=e2b08c9b-7a5a-4837-a1fc-5e72c94db102> [3 May 2013]

include Irish cookbooks, ethnic cookbooks, cookbooks written by the most legendary chefs (or by any passionate foodie who has never spent a day in a professional kitchen), Modernist Cuisine cookbooks, or old style re-printed cookbooks such as Maura Laverty's *Full and Plenty*. The era of 'hyperchoice' has definitely arrived. Given the popularity of cookery-based programmes and books, the question remains: why have Irish people become so enthralled by what had long been considered a peripheral matter?

Our relationship with food reflects many things about ourselves. Indeed, Brillat-Savarin's adage, 'Tell me what you eat and I will tell you what you are', should perhaps be slightly modified. Undoubtedly, it fails to convey the truth that human beings are first and foremost defined by the way they treat, regard and prepare food, and only then by *what* they eat. The rituals of cooking and eating – a reflection of our creeds, of our state of mind – evolve constantly, as does the society we live in. The time when Monica Sheridan licking her fingers on television would shock her audience is long gone. And this takes us to our next point: is a more liberal and secular society a possible reason for the current success of food-related matters?

To understand this change, we need to consider the current religious context. While over 84 per cent of the Irish population still claims to be Roman Catholic (Census 2011), weekly church attendance is declining dramatically – to 35 per cent, according to a survey commissioned by the Association of Catholic Priests in 2012. More generally, this decline in Mass attendance is mirrored by changes in people's attitude towards Church teaching. Principles such as fasting, privation, gluttony and other matters pertaining to the flesh have acquired a totally different meaning. Concupiscence, stemming from Adam and Eve's capitulation to temptation and eating the apple, symbolises Man's natural inclination to sin. Moreover, overeating and rich foods have long been associated with the deadly sin of gluttony. Beginning in the 1960s, the relaxation of moral standards would actually pave the way for a different approach to food. Children no longer fear God's wrath if they eat a few sweets during Lent. For the same reason, fish is no longer reserved for fast days. The way people regard their body has also significantly evolved. Current cookery programmes, for example *Nigella's Kitchen*, often display a sensuality which few viewers in the 1960s could have imagined. Of course, at the time, censorship was diligent enough to prevent this from happening. The term 'gastroporn' probably best epitomises this frequent association between food and sexuality. It refers to the way in which food is staged and photographed like an eroticised body, supposedly to seduce the eater. Today, the correlation between food and seduction is extensively used in the marketing of many products. The pleasure of the senses is promoted. In television cookery programmes, we encounter comments such as 'visually it looks so inviting', 'your food is just sexy', or 'if you weren't married, I'd be cooking with you tonight'.[9]

As mentioned previously, Monica Sheridan, remembered for her wit, dominated the culinary scene in the 1950s and 1960s. As the first ever celebrity cook in Ireland, she broadened the Irish housewife's horizons. Irish women undoubtedly owe her a great deal with regard to the evolution of their role in society. In the column she wrote for *The Irish Times* from May 1954 entitled 'Good Cooking', she described her various experiences in France, travelling back and forth between *haute cuisine* restaurants and remote farms. She gave practical and modern advice to the Irish woman on how to organise her household. Cooking took on a new dimension. Still today, many women recall with fondness her programmes and cherish her cookbooks like little treasures preciously nestled between Jamie Oliver's *Naked Chef* and Rachel Allen's *Easy Meals*.

This invitation to travel, to discover new cuisines, different lifestyles, was not only reinforced by the cookbooks of British author Elizabeth David, but also by the growing popularity of holidays abroad. Irish people tried new ingredients; their palates began to grow accustomed to more exotic foods. Undoubtedly, immigration also played a role. Today, big-city dwellers can eat in a great variety of ethnic dining-venues, the Irish urban landscape being now home to Moroccan, Indian, Italian, Japanese, Chinese, Thai, Malaysian, Vietnamese, Korean, Argentinian, Cuban, Lebanese, Mexican, Nepalese, Spanish, Mongolian and even Tibetan restaurants. In Dublin, Asia Market in Drury Street and Eurasia supermarket on Fonthill Road for instance, primarily serve immigrant communities, but they also

---

9   Heard on *Masterchef Ireland 2011*. RTÉ 1. Episode 9, aired 4 October 2011.

offer Irish people new culinary experiences with access to an array of produce completely unknown to them until relatively recently.

Despite Ireland's deep economic downturn, food-related businesses are thriving. In fact, some even see the food industry as a possible solution to Ireland's problems. Recent research led by Good Food Ireland and Grant Thornton claims that food is 'the secret ingredient to Irish tourism and export growth'. It shows that two out of three Good Food Ireland-approved providers met earning expectations in 2011, and that four out of five expected growth in 2012 (Barry 2012). According to Suzanne Lynch of *The Irish Times*, 'food and drink exports increased by 12 per cent [in 2011], reaching close to €9 billion. [...] Irish agriculture embodies what is hoped will be the twin catalysts for the Irish economic recovery – exports and innovation' (Lynch 2012). Philip Boucher-Hayes draws a similar conclusion in his provocative essay *Basket Case* in which he argues that 'Irish food is a world-beating product. If Irish food producers are given better levels of support, there is enormous potential to exploit our natural resources and expertise in farming and food' (Boucher-Hayes and Campbell 2010, p. 236). In this regard, it is in Ireland's best interests to be a nation of foodies.

In addition to economic benefits, and in what may be perceived as one of the many contradictions of our hypermodern society, foodism also has environmental benefits. In reaction to the often inequitable policies pursued by major supermarket chains, most contemporary Irish foodies have a more respectful, environmentally friendly and sustainable approach to food. The economic recession has upset and transformed people's views on consumption. Today, the growing tendency (advocated by Bord Bia and Fáilte Ireland as previously seen) is to buy local produce, which in return enables producers to live from their land in a sustainable manner.[10] Many

10   See Origin Green Ireland, 'a unique sustainability development programme developed by Bord Bia [The Irish Food Board] to internationally demonstrate the commitment of Irish food and drink producers to operating sustainably – in terms of greenhouse gas emission, energy conservation, water management, biodiversity, community initiatives and health and nutrition'. <http://www.bordbia.ie/origingreen/pages/origingreenhome.aspx> [31 May 2013]

local producers are involved in the Slow Food movement, founded upon the concept of eco-gastronomy, which aims to 'counteract fast food life, the disappearance of local food traditions and people's dwindling interest in the food they eat, where it comes from, how it tastes and how our food choices affect the rest of the world'.[11] From farm (or garden) to fork, all the while minimising the distance between the two, such is the message delivered both in the media and on the ground by chefs like Darina Allen, Richard Corrigan or Clodagh McKenna. The popularity of farmers' markets and local food festivals, already mentioned, reinforces the idea that what people are looking for is literally to taste the place. Preserving one's *terroir* is unquestionably a struggle to preserve one's identity from galloping globalisation, which is progressively eroding unique national cultural characteristics.

It would, however, be wrong to close this chapter without acknowledging that for some people, food still equals survival. The term 'foodie' still predominantly characterises food enthusiasts from the upper-middle class. Not everyone can experience dining out on a regular basis, not everyone can buy a ticket to the Taste of Dublin (even if a 'recession-friendly' ticket was implemented in 2012), and the farmers' markets are not usually frequented by a low-income clientele. In 2010, one in five children reported going to bed hungry because of the lack of food in their household (Kennedy 2012). As a result, in order to overcome the realities of deprivation, another type of 'foodie' has emerged. While these people probably would not call themselves 'foodies', they are the proponents of 'good food' accessible to all. Many excellent initiatives have emerged from less affluent areas. Crosscare, a Catholic organisation working with the homeless and poor developed a food bank twenty years ago and since then many 'Community Food Initiatives' have flourished. They are 'projects to improve the availability, affordability and accessibility of healthy food for low-income groups at local level using a community development approach'.[12] Examples of such

11   <http://www.slowfoodireland.com/index.php/slow-food/what-is-slow-food.html> [5 April 2012]
12   <http://www.healthyfoodforall.com/what_is_a_cfi.htm> [20 April 2012]

initiatives include food co-operatives, community food-growing projects in communal allotments, actions led by the Grow It Yourself (GIY) movement, breakfast clubs in community cafés, educational projects (i.e. the 'Cook it!', and the 'Healthy Food Made Easy' programmes funded by the Health Service Executive) and many others. As these initiatives remind us, food should be available to anyone, especially in a country endowed with so much high-quality produce.

Freed from constraining religious principles, more open to other exotic societies, ready to experiment with more adventurous dishes, Ireland has seen an unprecedented interest in food in recent years. The media and the internet allow both a fast exchange of information and knowledge, and virtual culinary trips. Beyond experimentation, food can also be perceived as an object of fantasy. Furthermore, as a possible recipe for renewed economic success, culinary culture also participates in redefining Irish identity in these times of 'liquid modernity'.[13] Certainly, in economic terms, the tourism and food industries have clearly understood that they have to work hand-in-hand to promote Irish food. Far from the hectic cities, Ireland conveys an image of wonderful, lush green pastures, of a fertile land full of quality produce. In this regard, in order to oppose the dehumanisation process engendered by global trade and the 'McDonaldisation' of our hypermodern societies, foodism expresses increased environmental awareness and a desire to protect and promote Ireland's food heritage. Ireland has undoubtedly become a 'foodie' nation, and perhaps more importantly, has also developed a more reflective and responsible attitude towards food.

13   A term used by sociologist Zygmunt Bauman to describe the uncertainty, the short-termism and the ongoing fragmentation of the world we live in.

Works cited

A Taste of Ireland. <http://atasteof-ireland.com/2012/04/20/food-festivals-ireland-2012> [20 April 2012]

Association of Catholic Priests (2012). *Contemporary Catholic Perspectives.* <http://www.associationofcatholicpriests.ie/wp-content/uploads/2012/04/Contemporary-Catholic-Perspectives.pdf> [31 May 2013]

Barr, A. and P. Levy (1984). *The Official Foodie Handbook: Be Modern, Worship Food.* London: Ebury Press.

Barry, A. (2012). 'Food Sector "Pivotal in Irish Tourism"'. *Business ETC.* <http://businessetc.thejournal.ie/food-sector-pivotal-in-irish-tourism-426617-Apr2012> [24 April 2012]

Bord Fáilte (1974). *Irlande.* Dublin: Bord Fáilte.

Bord Fáilte (1978). *Bord Fáilte Review of 1978.* Dublin: Bord Fáilte.

Bord Fáilte (1987a). *Irlande.* Dublin: Bord Fáilte.

Bord Fáilte (1987b). *Reports and Accounts for the year ended 31st Dec 1987.* Dublin: Bord Fáilte.

Boucher-Hayes, P. and S. Campbell (2010). *Basket Case: What's Happening to Ireland's Food?* Dublin: Gill & Macmillan.

Brillat-Savarin, A. (1982). *Physiologie du goût.* Paris: Flammarion – Champs classiques.

Census (2011). <http://www.cso.ie/en/media/csoie/census/documents/census-2011pdr/Pdf,8,Tables.pdf> [27 May 2013]

Collins Dictionary Online. <http://www.collinsdictionary.com/dictionary/english/foodie> [4 April 2012]

Corr, F. (2006). 'Training for Tourism', *Ireland of the Welcomes*, vol. 55, no. 5, September–October 2006.

Deegan, G. (2011). 'Culinary visitor centre planned for Meath', *The Irish Times*, 26 November.

Digby, M. C. (2012). 'Food File', *The Irish Times*, 5 May.

Fáilte Ireland (2007). *Fáilte Ireland National Tourism Development Authority, Tourism Product Development Strategy, 2007–2013*, Dublin: Fáilte Ireland.

Fáilte Ireland (2011). *National Tourism Implementation Framework 2011–2013.* <http://www.failteireland.ie/FailteCorp/media/FailteIreland/documents/Business%20Supports/Tourism%20Sector%20Development/Food/49993_FailteIreland_Strategy.pdf> [4 March 2012]

Fáilte Ireland (2013). *Food Tourism in Ireland.* <http://www.failteireland.ie/In-Your-Sector/Food-Tourism-in-Ireland.aspx> [21 May 2013]

Fischler, C. (2001). *L'Homnivore*, Paris: Odile Jacob.

Gittens, G. (2011). 'Neven's flavour of the year as top TV chef', *Herald.ie*, 13 December. <http://www.herald.ie/news/nevens-flavour-of-the-year-as-top-tv-chef-2961721. html> [5 April 2012]

Goldstein, D. (2011). 'What's in a Name?' *Gastronomica: The Journal of Food and Culture*, vol. 11, no. 2 (Summer 2011), pp. iii–iv.

Greene, G. (1980). 'What's Nouvelle? La Cuisine Bourgeoise', *New York Magazine*, 2 June.

Hunt, J. (2011). 'Producers urged to tell the story of their brand', *The Irish Times*, 23 November.

Irish Food Tours. <http://www.irishfoodtours.ie> [22 May 2013]

Kennedy, S. (2012). 'Time to revive poverty agency', *The Irish Times*, 5 May.

Lipovetsky, G. (2005). *Hypermodern Times*. Translated by A. Brown. Cambridge: Polity Press.

Lynch, S. (2012). 'Ireland reaping the rewards as agri-food industry keeps growing', *The Irish Times*, 20 April.

Mac Sorley, J. (1955). 'Eating in Ireland', *Ireland of the Welcomes*, Vol. 4, no. 2, September–October 1955, pp. 17–20.

Mehta, G. (2007). *The Welcome Business: Tourism and Travel in Ireland*. Dublin: Gill & Macmillan.

Mullally, U. (2012). 'You are what you eat', *The Irish Times*, 4 February.

Oxford Dictionary Online. <http://oxforddictionaries.com/definition/foodie?q= foodie> [4 April 2012]

Restaurants Association of Ireland. <http://www.rai.ie> [20 April 2012]

Seanad Éireann (1988). 'Special Restaurant Licence (Standards) Regulations: Motion'. Volume 120 no. 9, 28 June 1988. <http://debates.oireachtas.ie/ seanad/1988/06/28/00011.asp> [23 May 2013]

Tannery Cookery School. <http://www.tannery.ie/classes.html> [5 April 2012]

Taste of Dublin. <http://www.tasteofdublin.ie/exhibitors/why-choose-taste-2> [22 May 2013]

The Cook Book Club. <http://www.thecookbookclub.com> [5 April 2012]

Walsh, J. (2013). 'Irish chefs Zack Gallagher and Wendy Kavanagh start new all-Ireland culinary tour business', *Irish central.com*, 21 May. <http://www.irishcentral. com/business/Irish-chefs-Zack-Gallagher-and-Wendy-Kavanagh-start-new-all-Ireland-culinary-tour-business-208275961.html> [22 May 2013]

JOHN MULCAHY

Transforming Ireland through Gastronomic Nationalism

In 2005, the UN general assembly heard that 'the very best solutions come when business, governments and civil society work together' (Blanke and Chiesa 2008, p. 98). Ireland is a country in need of solutions, and gastronomy is one that could be profitably exploited. Ireland can be reinvigorated and redefined through each person's need to eat several times a day. Gastronomy has significance for all at some level, and it can transform Irish life – each citizen and organisation doing their part, so that, collectively, the nation benefits. This national activism will not be found in elitist or high profile restaurants, but in the authentic gastronomy of Irish domestic and workplace kitchens, grown by, purchased from, prepared and eaten by, Irish residents, supported and promoted by both a proactive business community and an engaged public service. This intuitively reflects Irish history, geography, culture, landscape, and all the other components that uniquely make Ireland what it is, thereby providing compelling reasons to engage, to visit, to do business here.

Ireland is not the first country to embark on this path, despite the globalisation of food, facilitated by transportation and technological innovation, and international tourism. Food, cuisine and gastronomy are tied to place. À la France (the archetypal culinary nation), culinary distinction is utilised as a marker of identity in places such as Norway, Singapore, New Zealand and Scotland in order to promote both tourism and exports. So this is about creating, in Ireland, an imagined community of gastronomy that accommodates and balances innovation and tradition, individual creativity and time-honoured conventions, the singular and the collective.

Against that backdrop, this chapter argues that a gastronomy-driven economy is realistic, viable and sustainable, as gastronomy offers a scalable,

cost effective means of local and regional development, with the potential to
strengthen identity, enhance appreciation of the environment, and encourage the regeneration of local heritage and the local economy. Ireland has
a significant opportunity to capitalise on gastronomic nationalism worth
approximately €2–€3 billion annually from tourism alone, which provides
a powerful momentum. Such a commerce-focused business case is likely
to attract the attention of policy makers and enterprises unaware of the
centrality of gastronomy to Ireland's economic strategy and indigenous
profitable enterprises, and creates the necessary awareness and buy-in for
success at national and local levels.

The evidence for this approach is assembled in two stages. Firstly, by a
focus on how gastronomy reflects the interaction of food, the environment
and society at multiple levels, often in unexpected ways, but with economic
development as the output. Secondly, by looking at some existing examples
of success that confirm how collaboration at multiple levels results in a
significant return on investment not just of economic capital, but also of
social, cultural and symbolic capital (Swartz 1997, p. 80).

Gastronomy in society

As a philosophy in the broadest sense, gastronomy can be traced back to
Archestratus (fourth century BC) who perceived it as 'the pleasure of taste
pursued according to a gastronomic code or set of rules' and wrote what
might be considered the world's first eating guide called 'Gastronomia' –
literally, rules for the stomach (Santich 1996, p. 176). In 1825, Jean-Anthelme
Brillat-Savarin, the modern champion of gastronomy, defined it as the 'reasoned knowledge of everything pertaining to man, insofar as he nourishes
himself' (cited in Flandrin, Montanari, and Sonnenfeld 1999, p. 432). A
contemporary observation from Barbara Santich is that 'gastronomy is
the reasoned understanding of everything that concerns us insofar as we
sustain ourselves' (Scarpato 2002, p. 54). Signalling how germane food and

its consumption is to human existence, the philosopher Terry Eagleton has observed: 'Genuine eating combines pleasure, utility, and sociality, and so differs from a take-away in much the same way that Proust differs from a bus ticket' (Eagleton 1997). No longer a survival necessity (in some developed economies, anyhow), food is, at a philosophical level, 'the thesaurus of all moods and all sensations' (Ellmann 1993, p. 112), and it is not only an important signifier within culture and the symbolic order, but it also plays a vital role in our sense of self. People's food preferences and their ability to discriminate aesthetically is deeply ingrained and socially embedded so that it seems natural, even though it is learned rather than innate (Mennell 2005, p. 469). Regardless of the variety of food presented to them, people (locals or tourists) consistently make food choices in keeping with their class identity, which in turn reproduces socioeconomic hierarchies of power and control (Everett 2009, p. 28). Thus, the relationship between people and their food is quite distinctive. Consequently, the selection of food by a person and how it is consumed becomes a marker of identity and difference (Richards 2002, p. 5). These perspectives suggest, at a human level, that food is not only fuel for the body, but, also a gastronomic foil for philosophy, socialising, and a means of simultaneously enriching experiences, expressing personal identities, and adding to quality of life.

However, at a national or regional level, food heavily influences (and is influenced by) the farming landscape and other environments through its production (Sage 2005). These are elements of every destination, providing it with its own unique character and authenticity (Yeoman, Brass and McMahon-Beattie 2007, p. 1135). Consequently, there are national and continental differences in relation to food, its production and its consumption that, although not obvious, have implications for the provision and consumption of gastronomic experiences. Within Europe, there appear to be significant differences in the agriculture systems; industrial level efficiency is the foundation of food production in Northern Europe, while 'terroir' and tradition dominate in Southern Europe (Parrott, Wilson, and Murdoch 2002, p. 242). There is a similar polarisation in France, Italy and the Mediterranean countries where eating out patterns are predominantly based on traditional food and regional cuisines, while the UK and the US are leaning towards creolisation and internationalisation through the proliferation of exotic and ethnic cuisines (Miele and Murdoch 2002, p. 314). Similarly, Paul Rozin has observed that: 'The food-pleasure attitude of the French, in comparison to the food-poison attitude of Americans presumably leads to the popularity of all types of foods modified to be "healthier" (low fat, low salt, no additives) in the United States' (Rozin 1999, p. 20). Clearly, food seems to have quite a functional role in Northern Europe, the UK and the USA, with related consequences for areas of economic activity. This reflects what has been a dominant narrative – in modern societies, food has always been considered as inconsequential (Scarpato 2002, p. 55). Not only is food invisible, but the issues that affect it have become invisible also (Symons 1998, pp. ix–xi).

Happily, various case studies demonstrate how food can combat parochialism and offer commercial benefits. Indigenous cattle breeds in Italy have been shown to have additional social and cultural value as custodians of local traditions (Gandini and Villa 2003). The 'adopt a sheep' project in Italy's Abruzzo National Park both demonstrate food's wider role in tourism, business and the economy (Holloway et al. 2006). In Sweden, the historical and rural context of local food was reinterpreted to achieve not only commercial business goals for rural food businesses, but also to serve a tourist agenda (Tellstrom, Gustafsson, and Mossberg 2005). The French concept of 'Cuisine de Terroir' demonstrates how food preparation and consumption must be grounded locally, how the gastronomic relationship goes beyond eating out, and how a shorter supply chain creates a fundamentally different type of relationship between larger numbers of producers and consumers (Chossat and Gergaud 2003). Essentially, food reaches the consumer 'embedded with information at the point of sale' so that the consumer can make connections (an economy of regard) with the place of production, the methods employed and the values of the people involved (Sage 2003, pp. 48–49). This, in turn, both creates and reinforces the affiliation that consumers seek with their environment, inevitably increasing their gastronomic expenditure. These and other initiatives have had a multiplier effect resulting in several types of economic returns from food, particularly in terms of rural development by protecting and creating employment, resulting in social and environmental benefits to communities (Boyne, Hall, and Williams 2003). Food, therefore, is not only an instrument of regional development, but also of general economic development (Henderson 2009, p. 321).

Gastronomy creates capital

Bourdieu's (1984) study of class in French society showed how a person's preference for food is a demonstration of cultural capital, as prestige and success are functions of gaining access to this capital, which is highly valued by society. Some argue that simply buying organic food at a market is an expression of cultural capital (Watts, Ilbery and Maye 2005, p. 30). Such a purchase entails a high quality personal interaction with an alternative form of value (the economy of regard) where there is a significant moral content to transactions beyond the exchange of products for cash. Cultural capital is also evident in the wide variety of ethnic cuisines consumed by middle to high-class consumers who are economically and socially confident enough to be able to order it – and have probably experienced it as tourists as well. Such experience, accumulated along with other travel experiences, is used to exhibit cultural capital when relating those experiences to others. The outcome is that gastronomy is one of the 'new' forms of independent and sustainable activities that enable each person to enhance their cultural capital.

Scotland has already identified the need for cultural capital in their visitor profiles. Scenario planning has demonstrated that Scottish gastronomic tourism can gain cultural capital and social cachet as tourists (and locals) trade up, and that food creates its own cultural capital, along with commercial opportunities (Yeoman, Brass and McMahon-Beattie 2007). Swedish enterprises have already commercialised the cultural capital of local rural food through narrative in order to create competitive advantage for their businesses (Tellstrom, Gustafsson and Mossberg 2005). A 'gastronomic centre of higher cultural capital' has even been proposed, underpinned by the idea that one should consume less, and consume better,

to support the view that products from small-scale high quality producers
yield more satisfaction per unit consumed, so that consuming better in
terms of quality may actually lead to consuming less in terms of quantity
(Askegaard and Kjeldgaard 2007).

Therefore, enterprises can 'out local' global competition by leveraging
on and sustaining, maintaining, developing/constructing local cultural
capital. This perspective should inspire public administrators, policy makers,
research institutions, and businesses to collaboratively focus on cultivating
local cultural capital and resources rather than alternative systems of belief
in global economics.

Gastronomy at work – examples of success in tourism

These case studies show that gastronomic tourism, at several levels, has
the capacity to create interdependencies that influence the development
and acceptability of both a destination and its gastronomy to a visitor.
From a business perspective, it should also be evident that gastronomic
tourism's primary advantage lies in its ability to adapt to and react to the
effects of phenomena such as globalisation, localisation, or creolisation,
mostly because the adjacent living culture changes (Richards 2002, p. 16).
Inevitably, this results in greater economic activity and returns.

Ireland – the success of the Fuchsia Brand in West Cork

The Fuchsia Brand in West Cork is an initiative of the West Cork LEADER
Co-operative Society (Dempsey 2008). A review in 2007 demonstrated
a strong local economy driven by food as a high value product. While the
geographic size of the area was small, the review showed that, of the total
direct value of output (€106.97 million), 54 per cent was associated with
the food and beverages sector, and 33 per cent with the accommodation

and catering sector (O'Reilly 2001). Critical to these figures is not only a highly integrated indigenous food industry in the region, but also the fact that the local gastronomy forms an important component of the touristic experience (Sage 2003). The tourists associated high quality local food with a natural environment in the region, and this was discussed when they returned home. Both the region and food products benefited, which facilitated the growth of wider economic benefits in the context of food exports to the tourist's place of origin, while also keeping imports in West Cork to a minimum, thus having a significantly positive spending multiplier effect. In Fuchsia's case, of the €106 million output, €69 million remained in the region and supported 1,131 jobs by contributing €88 million to the West Cork economy.

In that context, consider that tourists spent €2 billion on food and beverages in Ireland in 2009 (Fáilte Ireland). Food and drink represents the largest component of visitor expenditure in Ireland and exceeds the average spent on 'bed and board'. This should be a powerful motivator for both government and enterprise – the economic linkages are very obvious between the hospitality sector, agriculture providers, value-added providers and distributors. Given the Fuchsia example, revenues of this magnitude can provide a considerable opportunity for development and growth, and all that this entails (maximised return on investment, regional spread, increased employment in agriculture and services, and contribution to economic, social and environmental sustainability).

It is worth noting that the Irish percentages (of visitor expenditure on food) stand up well in comparison with international experience. An estimated 36 per cent of visitor expenditure is on food and drink outside of accommodation (Fáilte Ireland). In comparison, tourists in Canada spent, on average, one third of their travel expenses on food (Hashimoto and Telfer 2006, p. 37), while the proportion drops lower in South Africa and Australia where the amount spent by tourists on food ranged between 8 per cent to 26 per cent (Hall and Sharples 2003, p. 3).

Austria – integrating agriculture and gastronomic tourism

Austria considers itself to have the reputation of being 'Europe's Deli Shop' based on its 18,500 eco-farms and the fact that cattle farming contributes 30 per cent of agricultural value-added business (Austrian National Tourist Office). Of the 137,000 farms in Austria, almost 33 per cent were engaged in 'economic activity other than agriculture', over 8 per cent were involved in tourism, and over 11 per cent were processing farm products (Loverseed 2007, p. 25). Government policy seeks to ensure that these small farming communities are provided with relevant support in order to make a living. Marketing and selling local produce is seen as a central feature of that policy, and the vast majority of hotels in ski and hiking resorts work closely with local farmers and use their products. The emergence of several Michelin and Gault-Millau rated restaurants in the Salzburg province is evidence of the popularity and quality of the local ingredients available (Loverseed 2004, p. 17). Recognising that tourists expect to find rural landscapes of communities farming local breeds producing local products and local culture, some Austrian villages and businesses subsidise farmers to ensure that these desired features do not decline, thereby attributing a market value to local breeds (Loverseed 2007, p. 11).

Norway – 'scary food' as an economic driver

Voss is a small farming community of 13,500 on the West coast of Norway, where farming traditions are based on milk and meat production from sheep and cattle. It has established a niche in the market mainly by relying on nature based and extreme sports as part of its image. A traditional Norwegian meal, *Smalahove*, has become part of that destination brand. Described as a 'relic of Nordic gastronomy' a salted, smoked, and cooked sheep's head is split into two halves for service. In essence, a national traditional food, dating from 1300, has become a lifestyle commodity – admittedly for a specific tourist market segment. The main features of the product are as follows (Gyimóthy and Mykletun 2009):

- A unique, quality certified, industrial unit which processes 60,000 sheep's heads a year (120,000 meals). Approximately 90 per cent are sold to supermarket chains and catering companies, while the other 10% services retail customers locally and abroad.
- The sheep's head meal has evolved into a special occasion.
- Developed specifically around the meal, a microbrewery beer and an aquavit have replaced the traditional accompaniment of sour milk. Other product augmentation featuring sheep's heads include jewellery (e.g. tie pins, earrings, and cufflinks), cutlery, tableware, glasses and books featuring sheep's head songs, cartoons, or, for strangers and those attending the meal for the first time, codes of conduct. An internet portal maintains a virtual community with songs, pictures, and stories (www.smalahove.no).
- A farm restaurant serves over 6,000 sheep's head meals a year. The meal includes storytelling, a guided tour of the farm and the unique production facility, a home brew, and a specially grown Voss potato.
- A Voss hotel has been offering the meal since the 1960s with an emphasis on exclusivity achieved by limited availability, a dress code, and various rituals or ceremony during the evening. These include entitlement to a symbolic membership of an unusual gourmet community on receipt of your sheep's head jawbone, which has been cleaned, and your name burned into it.
- In 1998, Voss launched a two-day 'Sheep's Head Release' festival similar to the Beaujolais Nouveau event in France. Based on a traditional sheep auction and exhibition, it celebrates local food and tradition. It includes a 'lambs run' for children, wool shearing contests, a sheep's head eating contest (requiring style and aptitude as well as speed), a food fair primarily showing local food producers, and the climax is a community feast for 850 at long tables in a festival tent.
- Voss, also known for its Extreme Sports Festival every June, includes a 'try it' package where the sheep's head meal is one of ten 'extreme activities' which visitors can undertake (<http://www.ekstremsportveko.com>).

In spite of its arguably bizarre nature, the evolution of this traditional dish into a modern consumer product has greatly contributed to the image of Voss as a tourism destination. The meal, with its invented ceremonies, accessories, and merchandise, manages to perform several gastronomic and tourism roles at once – as a traditional harvest-type festival, a staged atmosphere such as the rural farm, as a community feast, a trophy event, an extreme adventurous experience, or a commercial food product with scale. The dish illustrates the ways that aspects of gastronomy such as food tradition, food adventures, culinary arts, and entrepreneurial activities interact when creating business successes.

The sheep's head meal renaissance is a creation achieved by individual entrepreneurs and entrepreneurial networks, which has contributed to growth and distinctiveness of the area and its branding as a destination. Moreover, the meal has inspired other entrepreneurs within farming and elsewhere to supply other products and services.

A possible framework for gastronomic nationalism in Ireland

Ireland already has a significant presence through high quality foods or ingredients, or the products derived from them, which are exported in vast amounts (e.g. milk powder, cheese, meat, Kerrygold butter, Bailey's Irish Cream, Jameson whiskey) and this export market shapes Ireland's image internationally. In the face of the industrialisation of food that such exports require, the consequence is that Ireland is failing to take advantage of some of its prime food ingredients domestically. It risks permanently losing assets associated with food – examples include the Kerry cow, Iveragh lamb (some recent initiatives exist, but compare it with the success of Shetland lamb) and varieties of fruit and grains, the loss of which impacts – at the very least – local, regional and national cultures, economies, landscapes, and environments.

Generating integrated solutions to such problems across economic sectors and geographical regions is complex, not least because most citizens, policy makers, politicians, or enterprise owners tend to look at food, eating, gastronomy (i.e. some sort of food experience), through their own 'lens'. They may not even have any personal interest in food as anything other than fuel, so food may not be taken seriously or understood, as it has no obvious commercial or cultural value to this audience. In contrast, the 'lens' should be food itself, if a range of desirable outcomes is to be achieved, particularly when policy, strategy, economics, habits, and perceptions are to be influenced effectively. If so, an important means of enthusing key influencers is to demonstrate food's capacity to add value by driving demand, increase business profitability, and achieve a return on investment for those that commit to food opportunities in addition to significantly enhancing activity in the Irish economy.

A possible framework to achieve this must include three groupings, the government, the public, and the business community.

The government

The government can exert influence in various ways:

- Integrated policy across all government departments
  - Agricultural policy acting locally. Policy that facilitates *both* exports and domestic production would be desirable.
  - The development of public health policy that facilitates local food production, distribution and sale, rather than hinders it.
  - Food must be a core feature of the education system and in tourism development.
- Procurement policies, within EU legislation, which are biased towards the award of local and small contracts by large State institutions, and by insisting on a verifiable Irish provenance on all foods;
  - The State operates some of the largest food purchasing budgets through, for example, the defence forces, health institutions, educational facilities, justice facilities such as the prison service and a range of semi-state bodies. Their change in food emphasis would have an immediate effect on food provision,

although the effect would be so great, a gradual roll out would
be necessary to allow various sectors to catch up in terms of
production capacity.

- As the largest employer in the State, the civil and public service
  has the opportunity to directly influence, in a positive manner, the
  socialisation of gastronomy.

- A proactive approach to protect the intellectual property embedded in Irish food culture in order to maintain competitive advantage and the distinctiveness of products in the face of increasing
  competition from other countries. For example, producers of food
  and tourism products could be encouraged to take an interest in
  gastronomic heritage and intellectual property rights. This might
  include the preservation of indigenous food types and varieties
  (such as breeds of cattle or varieties of apples), recipes, food com-
  binations, and local life and traditions related to eating and drinking (opening hours, working days, festivals, fêtes), all of which knit
  together to become a unique local, regional or national gastronomic
  culture. A key resource would be a gastronomic inventory of all
  the features that make up an area's identity – it would help to
  profile, contrast, distinguish, and emphasise its uniqueness. This
  implies concentrating on building local capacity – i.e. strengthen
  the knowledge, skills, and attitudes of local people for establishing
  and sustaining gastronomic awareness within an area.

The public

The public, as consumers, would need to be convinced, through a public
advocacy campaign, of the importance of their role in finding, purchasing, preparing and enjoying Irish food, and how that would contribute to
the common cause. The key message would not be the commodities or
the food, but how being loyal to Irish gastronomy through modern Irish
cuisine would generate jobs in a wide range of sectors, such as agriculture,
milling, dairy production, distribution, retail, catering, tourism and so on.

Business

Business, as a result of the demand created by the government and the public would need to identify the range of local opportunities emerging from a food nationalism campaign. Ideally, these should not be national or international sized businesses, but small and medium sized enterprises attuned to the needs of their locality and who source their raw materials locally, so that all concerned stand to gain. The implementation of the framework would have to be dovetailed with the refocusing of the government targets so that demand and business provision scales up at the same time.

Conclusion

There is a substantial economic, social, and developmental rationale to argue for the viability and sustainability of gastronomic nationalism in Ireland. Gastronomy's primary advantage lies in its ability to adapt to and react to the effects of phenomena such as globalisation, localisation, or creolisation. This occurs because food is close to changes in local culture, especially in cuisines where culinary vitality depends on adaptability and flexibility, and has been shown to be a highly sensitive marker for much broader social, political, and economic changes in society. It therefore becomes a very effective argument in policymaking, as it is a cost effective, profitable option. Enterprises can 'out local' global competition by leveraging on, and maintaining/sustaining, or developing/constructing local cultural capital through gastronomy. This perspective should inspire public administrators, policy makers, research institutions, and businesses to collaboratively focus on cultivating local food capital and resources, thus avoiding sectors and regions acting independently. It should also encourage a predisposition to the holistic nature of gastronomy. Such collaborative community action led by those who can demonstrate social and cultural capital has been critical to success both in Ireland and abroad. While these champions of food might have economic capital, they seem to be instinctively aware that some in the community will think differently, and that for any one project to work, it must benefit the entire community in multiple ways through sharing, communication, openness, and good management. This approach also identifies and protects local food assets and exploits them appropriately.

From a business case perspective, the most compelling and logical argument is that Irish gastronomy is a people business – both in terms of those who provide and consume the experience. The possession of economic capital allows and facilitates investment in cultural capital through allowing the investment of time. Yet built into that transaction, and because of it, are other transactions of cultural capital (on the part of the citizen, acquiring and displaying it) and social capital (on the part of the service provider in assembling and providing the experience), all of which generates further capital, especially economic capital, thus creating a virtuous circle for all. Gastronomic nationalism is therefore a credible driver of the wider economy.

Works cited

Askegaard, S. and D. Kjeldgaard (2007). 'Here, There, and Everywhere: Place Branding and Gastronomical Globalization in a Macromarketing Perspective'. *Journal of Macromarketing*, no. 27 (2). pp. 138–147. doi: 10.1177/0276146707300068.

Austrian National Tourist Office (2012). 'Austria'. <http://www.austria.info/us/about-austria/trade-industry-1140668.html> [2 May 2012]

Blanke, J. and T. Chiesa (2008). *The Travel and Tourism Competitiveness Report* 2008. Geneva: World Economic Forum.

Bourdieu, P. (1984). *Distinction: A Social Critique of the Judgement of Taste* (trans. R. Nice). London: Routledge.

Boyne, S., Hall, D. and F. Williams (2003). 'Policy, Support and Promotion for Food-Related Tourism Initiatives: A Marketing Approach to Regional Development'. *Journal of Travel & Tourism Marketing*, no. 14. pp. 131–154.

Chossat, V. and O. Gergaud (2003). 'Expert Opinion and Gastronomy: The Recipe for Success'. *Journal of Cultural Economics* (27). pp. 127–141.

Dempsey, I. (2008). 'The Evolution of the Fuchsia Brand'. In *Perspectives on the West Cork Regional Brand*, eds I. Dempsey and S. O'Reilly. Clonakilty, Co Cork. <http://www.westcorkaplaceapart.com/en/about-fuchsia-brands/publications>.

Eagleton, T. (1997). 'Edible ecriture'. *The Times Higher Education Supplement*, 13 March, p. 25.

Ellmann, M. (1993). *The Hunger Artists: Starving, Writing, and Imprisonment.* Cambridge, Mass.: Harvard University Press.

Everett, H. (2009). 'Vernacular Health Moralities and Culinary Tourism in Newfoundland and Labrador'. *Journal of American Folklore*, no. 122 (483). pp. 28–52.

Fáilte Ireland (2011). *National Food Tourism Implementation Framework 2011–2013.* Dublin.

Flandrin, J., Montanari, M. and A. Sonnenfeld (1999). *Food: A Culinary History from Antiquity to the Present.* New York; Chichester: Columbia University Press.

Gandini, G. C. and E. Villa (2003). 'Analysis of the cultural value of local livestock breeds: a methodology'. *Journal of Animal Breeding & Genetics*, no. 120, pp. 1–11.

Gyimóthy, S. and R. J. Mykletun (2009). 'Scary food: Commodifying culinary heritage as meal adventures in tourism'. *Journal of Vacation Marketing*, no. 15 (3), pp. 259–273. doi: 10.1177/1356766709104271.

Hall, C. M. and L. Sharples (2003). 'The consumption of experiences or the experience of consumption? An introduction to the tourism of taste'. In *Food Tourism Around the World: Development, Management and Markets*, eds C. M. Hall, L. Sharples, R. Mitchell, N. Macionis and B. Cambourne, pp. 1–24. Oxford; Boston: Butterworth-Heinemann.

Hashimoto, A. and D. J. Telfer (2006). 'Selling Canadian culinary tourism: branding the global and the regional product'. *Tourism Geographies*, no. 8 (1). pp. 31–55.

Henderson, J. C. (2009). 'Food tourism reviewed'. *British Food Journal* no. 111 (4–5), pp. 317–326. doi: 10.1108/00070700910951470.

Holloway, L., Cox, R., Venn, L., Kneafsey, M., Dowler, E. and H. Tuomainen (2006). 'Managing sustainable farmed landscape through alternative food networks: a case study from Italy'. *Geographical Journal*, no. 172, pp. 219–229.

Loverseed, H. (2004). 'Gastronomic tourism – Europe'. *Travel & Tourism Analyst*, Mintel International Group Ltd.

Loverseed, H. (2007). 'Rural Tourism'. *Travel & Tourism Analyst*, Mintel International Group Ltd.

Mennell, S. (2005). 'Conclusions, Culinary transitions in Europe: an overview'. In *Culinary cultures of Europe: identity, diversity and dialogue*, eds D. Goldstein and K. Merkle, p. 469. Strasbourg: Council of Europe Pub.

Miele, M. and J. Murdoch (2002). 'The Practical Aesthetics of Traditional Cuisines: Slow Food in Tuscany'. In *Sociologia Ruralis*, no. 42 (4), pp. 312–328.

O'Reilly, S. (2001). 'FUCHSIA BRANDS LTD: A case study of networking among the Food Producer Members'. Cork: Department of Food Business & Development, University College Cork.

Parrott, N., Wilson, N. and J. Murdoch (2002). 'Spatializing Quality: Regional Protection and the Alternative Geography of Food'. *European Urban and Regional Studies*, no. 9 (3), pp. 241–261. doi: 10.1177/0969776402000900304.

Richards, G. (2002). 'Gastronomy: an essential ingredient in tourism production and consumption?' In *Tourism and Gastronomy*, eds A. Hjalager and G. Richards, pp. 3–20. London: Routledge.

Rozin, P. (1999). 'Food Is Fundamental, Fun, Frightening, and Far-Reaching'. *Social Research*, no. 66 (1), p. 20.

Sage, C. (2003). 'Social Embeddedness and Relations of Regard: Alternative "good food" Networks in south-west Ireland'. *Journal of Rural Studies*, no. 19 (1), pp. 47–60.

Sage, C. (2005). 'Food for Thought'. *The Irish Times*, 28 June, p. 10.

Santich, B. (1996). *Looking for flavour*. Kent Town, South Australia: Wakefield Press.

Scarpato, R. (2002). 'Gastronomy as a Tourist Product: The Perspective of Gastronomy Studies'. *Tourism and Gastronomy*, eds A. M. Hjalager and G. Richards, pp. 93–106. London: Routledge.

Swartz, D. (1997). *Culture and Power: The Sociology of Pierre Bourdieu*. Chicago: University of Chicago Press.

Symons, M. (1998). *The Pudding that took a thousand Cooks: The Story of Cooking in Civilisation and Daily Life*. Ringwood, Vic.; Harmondsworth: Viking.

Tellstrom, R., Gustafsson, I.-B. and L. Mossberg (2005). 'Local Food Cultures in the Swedish Rural Economy'. *Sociologia Ruralis*, no. 45 (4), pp. 346–359.

Watts, D. C. H., Ilbery, B. and D. Maye (2005). 'Making Reconnections in Agro-Food Geography: Alternative Systems of Food Provision'. *Progress in Human Geography*, no. 29 (1), pp. 22–40. doi: 10.1191/0309132505ph526oa.

Yeoman, I., Brass, D. and U. McMahon-Beattie (2007). 'Current issue in tourism: the authentic tourist'. *Tourism Management*, no. 28 (4), pp. 1128–1138.

Drink and Be Merry – Beer, Pubs and the Irish Psyche

TARA MCCONNELL

'Brew as much as possible during the proper season': Beer Consumption in Elite Households in Eighteenth-Century Ireland

The level of wine consumption by the gentry and nobility of Georgian Ireland attracted generally negative commentary from visitors to the king-dom's shores (Bush 1769, pp. 26–27; Melville 1811, p. 85). Lord Chesterfield,[1] during his tenure as Lord Lieutenant in Ireland (January 1745–November 1746), famously deplored the excessive expenditure by gentlemen on claret in particular (Chesterfield cited in Clarkson 1999, p. 84). Bishop Berkeley[2] joined him in inveighing heavily against this ruinous tendency – to little or no apparent effect, it must be noted. Certainly, the bishop's proposed alternative tipple – tar water – was never likely to attract many converts in a land where claret was consumed 'cold, mulled, and buttered' (Barrington 1826, p. 43) as well as being an integral element of elite hospitality (Maxwell 1946, p. 101). That wine was associated with the elite is not surprising. Mrs. Delany[3] observed in 1752 that even 'private gentlemen of £1000 a year or less' were in the habit of regularly giving dinners that featured the wines of 'Burgundy and Champagne' (Delaney cited in Cahill 2005, p. 77). Less well known, perhaps, is the fact that beer and ale not only formed a necessary element of the daily nutritional intake of servants and workers, but also

---

1   Philip Dormer Stanhope, 4th Earl of Chesterfield (1694–1773). English statesman and author of a series of famous letters to his son, published after the latter's death.
2   George Berkeley, Bishop of Cloyne (1685–1753). Irish philosopher and tar-water enthusiast. See queries 154, 157, 498 in J. Johnston. (1970). *Bishop Berkeley's Querist in Historical Perspective*. Dundalk: Dundalgan Press (W. Tempest) Ltd.
3   Mary Delany née Granville (1700–1788). Her published letters provide astute obser-vations of mid-Georgian Irish society.

found a place on the sideboards of the privileged classes in this period. This
chapter examines the place of beer in aristocratic and gentry households in
Georgian Ireland. The different characteristics of ale, beer, and small beer
are explained, and an overview of tastes in beverages and serving practices
relating to beer is provided. The chapter also explores links between social
position and beer drinking.

The nature of beer in eighteenth-century England and Ireland

The meanings attributed to the terms 'ale' and 'beer' have altered over
time. Prior to the seventeenth century, 'ale' was the word used to describe
unhopped, fermented malt liquor. The term 'beer' described hopped malt
liquor, a style unknown in England until its arrival there – via the Low
Countries – in the fifteenth century. By the eighteenth century, 'ale' generally described 'a light-coloured drink typically brewed in the provinces,
as opposed to "beer", the darker, thicker drink of the cities' (Sambrook
1996, p. 17). However, in her extensive study of country house brewing
in England between 1500 and 1900, Sambrook (1996) notes that these
terms applied somewhat differently to the products of eighteenth-century
country house or estate brewing. Her research indicates that 'ale', in this
specific rural context, applied to malt liquor of high strength, with 'beer'
describing various brews of weaker strength, e.g. small beer[4] (Sambrook
1996, p. 18). Barr (1998, p. 250) states that there was significant variation
in the strengths of different beers in this period, but that small beer was
generally between two to three percent alcohol and that porter, at seven
percent alcohol, would have been at the top end of the spectrum in terms
of alcoholic potency.

---

4   Small beer was usually made after ale, using the same charge of malt (Sambrook 1996,
     p. 119).

For centuries, beer provided a nutritious and wholesome alternative to unsafe water supplies, especially in urban areas. Prior to the arrival of tea and coffee in seventeenth-century Europe, and the eventual democratisation of these commodities over the next century or so, it was common for workers and servants to break their morning fast with bread, and perhaps a pat of butter, washed down with beer. A 1737 manuscript account of viceregal household staff at Dublin Castle, which shows daily allowances of food, drink, and other commodities, reveals that certain unnamed servants (to various important household staff members, e.g. the steward and comptroller) were each allocated a quart of beer *per diem*, along with 'a pat of butter in the morning' (Vernon Barton Papers, NAI/PRIV/1230/2006/153/3: 40). The 'ale butler' was a member of the household of successive viceroys throughout the eighteenth century, and he required an assistant to execute his duties. The important role of this assistant is evident when the quantities of ale and small beer dispensed to certain members of the Duke of Devonshire's[5] household staff at the Castle, in 1737, are examined. Certain upper-staff members were permitted to 'eat at the several tables'.[6] Amongst these, the tables of the Steward, the Gentleman and Pages, the Officers and the Battleaxes were collectively provided with a daily allowance of sixteen gallons[7] of beer. This quantity was divided, not strictly equally, between fifty-two individuals. Eleven battleaxes, for example, received an allocation of three gallons. Three 'Turnspits' – clearly not seated at table – were expected to slake their respective thirsts with a group allotment of one and a half gallons of ale, and two gallons of small beer – clearly pointing to the dehydrating nature of their work. The 'State Coachman when he goes out with the Coach' was allocated six quarts of ale, and the

5   William Cavendish, 3rd Duke of Devonshire (1698–1755), Lord Lieutenant of Ireland, 1737–1744.

6   These refer to the following individual tables: 'the Steward's, the Gentleman & Pages, the Officers, the Footmen, the Porter, the Battleaxes, and the Sentrys' (Vernon Barton Papers, NAI/PRIV/1230/153/3: 33).

7   According to Sambrook (1996, p. 273): 'Gallons were standardized into the imperial system in 1824. Imperial gallons represented a reduction from the previous measures of 1.6 percent.'

'Confectioner & his Maid' received one gallon daily; presumably, the confectioner drank the lion's share of this allocation (Vernon Barton Papers, NAI/PRIV/1230/2006/153/3: 33, 38–40).

The nutritional value of beer in the context of the overall diet of any but the truly poor in Georgian Ireland was significant. In important households, a stated allowance of beer, frequently formed part of an individual's remuneration, as did a specific allowance of other commodities such as bread, candles, and coal. It has been suggested that in England, between the sixteenth and early eighteenth centuries, the daily average intake of beer amongst men, women, and children was one quart. Labouring men, of course, would have had the highest intake and children (ideally) the lowest. Barr (1998, p. 250) provides the following useful examples to illustrate the nutritional benefits of beer drinking. A colleague of Benjamin Franklin's, in the days when Franklin worked at the printing press, consumed six pints of beer daily, providing 1,500 calories. In the 1730s, men performing heavy physical labour would drink as much as a gallon of beer each day, thereby consuming 2,000 calories. An individual would have had to consume an indigestibly large quantity of bread to obtain that same level of caloric energy. Thus, beer was not only healthful and hydrating, but also provided essential energy quickly and in an easily digestible form.

Brewing and beer consumption at the 'big house'

Sambrook (1996, p. 198) notes that 'the consumption of ale at the wealthy dinner table took a new lease of life in the early years of the eighteenth century, when there developed a fashion for extremely strong ale'. She attributes this fact to the effects of the provisions of the Methuen Treaty (1703) on English drinking habits. According to the treaty's terms, Portuguese wines attracted significantly lower rates of duty than French wines (£7 per tun versus £55) in exchange for the lifting of a Portuguese ban on the importation of English woolens. Hence, the market for rough Portuguese wines expanded not because English taste in wine changed, but due to the fact that French wines were priced beyond the reach of all but the wealthy (Barr 1998, pp. 33, 201). Port wine, dry and often made harsher by the addition of brandy, did not go down as smoothly as claret, and even society tipplers welcomed the new, strong ale as an alternative to coarse wine. The well-heeled Georgian, however, always concerned with 'politeness', drank ale from small, elegant ale glasses with a capacity of no more than four fluid ounces. Nonetheless, elite householders did drink low-strength beer such as small beer. In fact, some great houses in England provided two different qualities of small beer, i.e. best and common, which Sambrook (1996, p. 199) posits were likely to have been consumed by those of different ranks.

In Ireland, long-established trade links with French wine houses, many of which – (particularly in Bordeaux) were run by *Hibernois*[8] – helped claret to retain pole position as the most popular wine in the kingdom. The Irish-Portuguese trade dispute that flared up in 1781 as a result of a Portuguese embargo on Irish textiles had the added effect of souring the taste for port wine for Irish wine drinkers (Kelly 1989, p. 99; Lammey 1986, p. 31). The predilection for claret did not preclude wealthy Ascendancy landowners from following the development of ale as a fashionable drink in England. The Marquis of Kildare, later 1st Duke of Leinster, and his elegant English wife drank the beer brewed at their country estate, Carton House. A copy of the marquis of Kildare's household book, 1758, is now in the public domain as a reproduction (Dooley 2009). This fascinating document provides information about consumption practices, conditions of employment, and household regulations that falls into the 'hen's teeth' category in relation to the 'big house' in Georgian-era Ireland. Kildare was married to Emily Lennox, second daughter of the 2nd Duke of Richmond (1701–1750) and great-granddaughter[9] to Charles II. In her published letters, Lady Emily frequently adverts to household issues, and it would appear from his replies that her husband was keenly interested in such details. The detailed rules

---

8   The name given to Irish who emigrated to France in the course of the sixteenth, seventeenth and eighteenth centuries, such as the Jacobite refugees who accompanied James II into exile there.

9   By his French mistress, Louise de Kérouaille, Duchess of Portsmouth (1649–1734).

and requirements that the marquis set forth in his household book show that he turned a percipient mind to the regulation of his household.

When the marquis first set down his household rules in 1758, responsibilities relating to the management of brewing and to the maintenance and service of beer stocks at the Kildare's country estate, Carton, were initially assigned to the steward and butler, respectively. Dooley (2009, p. 192), notes that the Marquis of Kildare's steward was given exacting instructions relating to all brewing matters on the estate. Amongst these appear various stipulations requiring him to concern himself directly with the keeping, milling, and malting of all grain destined for the brewing process. He is also enjoined to 'brew as much as possible during the proper season' and to 'take good care of the Brewing, and not to trust it to any person'. At a cursory level, this appears to indicate that the steward also functioned as brewer at Carton.

Nonetheless, at this period in England, it was common for a full-time brewer to be engaged at an estate as large as Lord Kildare's. Even at lesser estates, practical brewing – if not part of the butler's remit – was often carried out by some other estate worker or even a tenant farmer (Sambrook 1996, pp. 175–176). Carton's steward might possibly have acted as the estate's brewer, or the stated rules may have been intended to emphasise the degree of attention he was expected to direct towards both the brewing process and anyone working under him in the capacity of brewer. The marquis may have wished to underscore the point that the quality of beer produced at Carton was the sole responsibility of the steward, irrespective of the number of underlings involved in the overall process. It does seem unlikely that the steward at one of Georgian Ireland's premier estates would have been charged with executing the actual brewing process. In view of the high status of a steward in the hierarchy of servants and the extensive scope of his duties – ranging from 'turning out idlers' to being charged with 'the care of everything belonging to the House and Stables (except what regards the Housekeeper)' when the family was away from the estate – it would certainly have been unusual for him to have functioned as brewer. Finally, a later addition to the marquis's rules, dated 23 January 1760, is addressed 'To the person who has the care of the brewing' (cited in Dooley 2009, p. 205). This suggests that the steward was no longer in charge of the actual brewing process, or at least that the responsibility for that operation could change as dictated by necessity.

Another curious element that arises in the household rules for Carton is the direction to the steward to hold the keys of 'the Malt Liquor Cellars' and 'not to suffer any Person to tap a Vessel of Malt Liquor but himself upon any account' (Dooley 2009, p. 193). Normally, these responsibilities would have been assigned to a butler. Elsewhere in the document of instructions, however, a section headed 'Rules and orders for delivering out malt liquors at carton [sic] to be observed by the person who is entrusted with the key of the ale and small beer cellars' was added at a later date. This suggests that it may not have proven practical for the steward to have sole charge of these cellars, prompting the marquis to agree to allow him to entrust a different servant, e.g. the butler, with the responsibility. The eighteenth-century butler was usually tasked with overseeing the provision, care, and service of beverages and, additionally, with the care of household plate and glassware (Sambrook 1996, p. 173). Doubtless, caution would have been exercised in relation to the devolution of the responsibility of key-holder from the steward to any other servant.

Jonathan Swift, in his satirical *Directions to Servants* (Swift 1745, p. 32), presumes that it is a butler's responsibility to tap ale and small-beer in the cellar (indicating that this was, indeed, the norm). Swift 'directs' this fictional butler, who has free access to his master's beer cellar, as to the best means to pollute and waste the stock therein unhindered. Putting the Dean's satire aside, the spoilage and wastage of household beer would have been a serious matter for a master. Brewing for private consumption was an expensive process. Simply obtaining the necessary grain and preparing it for the brewing process, e.g. growing, harvesting, malting, and milling barley, would have been costly. Considering the cumulative cost of raw materials, manpower, and necessary accouterments (e.g. coppers, mash tubs and barrels), it is little wonder that an estate owner like Lord Kildare concerned himself with all matters relating to the beer produced, dispensed, and consumed at Carton – from the accounting of grain right through to the allocation and waste of beer throughout the household. Certain rules instruct the steward to keep a close account of all grain, malt, and hops, and to ensure that none is embezzled. A subsequent rule – addressed to an unspecified party in charge of the key to the malt liquor cellars – directs that 'If any person waste any Malt Liquor willfully, Lord or Lady Kildare must be informed of it as soon as possible' (cited in Dooley 2009, p. 197).

To modern eyes, it may appear that the rules Carton's servants were expected to follow were unreasonably exacting. Yet a great estate such as Carton entailed equally great responsibilities for its owner and was expensive to run; so Lord Kildare's assiduousness was, in fact, not only practical, but also commendable. The rules in the household book actually indicate that although the marquis abhorred waste, he was a generous employer. Several rules relating to ale and small beer allocations to 'the Family' (i.e. all members of the household) make it clear that servants were not stinted beer – e.g. 'no person of the Family to be refused Small Beer as much as they shall drink till six o'clock in the Evening, after which time, it may be refused till the bell rings for the Servants' Supper' (cited in Dooley 2009, p. 196).

The Kildare's butler was expected to ensure that ale and beer in sufficient quantity were ready to be served at dinner, and that any 'left over after my Lord and Lady has dined must be carried to the 2nd Table' (cited in Dooley 2009, p. 191). This rule was qualified further by a later addition:

> A Pint of Ale or Strong Beer with a necessary Quantity of Small beer to each person who dines at the second Table and what is left of each kind of Malt Liquor after the Duke and Dutchess [sic] of Leinster have dined and which is to be carried to the second Table and not to be included in the first mentioned Quantity.
>
> (Dooley 2009, p. 214)

These rules imply that ale and beer were served at the noble couple's table on a regular basis. Lady Emily, in a letter dated 14 December 1762, in remarking to 'her dear Jemmy' that she has cause to avoid ale and beer, tacitly highlights this avoidance as an anomaly. Upon returning home to Carton from a visit to her sister, Lady Louisa Connolly, at the neighboring estate of Castletown,[10] she writes to her husband that although she is delighted

---

10   Castletown House, Celbridge, County Kildare, was home to Thomas Connolly and
     his wife, Lady Louisa. It was Ireland's first Palladian mansion and as grand as the
     Kildares' Carton House.

to feast again upon their own butter and cream – finding it superior to that produced at Castletown – recent stomach trouble has prevented her from venturing on 'the ale and small beer' (Fitzgerald 1949, p. 155).

Beer service at the grand table

The way in which beverages were served at elegant tables such as the Kildare's differed greatly from today's style of service. Bottles were not left to stand on the dining table and there was no question of 'self-service'. A text of 1791, setting out matters of table service and etiquette, provides a servant with 'Rules for waiting at table'. Three of those rules focus on the correct manner of serving beverages:

> 8. To give [sic] the plates, &c. perfectly clean and free from dust, and never give a second glass of wine, in a glass that has been once used. If there is not a sufficient change of glasses, he should have a vessel of water under the sideboard, to dip them in, and wipe them bright.

> 9. It is genteel to have thin gill-glasses, and the servant should fill them only half full, this prevents spilling, and the foot of the glass should be perfectly dry, before it is given.

> 10. To give nothing but on a waiter, and always to hand it with the left hand, and on the left side of the person he serves. When serving wine, to put his thumb on the foot of the glass, this will prevent its over-throw.

> (Trusler 1791, p. 13)

However complicated matters may have seemed for servants, they were equally complex for the thirsty diner. In order to slake one's thirst, it was first necessary to attract the attention of a footman. The variety of dishes presented *en masse* meant that wine and beer could be drunk at any time throughout the meal. Nevertheless, custom of the period dictated that one had to be 'challenged' before one could put a glass to one's lips. A lady had to be directly solicited to drink by a gentleman, who would first drink to her, then to the hosts, and thereby work his way through everyone at table. To do otherwise, one observer noted, was considered 'undecorous' [sic] (Paston-Williams 1993, p. 258). Prince Pückler-Muskau, a German noble-man, identified in this system a slight obstacle to efficient personal hydra-tion: 'It is esteemed a civility to challenge anybody in this way to drink ... If the company is small, and a man has drunk to everybody but happens to wish for more wine, he must wait for dessert (after which he could drink freely)' (Pückler-Muskau (1828) cited in Paston Williams 1993, p. 258).

The comical events depicted in Swift's *Directions to the Butler* (1745, pp. 21–36) indicate that the Dean had become quite expert at recognis-ing the ways of incompetent butlers. His satirical manual of instruction, *Directions to Servants in General* (1745) are viciously amusing, with the humour therein evidently born of frustration and disappointment. Swift lays bare all possible shenanigans by wayward servants, but does not spare foolish masters from pillory-by-prose as well. Swift's caricature 'servants' are outrageously slovenly and dishonest, but many of the infractions recounted – albeit exaggerated – ring true. The butler is, from the outset, advised thus:

> In waiting at the Side-board, take all possible Care to save your own Trouble, and your Master's Drinking Glasses: Therefore, first, since those who dine at the same Table are supposed to be Friends, let them all drink out of the same Glass, without washing, which will save you much Pains ... give no Person any liquor until he hath called for it thrice at least ... If any one desires a Glass of Bottled Ale, first shake the Bottle ... then taste it, to see what liquor it is, that you may not be mistaken: and lastly, wipe the Mouth of the Bottle with the Palm of your hand, to shew your cleanliness ...
>
> If any one [sic] calls for Small-beer towards the end of Dinner, do not give yourself the Pains of going down to the Cellar, but gather the Droppings and Leavings out of several Cups and Glasses and Salvers into one: but turn your Back to the Company for fear of being observed.
>
> (Swift 1745, pp. 21–22)

It is to be hoped that, at a later date, Swift's 'servants' turned their atten-tion to Trusler's *The Honours of the Table*. Bald satire aside, these 'direc-tions' help to confirm that, in Georgian Ireland, beer was as much a part of gentry meals as was claret.

Beer fit for a bishop

The letters of Edward Synge[11] provide further proof of the prominent place of beer on elegant sideboards throughout the country. Mrs Delaney, who disapproved of 'high-living' amongst clerics, noted that 'the Bishop [of Elphin] lives constantly very well', but she graciously conceded that, in his case, 'it becomes his station and fortune' (cited in Cahill 2005, p. 77). Whilst at his palace in Roscommon in the summer months, over a six-year period the bishop wrote virtually daily to his daughter, Alicia, who remained at their Dublin town house. In addition to endlessly correcting Alicia's inventive orthography and grammar, her father discussed all manner of household matters with her, and beer and brewing were topics he often turned to in his correspondence. On 11 July 1749, the bishop sent his daughter an account of a most unhappy discovery he had made the previous day. He had dispatched Shannon, the butler at Elphin, to check on the ale cellar. It was thereupon discovered that the housekeeper, Mrs Heap, who was in charge of the brewing, 'had almost totally neglected the affair'. The resulting ale, 'bitter beyond sufferance' and 'not one drop ... clear', was a source of distress to Synge. He was particularly upset because the malt used, he lamented, was 'from mine own Barley, the Crack of the whole Country ... all I have to comfort me in this distress, is, that Mine own small Beer, which I have made them Brew, answers mighty well, and gives great content' (Legg 1996, pp. 133–134).

The bishop's letters show that he was an aficionado of beer: he discusses ale, strong beer, and small beer, and he knows what he likes. He requests that Alicia 'prevail on [a Dublin brewer] to brew some Ale on purpose, such as you know I like, pale, soft, smooth, and not too bitter, and lay in some three or four half Barrels, as soon as brew'd ... Give like orders about Small Beer' (Legg 1996, p. 150).

Synge's guests were also partial to malted liquors. The bishop enjoyed recounting the following amusing anecdote about a female visitor:

11　Edward Synge (1691–1762), Bishop of Elphin from 1740 to 1762.

She often makes me laugh in my sleeve. I have some malt drink here, which she
likes very much ... At the beginning of diner [sic] she calls for Cyder. I say, Drink a
glass of beer. Oh! It is too strong, I am afraid of it. However, she's prevail'd on, and
when once enter'd, she calls for three or four more without hesitation. She never
exceeds, but the doo [sic] that she makes, occasions her drinking that manly liquor
to be more notic'd.

(Synge cited in Legg 1996, p. 457)

Conclusion

Bishop Synge may have been amused by the initial reluctance of a lady
guest to enjoy the beer he offered, but he was as serious about brewing operations and the management of his beer stocks as Lord Kildare
was about those same activities at Carton. Both men held a high social
position in Georgian Ireland, both maintained households in town and
country, both had a great fortune, and both – Synge in his letters to his
daughter and Kildare by the rules he devised for his household – showed
a commitment to careful management of their fortunes and properties. In
keeping with the custom at the time, the many servants employed in their
households were categorised as 'family'. As in the case of blood relatives,
it was usual to feed, clothe, and house servants, albeit on a more modest
scale. Although beer, like bread, was an important dietary element of
eighteenth-century gentry and noble Irish households, it was also a beverage to be enjoyed at meals and amongst friends. Class divisions were
sharply delineated in Georgian Ireland, but beer, that most democratic of
beverages, provided welcome refreshment in servants' halls and elegant
dining rooms alike.

Works cited

Barr, A. (1998). *Drink: A Social History*. London: Pimlico.

Barrington, J. T. (1826). *Recollections of Jonah Barrington*. Dublin: The Talbot Press Limited.

Bush, J. (1769). *Hibernia Curiosa: A Letter from a Gentleman in Dublin to his Friend at Dover in Kent*. Dublin: J. Potts and J. Williams.

Cahill, K. (2005). *Mrs. Delany's Menus, Medicines and Manners*. Dublin: New Island.

Clarkson, L. A. (1999). 'Hospitality, housekeeping and high living in eighteenth-century Ireland'. In *Luxury and Austerity*, eds J. Hill and C. Lennon, pp. 84–105. Dublin: University College Dublin Press.

Dooley, T. (2009). 'Copy of the marquis of Kildare's household book, 1758', *Archivium Hibernicum*, 62: 183–220.

Fitzgerald, B. (ed.) (1949). *Correspondence of Emily, Duchess of Leinster (1731–1814)*, Volume I. Dublin: Irish Manuscripts Commission.

Lammey, D. (1986). 'The Irish-Portuguese Trade Dispute, 1770–90', *Irish Historical Studies*, 25, 97: 29–45.

Legg, M.-L. (ed.) (1996). *The Synge Letters: Bishop Edward Synge to his Daughter Alicia, Roscommon to Dublin, 1746–1752*. Dublin: The Lilliput Press Ltd.

Kelly, J. (1989). 'The Anglo-French Commercial Treaty of 1786: The Irish Dimension', *Eighteenth-Century Ireland/Iris an dá chultúr*, 4: 93–111.

Maxwell, C. (1946). *Dublin Under the Georges, 1714–1830*. London: Faber and Faber Limited.

Melville, E. (1811) *Sketches of Society in France and Ireland, Years 1805–6–7*, Dublin: Printed for the Author.

Paston-Williams, S. (1996). *The Art of Dining: A History of Cooking and Eating*. Oxford: Past Times.

Sambrook, P. (1996). *Country House Brewing in England, 1500–1900*. London: The Hambledon Press.

Swift, J. (1745). *Directions to Servants In General*. London: R. Dodsley and M. Cooper.

Trusler, J. (1791). *The Honours of the Table*, Second Edition. London: Printed for the Author.

The Vernon Barton Papers. National Archives Ireland. NAI/PRIV/1230.

BRIAN MURPHY

The Irish Pub Abroad:
Lessons in the Commodification of
Gastronomic Culture

In January 2012, the *Lonely Planet* released the latest edition of their guide to Ireland. It suggested that 'the pub remains the number one attraction for visitors coming to Ireland and it is still the best place to discover what makes the country tick' (cited in McGreevy 2012, p. 7). The links between the pub and Irish identity are strong and in recent years the expansion of Irish pub culture beyond national borders has influenced how people abroad view our gastronomic identity. Such commodification of Irish gastronomic culture has managed to successfully expose Ireland's sense of place to people outside of the country. Though not always positive, this 'place exportation' has affected the image of Ireland and the Irish. One might reasonably ask how interactions with this type of commoditised sense of identity might encourage people to form a long-lasting bond with a particular region/place and how this might colour their attitudes to products particularly associated with that region.

In that same edition of the *Lonely Planet*, one of Ireland's most popular tourism attractions, the Guinness Storehouse, is referred to as being 'really about marketing and manipulation'. Therein lies the perennial difficulty with the commodification of gastronomic culture. How can the exportation of a gastronomic identity play a role in improving people's relationship with a place without it being perceived as false and inauthentic? This difficulty surrounding the commodification of gastronomic culture can be even more pronounced when we examine how something as traditionally Irish as the pub is exported beyond our country's borders. McGovern (2002, pp. 78–79) argues that the:

> Irish Theme Bar is a commodified cultural form that has mobilised a series of signs
> and symbols associated with an alcohol-centred stage Irish identity ... The cultural
> reproduction of such ethnic signs represents a reification of their meaning. As a
> consequence an essentialised conception of ethnicity is constructed, commodified
> and consumed.

It is the consumer's perception of such commodification that has the potential to shape their attitudes to that culture and one can argue that this
commodification offers us the opportunity to influence attitudes in both
a positive and a negative way. Positive, if the consumer perceives the experience of the Irish pub abroad as being both enjoyable and a fair reflection
of Irish culture. Negative, if the Irish pub is deemed too exploitative and
perhaps overly stage 'oirish'. According to Cole (2007, p. 946), cultural
commodification is often viewed as very unattractive in Western society.
Even though Cole is referring to quite extreme examples in Indonesia, it
is fair to say that many writers are prone to mock the concept of cultural
commodification and look upon it as a betrayal of cultural integrity for the
purposes of that dirty word, 'profit'. Cole, however, is keen to stress that
from the commodity providers' perspective there are benefits. MacDonald
(cited in Cole 2007, p. 956) argues that 'many people can use cultural commodification as a way of affirming their identity, of telling their own story,
and of establishing the significance of local experiences'. Therefore cultural
commodification in some cases may lead to an enhancement of identity,
perhaps to a level that sometimes seems extreme to people originally from
that culture. This might go some way towards explaining that intense 'oirishness' that is sometimes evident in Irish pubs abroad.

In the oenological domain, certain wine regions are also commoditis-
ing their gastronomic culture and exposing elements of this culture to an
outside audience. In recent years there have been substantial efforts made
by representative bodies from French wine regions such as Cahors, the
Rhone and Beaujolais to expose their wine culture to audiences outside their
immediate boundaries. Very few of these regional French examples have
had anything like the consistent success the Irish pub has had in influencing
attitudes to their own gastronomic identity, particularly among communities abroad. It is with this in mind that I explore the unprecedented success

of the Irish pub as a marker of Irish identity. The Irish pub abroad offers us one of the clearest examples of this exportation of 'place' to countries and markets far removed from the product's original home. It is this commodification of place and identity that benefits the perception of specific places. It creates positive feelings that foreign consumers have towards the 'place' and its associated gastronomy, be they tangible, in the form of food and drink, or intangible, in the form of services and attitudes.

Barbara O'Connor (1993, p. 68) suggests that 'cultural and national identities are constructed from the representations which certain people both inside and outside our culture produce for us'. She likens this to how personal identities are developed through interactions with others and goes on to explore tourist images of Ireland and the sense of identity which is engendered by such representations. In a similar way, it is feasible to explore how associations with 'place' might be used to encourage relationships between actual gastronomic products and consumers. There are many instances of this exportation of gastronomic culture and identity to a place other than the location normally associated with the product in question. O'Connor uses Irish tourism as an example, suggesting that a number of writers agree that there are a variety of tourism 'markers' which represent how people abroad view Ireland. In many cases these images of what O'Connor refers to as 'paddy whackery' are what shape people's views of Irish identity (1993, p. 70).

It is valid to also view the existence/role of the Irish pub abroad as offering a certain representation of Irishness, at least as this phenomenon is perceived by the external viewer. Many would argue, perhaps with some validity, that the Irish pub, particularly abroad, is a somewhat contrived reflection of Irish culture. Indeed Honor Fagan (2000, p. 137) argues that: 'What passes for Irish culture today – the musical dance show Riverdance, the supergroup U2, or the ubiquitous global Irish pub – does not spring from the eternal wells of the Irish soul. Rather these phenomena are, to a large extent, manufactured by the global cultural industry.'

One might counter such arguments by citing numerous examples that show the importance of the modern Irish pub in framing, in particular outside of Ireland, people's view of certain aspects of Irish culture. Coverage of President Obama's recent trip to Ireland heavily featured his visit to

Hayes' Pub in Moneygall. The iconic image of Obama drinking a pint of Guinness attracted worldwide attention. Similarly, Queen Elizabeth and Prince Philip's visit to the Gravity Bar in the Guinness Storehouse was given serious attention by the international media. These visits are usually very contrived, as in the case of Obama's more recent 'surprise' St Patrick's Day visit to the Dubliner Pub in Washington. While such examples may no longer spring from Fagan's 'eternal wells of the Irish soul', nevertheless Irish culture is not a stagnant concept and although some may find it quite unpalatable, modern Irish pubs abroad can be as valid in reflecting Irish culture as any struggling 'authentic' rural Irish pub in today's rapidly changing economy. Neville (2007, p. 154), however, is keen to offer some words of caution in this regard: 'In all this we are in danger of believing our own hype, of crossing to the other side of the mirror to reawaken as the cast of advertisements and films.' She cites her own presidential example of Bill Clinton's visit to the Guinness Brewery in 2001 asking whether we have 'finally gone mad and joined the cast of some giant Guinness advertisement'. The photographs, taken ten years later, of both Obama and Queen Elizabeth consuming, or in close proximity to, Guinness, perhaps suggest a certain prophetic quality to her comments. There continues to be a notable blurring of the lines between the promotion of our authentic Irish culture and the marketing of that same culture abroad. We are right to be concerned about whether we are looking into, or out of, 'Neville's mirror'.

McGovern (2003, p. 83) has also emphasised the importance of the domestic Irish pub as a key marketing 'motif'. He confirms the *Lonely Planet* view and suggests that the average tourist regards the Irish pub as a very attractive element in Irish society. It is used as a condensed version of Irish identity, one that can be explored and sampled by the typical tourist and which offers a somewhat stylised version of our culture. While some might suggest that the power of the Irish pub as a signifier of Irish identity has been diminished over the years, the recent examples in the *Lonely Planet* guide dispute this. O'Connor (1993) discusses how inbound tourists view the tourist product as a reflection of Irish culture and society, but it is McGovern who takes the argument outside Ireland's borders and relates Irish identity to the explosion of the Irish theme bar on a global scale that has happened in recent decades.

The important role of the Irish pub abroad in shaping people's perception of Irish culture and society has ultimately benefited Ireland through tourism, improved intercultural relations and a general affection towards things Irish. This has been achieved by consumers interacting with the culture of the Irish pub through McGovern's concept of 'tourism without travel'. It involves exposing people abroad to elements of Irish identity while located in their own country. There are other notable examples. These include a wide variety of hosted events that take place regularly in an effort to promote elements of one culture to another. One can think of the celebration of the Chinese New Year in many countries outside of China, or, to use a gastronomic example, the worldwide exposure that Beaujolais Day receives on the third Thursday of November each year. Perhaps the most noteworthy example we can relate to in Ireland is the celebration of St Patrick's Day on a now global scale where Irish culture is promoted on one particular day during the year. While certain commentators might consider that the recent extent and scale of such celebrations portray Ireland in a negative way, almost causing a 'coca-cola-isation' of Irish culture, one cannot deny its importance in promoting Irish identity abroad. Inglis (2008, p. 95) describes St Patrick's Day as 'a display of Irish cultural capital' and something that is unique in the world in terms of scale. There are celebrations and parades held not only in every town in Ireland but in almost every part of the United States as well as numerous other countries. Inglis (2008, p. 95) makes the interesting point that St Patrick's Day celebrations are actually an import into Ireland with the first recorded celebrations taking place in Boston in 1737. Even our enhanced contemporary celebrations reflect this importation according to a recent article in *The Irish Times*:

> Then there's the depressing embrace of garish cod-Irish iconography. In a weird post-modern swivel, perfectly decent Irish bars take on the character of those Massachusetts taverns that – all leprechauns and shillelaghs – perennially strive and fail to look like perfectly decent Irish bars. It won't be long before we start eating corned beef and cabbage and wishing each other 'top of the morning'.
>
> (Clarke, 2013)

One of the things, however, that makes the Irish pub abroad different from the cultural events such as these is that it acts as a permanent presence in the host countries' environment. One might regard it as a 'cultural ambassador'. Munoz and Wood explore the role of these cultural ambassadors in the context of themed restaurants in host countries. In their article, they cite Bailey and Tian (2007, p. 243) who suggest that these themed ethnic restaurants 'function as a "cultural ambassador", providing, for some, an initial exposure to and means of evaluating a country's food and people'. They also cite Spang, suggesting that such themed restaurants may become a 'stand in for travel or an enticement to it' (2007, p. 243), which echoes McGovern's view that the Irish Pub abroad provides that important function of 'tourism without travel', as already mentioned above.

It is difficult to calculate how prolific the Irish pub has become throughout the world. EuropeanIrish.com (2011), an organisation that links people interested in Irish culture and activities to Irish resources in Continental Europe, lists 2,472 separate Irish pubs on its website. Irishabroad.com (2012) lists another 2,292 outside of Europe. The Irish pub has a long history in many countries but it was really the expansion of the Irish theme bar on a global scale during the 1990s and early 2000s that has caused it to become a truly global phenomenon. In 1991, The Irish Pub Company was appointed by Guinness and since then has become the largest supplier of Irish pubs throughout the world. According to its own company profile, it has to date designed in excess of 1,000 and built in excess of 500 Irish pubs throughout the world (Irishpubcompany.com, 2012). They attribute their success to the fact that they have researched Ireland's pubs in great depth in terms of their origins, history and styles and their role in Irish culture.

The pub is at the very heart of Irish society. In its typically perceived setting, it is often the focal point of the local community, a meeting place, a place in which to gossip, a supporter of local events, a haven from the trials of the everyday work environment. Ray Oldenburg has written extensively on what he refers to as the 'Third Place'. This is a place that exists outside of both the home (The First Place) and the work environment (The Second Place). Oldenburg is keen to stress that Third Places 'exist on neutral ground and serve to level their guests to a condition of social equality' (Oldenburg 1998, p. 42). He feels that Third Places are in short supply in America, for example, which forces one to look to Europe, where he feels Third Places are well-catered for. He suggests that 'in the absence of an informal public life, Americans are denied those means of relieving stress that serve other cultures more effectively' (1998, p. 10). The essence of Oldenburg's argument is that Americans can look to European culture to find examples of successful Third Places:

> Thus, while Germans relax amid the rousing company of the *bier garten* or the French recuperate in their animated little bistros, Americans turn to massaging, meditating, jogging, hot-tubbing or escape fiction. While others take full advantage of their freedom to associate, we glorify our freedom not to associate.
>
> (Oldenburg 1998, p. 10)

Interestingly Oldenburg's examples of good Third Places include the English pub, the French café and the German/ American beer gardens, but for the most part exclude the Irish pub. And yet, according to Share (2003), it appears that the Irish pub fits very well into Oldenburg's conception of a Third Place. He enumerates a range of phenomena that qualify a location to be classed as a Third Place. They share the following traits:

> The 'Third Place' has to be on neutral ground.
> The 'Third Place' is a leveller.
> Conversation is the main activity.
> Regular customers are key.
> As a physical structure it often has a low profile.
> The mood is playful.
> It acts as a home away from home.
> (Oldenburg, 1998, pp. 20–42)

It is difficult to identify an entity that would be more suited than the Irish pub in terms of the criteria above and therefore it would seem eminently qualified to be considered a Third Place. Share (2003) goes on to explore these characteristics above and show how the Irish pub site is suited to its Third Place descriptor. It is the very fact that the Irish pub is a Third Place that has led to its suitability and success as an example of 'place exportation'. It is, in fact, the exportation of not only the physical structure of the

Irish pub but also of the majority of Oldenburg's Third Place characteristics that makes the Irish pub such an excellent example.

The craic: lost and found in Celtic Tiger Ireland

Grantham (2009, p. 257) explores the etymology of the word 'craic', noting its arrival, most likely from English/Scottish dialect, into Ireland in the 1960s. He cites Dolan (2002) who explains that 'the word "craic" in Hiberno-Irish is a noun and verb that can mean entertaining chat, sport; to have fun'. Grantham suggests that the '"craic" has become the quintessential term among the Irish for having a good time'. The Irish pub abroad is more than just a collection of artefacts and memorabilia. If it is to be successful, it must commoditise the associated 'craic' that comes hand in hand with the Irish pub concept. It is my contention that the 'craic' in an Irish pub abroad can only be achieved in the context of Irish staff and their innate sense of hospitality and warmth. It is an intangible aspect of Irish culture that is very difficult to plan for, or structure. Visitors from abroad have always perceived Ireland as a 'place' where the world famous 'hundred thousand welcomes' could always be found. This perception allowed many of our emigrants to bring with them this reputation for hospitality as they travelled throughout the world and many of them progressed to high-level positions within the international tourism industry. In a sense they exported the culture of the Irish welcome across the globe. It is this same interaction between Irish staff and customers that has led to such a renowned atmosphere or 'craic' in Irish pubs abroad. Oldenburg's Third Place concept gives us a 'way to understand and value the type of activity that occurs in this social site' (Share 2003, p. 10). If we look at the characteristics previously mentioned, we can see that most are people-related and are associated with Irish staff operating the particular 'place'. It is the Irish staff who will ensure the place is inclusive, that conversation flows, that the mood is playful, etc. It is this personal aspect that is most important if an Irish pub abroad is to play the role of an authentic Third Place and offer that one hospitality trait so particularly associated with Irish identity, namely 'the craic'. According to Diageo:

> Although it is possible to recreate the feel of a true Irish pub without Irish staff – we don't recommend it. No Irish pub is complete without the friendly warmth, humour and advice of a true Irish bartender. To recreate the friendly service expected in Ireland, pub operators adhere to a simple rule: Know a customer's name by his second visit and his drink by the third.
>
> (Irishpubconcept.com, 2012)

It is clear from this that Diageo are also keen to emphasise the importance of having Irish staff if the pub abroad is to be successful. Grantham (2009, p. 258) is quick to point out Diageo's flagrant stereotyping by suggesting that 'the "true Irish bartenders" on the Diageo site are from central casting, white, of course, and often red haired'. Even allowing for such blatant stereotyping, we can nonetheless see how important the staffing aspect of the Irish theme bar experience actually is. It is therefore ironic that the extravagance of our recent Celtic Tiger economy almost robbed us of our sense of hospitality and it was perhaps the Irish pubs abroad, during this time, which helped maintain and foster our reputation for 'one hundred thousand welcomes'. During the Celtic Tiger years our reputation for hospitality and service declined. Many would argue that we became so involved in our desire to become gastronomically superior that our general attitudes to service in our pubs, restaurants and hotels changed. Much social commentary during the early part of the new millennium revolved around the loss of our natural aptitude for hospitality and its replacement by a new avarice that went hand-in-hand with the Celtic Tiger. Any pretension towards our traditional welcome was frequently revealed to be based purely on the desire for profit. Thankfully, since the demise of that same Celtic Tiger, Ireland appears to have once more begun to understand the importance of traditional attitudes to customer service. Even though there is clearly still some way to go, we have at least started on the path of regaining a reputation for the '*céad míle fáilte*' that is rooted in such a strong historical legacy.

The '*briugu* or hospitaller' was one of the most important roles in ancient Celtic society (Molloy 2002, p. 14). Few would argue the very strong association that exists between Ireland and its reputation for traditional pubs. In more recent years, however, the concept of the typical Irish pub in Ireland has become somewhat diluted. Many rural pubs have closed down for a variety of reasons including land development opportunities and the shortage of transferable liquor licences. At the same time, many other pubs, particularly in large metropolitan areas, have morphed into 'superpubs' similar to the huge 'sports bars' in large American cities. These 'superpubs', with their numerous bars, smoking areas, food areas, are often far removed from the typical historical image of an Irish pub. They have often moved out of family hands and are controlled by chains and developers and there is no doubt that elements of identity were lost or sacrificed in the interests of expansion, development and increased profits. This phenomenon, how-ever, has not affected those Irish pubs outside Ireland's borders which have been, and continue to be, so important in influencing people's perception of Irish culture and identity.

McGovern (2003, p. 89) cites Jennifer Craik's assertion that the tour-ist perception of a particular destination is often formed in their original environment and culture. Thus, according to McGovern, the Irish pub abroad performs quite a specific role in shaping that perceived Irish iden-tity. If we accept that the actual product being referred to here is 'Ireland', we can begin to see how the concept of 'tourism without travel' has the potential to be used in similar ways to link other products to an associated gastronomic culture which can then be reified in a similar way with poten-tially beneficial outcomes. McGovern suggests that 'here is a way that the tourist can travel to a notional Ireland without having to go to the trou-ble of travelling to the real world' (2003, p. 91). Rojek and Urry (cited in McGovern 2003, p. 92) argue that 'cultures travel to and through the Irish Theme Bar, with its calculated design codes, its "authentic" Irish artefacts and most obviously through its imported Irish people the non-travelling tourist can have the craic delivered to his/her door'.

We should recognise that the average customer of the Irish pub abroad understands that the experience is often a staged one but this doesn't neces-sarily lead to a lack of enjoyment. Kelley (2006) explains that the consumer's enjoyment of the Irish pub abroad has been put together in a very calculated way. The article examines in particular the Irish Pub Company and their formulaic approach to the creation of this aspect of gastronomic culture. The opening line reads: 'Ireland, as much as the world knows it, was invented in 1991. That year the Irish Pub Company formed with a mission to populate the world with authentic Irish bars' (Kelley 2006). Even though it would be naive to suggest that the consumers of the Irish pub experience abroad are unaware of the fake element associated with the concept, there are many who find the commodification and exportation of such Irish identity as a very negative thing. This is, perhaps, more true in recent years since the rapid decline of the Irish economy and the inherent damage that has been done to the Irish image internationally. The rise of the Irish pub abroad, in a sense, reflected the economic rise of the Irish nation generally during the late 1990s and early 2000s, but so too the decline in Irish popularity might just have the potential to lead to a decrease in the popularity of Irish pubs abroad. Only time will tell.

During his exploration of the commercial phenomenon of the Irish pub worldwide, Grantham (2009) paints quite a negative picture of Irish pub culture. While there may be some merit in Grantham's suggestions – and there is undoubtedly a very negative side to the influence of the pub in Irish society – one would have to argue that there are also positive consequences from our close relationship with this most Irish of institutions. This is particularly true when one considers its role as a Third Place as elaborated by Share and discussed above. Authenticity is a crucial aspect of any themed environment. However, Munoz et al. (2006, p. 226) suggest that authenticity is 'a malleable construct that exists in the eye of the beholder. Expectations may differ between individual consumers and as such so too will perceptions of authenticity and evaluation of the environment.' However, they continue 'whereas consumers can differentiate the real from the fake, often the illusion of authenticity is good enough' (Munoz et al. 2006, p. 227). No one is suggesting that customers of an Irish pub accept that everything is authentic: on the contrary, they are aware of the stage 'oirishness' in many cases, but are prepared to embrace this and enjoy themselves regardless.

Conclusion

While actual travel can achieve a greater consumer affinity with a place-based product, and it is often an important outcome of the tourism experience (Bruwer & Alant 2009, p. 236), the exportation of a regional gastronomic identity, a form of McGovern's concept of 'tourism without travel', can also enhance the relationship between consumers and the product's regional identity outside its own natural borders. As long as it is enshrined and enveloped in the story of place, the Irish pub itself may in some way act as the cultural envoy and it has the power to enhance the relationship between the consumer and a delimited place of origin. Such an approach might provide opportunities in 'place exportation' that might benefit other parts of the gastronomic world. In the earlier part of this chapter, I suggested that it might have some applicability in particular to other nations' gastronomic culture. The Irish pub abroad template might suggest an opportunity, for example, for the regional French wine sector to steal a march on its major competitors by exporting its oenological sense of place outside its own borders. Just like the Irish pub, it could use the wine's entire story to build an emotional affinity between new consumers and its wine; a relationship based not only on the quality of the wine itself but also on its inherent gastronomic identity and infused with every feature of the story, place and cultural aspects that such an identity embodies. To that end, the totality of a consumer's wine drinking experience is every bit as important in creating that affinity between wine and consumer, something that the Irish pub abroad has successfully achieved by creating its own affinity between the consumer and Irish culture.

The success of the Irish pub in other countries has in general had a positive impact on how people relate to things Irish. In a sense it has provided an opportunity for people outside Ireland to experience elements of Irish culture in their home countries. Although the concept may not have originally been devised in a calculated way, it does affect the consumer's relationship with Ireland's products and services. The question is can the same process be repeated when it comes to regional French wines or other nations' gastronomic culture? Can we perhaps identify other 'places' that have the potential to operate in host countries with similar impacts, namely to allow consumers to form that same strong bond based around place, thus linking back to the original nation or region's gastronomic identity? The exact details of what such an entity might look like are beyond the scope of this chapter but we can identify particular traits based on the Irish pub abroad experience to date.

The Irish pub abroad acts as a consistent and permanent 'cultural ambassador' in the host country. This is achieved through its decor, its style of building, its atmosphere, its music, its theming. It has been argued that the Irish pub's promotion of the 'craic' is at least partly derived by being staffed by Irish individuals or people with strong ties to Ireland. The Irish pub abroad is much more than a simple selling or promotional opportunity and embraces many of the previously mentioned key elements that Oldenburg associates with a Third Place. Above all, any entity emulating the Irish pub abroad to promote its region's gastronomic produce should not be seen as just a blatant marketing opportunity, but should be viewed as an apparatus by which a particular region could form a strong emotional bond between it and consumers in the host country. Such a bond could be reinforced through associations with cultural events that reflect the home region or in an oenological example the annual release of Beaujolais Nouveau. In the Irish context, this occurs particularly on St Patricks' Day, Bloomsday and more recently with the growth of Arthur's Day, where new or annual customers join regulars in swelling the numbers in Irish pubs abroad. Any such a 'gastronomic place' could act as a communication hub for people interested in or tied to the region specified. It might run events such as live tasting experiences that are led by producers from the home region. Of course, this 'gastronomic place' would also provide an opportunity for sales just as the Irish theme bar abroad has done, but unlike the purely profit-driven Irish pub, the primary function should be about forming that bond between the patrons of the host place and the place itself. It is this long lasting bond, operating at an emotional level, that is so difficult to achieve in an increasingly homogenised and globalised environment. But it is also this bond that is so crucial if distinct and local gastronomic identities are to survive in that same world. Perhaps lessons from the often derided Irish pub abroad can help to point in the right direction when it comes to the reification and exportation of a unique gastronomic identity.

Works cited

ABC (2011). 'Prince Philip eyes Guinness during bar visit'. <http://www.abc.net.au/news/2011-05-19/prince-philip-eyes-guinness/2719622> [14 June 2013]

Bruwer, J. and K. Alant (2009). 'The hedonic nature of wine tourism consumption: an experiential view', *International Journal of Wine Business Research*, 21 (3), p. 236.

Clarke, D. (2013). 'St Patrick's Day stimulates the nation's need to be twinkly, drunk and sentimental'. *The Irish Times*, 16 March [online]. <http://www.irishtimes.com/culture/heritage/st-patrick-s-day-stimulates-the-nation-s-need-to-be-twinkly-drunk-and-sentimental-1.1327639?page=1> [24 June 2013]

Cole, S. (2007). 'Beyond Authenticity and Commodification', *Annals of Tourism Research*, 34 (4), pp. 943–960.

Dervan, C. (2011). 'Guinness cash in on Obama's Moneygall visit', *Irishcentral.com*. <http://www.irishcentral.com/news/Guinness-cash-in-on-Obamas-Moneygall-vist--122495959.html> [14 June 2013]

Dolan, T. (2002). *A Dictionary of Hiberno-English*. Dublin: Gill and Macmillan.

Europeanirish.com (2011). <http://www.europeanirish.com/pubs.php> [16 November 2011]

Grantham, B. (2009). 'Craic in a box: Commodifying and exporting the Irish Pub'. *Journal of Media and Cultural Studies*, 23 (2), April, pp. 257–267.

Honor Fagan, G. (2002). 'Globalisation and Culture: Placing Ireland'. *Annals AAPSS*, 581, pp. 133–143.

Irishabroad.com (2012). <http://www.irishabroad.com/pubs> [16 May 2012]

Irishpubcompany.com (2012). <http://www.irishpubcompany.com/company_profile.htm> [16 January 2012]

Irishpubconcept.com (2012). <http://www.irishpubconcept.com/why/critical.asp> [13 January 2012]

Independent.ie (2008). 'One for the road'. <http://www.independent.ie/irish-news/one-for-the-road-26500016.html> [14 June 2013]

Inglis, T. (2008). *Global Ireland*. New York: Routledge.

Kelley, A. (2006). 'Ireland's Crack Habit – Explaining the faux Irish Pub revolution', *Slate*. <http://www.slate.com/articles/arts/culturebox/2006/03/irelands_crack_habit.html> [20 January 2012]

McGreevy, R. (2012). 'Guide sings praises of Irish pub-but don't forget to get a round in', *The Irish Times*, 12 January, p. 7.

McGovern, M. (2002). 'The Craic Market: Irish Theme Bars and the Commodification of Irishness in Contemporary Britain', *Irish Journal of Sociology*, 1 (2), pp. 77–98.

McGovern, M. (2003). 'The Cracked Pint Glass of the Servant: The Irish Pub, Irish Identity and the Tourist Eye', in *Irish Tourism: Image, Culture and Identity*, eds M. Cronin and B. O' Connor, pp. 83–103. Clevedon: Channel View Publications.

Molloy, C. (2002) *The Story of the Irish Pub*. Dublin: The Liffey Press.

Munoz, C., Wood, N. and M. Solomon (2006). 'Real or Blarney? A cross-cultural investigation of the perceived authenticity of Irish pubs', *Journal of Consumer Behaviour*, 5, May–June, pp. 222–234.

Munoz, C. L. and N. T. Wood (2007). 'No rules, just right or is it? The role of themed restaurants as cultural ambassadors', *Tourism and Hospitality Research*, 7 (3–4) (June–September), pp. 242–245.

Neville, G. (2007). 'The Commodification of Irish Culture in France and Beyond', in *France and the Struggle against Globalization: Bilingual Essays on the Role of France in the World*, eds E. Maher and E. O'Brien, pp. 151–152. Lewiston: Edwin Mellen Press.

O' Connor, B. (1993). 'Myths and Mirrors: Tourist Images and National Identity', in *Tourism in Ireland: A Critical Analysis*, eds B. O' Connor and M. Cronin, pp. 68–85. Cork: Cork University Press.

Oldenburg, R. (1998). *The Great Good Place*. Philadelphia: Da Capo Press.

Share, P. (2003). 'A genuine Third Place? Towards an understanding of the pub in contemporary Irish Society', 30th SAI Annual Conference, Cavan, 26 April (available online at <http://staffweb.itsligo.ie/staff/pshare>).

EUGENE O'BRIEN

Bloomsday and Arthur's Day:
Secular Sacraments as Symbolic and Cultural Capital

> Select a clean, dry branded glass. Grab hold of the glass firmly, put your finger on
> the harp. Take it at 45 degree angle, grab hold of the tap, and in a nice smooth flow
> allow the beer to go into the glass. As the liquid goes into the glass, you hear that
> fantastic hiss. Straighten up the glass bring it up to the top of the harp and in a nice
> slow smooth stop bring the glass down and allow it to settle. Here's where you get
> that fantastic cascade and surge with the nitrogen bubbles, lying dormant in the beer
> now come out of the solution and they try to form a wonderful creamy head. This
> gives us this wonderful look and we can top up later on and create a dome across
> the top. Then, once settled, you take the glass back, hold it nice and straight, push
> the tap away from you and allow the beer to flow in nice and slowly and take the
> creamy head, proud at the rim, perfect in every way.
>
> (<http://www.guinness.com/en-ie/thebeer-draught.html>)

These are the words of one of Guinness Brewery's master brewers, Fergal
Murray, as he explains on the Guinness website how to pour the 'perfect
pint', and it is a set of instructions which forms Part 1 of what is termed
'The Guinness Experience'. The video explains what is termed the 'double
pour', where some three-quarters of the stout is poured first, and it is let
'settle', which means the creamy white head 'is created from the "initiation"
and "surging" of bubbles of nitrogen and carbon dioxide gas as the beer is
poured'. The video goes on to explain that it is the 'nitrogen that causes the
tight white creamy head' (<http://www.guinness. com/en-ie/faqs.html>).
There is a ritualistic and almost sacramental aspect to these instructions,
with set directions, fixed rituals and actions which will ensure the correct
transformation from brown surging liquid to the famous black and white
drink that is known throughout the world. One could almost view it as a
form of secular transubstantiation, as there is a clearly-defined change from
the frothing swirling motion of the liquid, the Brownian motion caused

by the rising of the nitrogen bubbles hitting off particles in the liquid, to the gradual, but almost inevitable, calm and stasis of the final stage of the pint, with a clean line dividing the black body from the creamy head. The time taken for this process is called, 'Guinness Time', and this has been measured at 119.5 seconds (<http://www.guinness-storehouse.com/en/pdfs/factsheets/factsheet_pdf_11.pdf>).

Sacraments are a significant way in religion to connect the immanent with the transcendent – they are a way of infusing holiness into the material (Fastiggi 2010, p. 31). What is being set out here are the correct conditions for the sacramental transformation to take place, what one might call 'the liturgical conditions, namely, the set of prescriptions which govern the form of the public manifestation of authority, like ceremonial etiquette, the code of gestures and officially prescribed rites' (Bourdieu 1991, p. 113). So putting the finger on the harp is sacramental in that it makes no difference to the material process of pouring but it makes a significant difference to the symbolic part of the process. It differentiates Guinness from other beers, in a manner that is paralleled by the 'Guinness Cloud' advertisement, which sees the cloud as different from other clouds because it is 'made of more'. At the end of this advertisement, at which point the miraculous cloud seems to have agency and direction, by moving around the cityscape, and miraculously quenching a fire, it then morphs into a pint of Guinness (<http://themill.com/work/guinness/cloud.aspx>).

Guinness has long been associated with Ireland and with Irishness. The harp icon on the Guinness glass is taken from the harp as a significant index and symbol of Irishness, and so there is an iconic parallel between product and nation from the outset. When American presidents arrive in Ireland, drinking a pint of Guinness is the iconic photograph that is flashed all over the world. Guinness has often been seen as a synecdoche of Irishness, and the connection between this drink and Ireland is one that has seldom been called into question. In this chapter, the modalities of that connection will be unpacked and explored, as there are a lot of ideological connections at work here, connections which are often oblique and occluded. The product, a globally manufactured, mass-consumption drink, has been marketed and fashioned to be a signifier of Irishness. This has been achieved through a very careful semiotic construction of the product in all of its modalities, from production, to preparation to consumption, to cultural status. This chapter will explore the construction of this sense of Guinness as a commodity fetish, through the use of advertising imagery associated with the sacred, through the association of the product with messianic time and through the attempt to make the production and consumption of the product into a secular sacrament, with its own feast day: Arthur's Day. It will also examine the overtly religious and sacramental associations that have been created around the advertising, manufacture and consumption of this product, a process of sacramentalisation which culminates in Guinness having its own secular feast day. Generally feast days are a way of integrating sacred time with secular time. So 17 March is another day on the secular calendar, but it is also especially marked as a celebration of the patron saint of Ireland, Saint Patrick; the same is true of 1 February, which in Ireland is known as Saint Bridget's Day, and one thinks of Christmas day and Easter Sunday in the Christian religions, as well as significant religious days and months, such as Ramadan, in other religions. In an Irish context there are two other 'feast' days which attempt to offer the same holiness or transcendence for their commodities as these do and they are Bloomsday, 16 June, and Arthur's Day, 27 September. The reason for this has been summed up by Frank McCourt who makes the telling point that Bloomsday, and its rituals, demonstrates that '*Ulysses* is more than a book. It's an event' (McCourt 2004, p. xiii), and Bloomsday ratifies this status as being something more than a book; as we will see, Arthur's Day has a parallel function with respect to Guinness, by suggesting that it is more than just a drink.

The notion of having a Guinness feast day, or Arthur's Day, is an example of sacramental time being interfused into secular time, and this is an ongoing trope in the narrative of Guinness. This is foregrounded by the clock advertisement, set in Český Krumlov in the Czech Republic in 1890, features a clock which changes time, and which refuses to be bound by time; it intervenes in secular, ordinary time in a manner similar to that of Arthur's Day. This idea segues with Walter Benjamin's idea of messianic time, a conception of the present as the 'time of the now', which is shot through with chips of messianic time (Benjamin 1968, p. 263). For Benjamin, whenever the present is separated from 'the continuous flow of events and objects through time, there occurs the messianic arrest in which history is brought to a standstill' (Ferris 2008, p. 132); it is a moment in time wherein we can reflect on time, and the Guinness clock enacts this slowing down of diurnal process so that the essentials can be grasped all the more fully. Accordingly, messianic time establishes 'a concept of the present as the now-time in which splinters of messianic time are interspersed' (Jennings 1997–2003, p. 397), and of course there is a religious context to the term, given the use of the signifier 'messianic'. Both Bloomsday and Arthur's Day access this notion of messianic time, by pausing normal time in order to achieve an altered perception.

The first Bloomsday took place in 1954, on the fiftieth anniversary of the events in the novel, when John Ryan and Brian O'Nolan (Flann O'Brien) organised what was to be a daylong pilgrimage along the *Ulysses* route. They were joined by Patrick Kavanagh, Anthony Cronin and A. J. Leventhal, Registrar at Trinity College. This day is now celebrated worldwide and has its own sacramental rites, practices and aura attached to it, as parts of the novel are read or acted out, and different food and drink from the novel are served and consumed, including, of course, plentiful supplies of Guinness. Guinness, as a product, is mentioned ten times in *Ulysses* as well as the two brothers of the Guinness family who became peers: Arthur Guinness, 1st Baron Ardilaun, is mentioned three times, including one where his name is used as a substitute for a pint of Guinness – 'Two Ardilauns' (Joyce 1989, p. 319) – while Edward Cecil Guinness, 1st Earl of Iveagh, is also mentioned three times. There are a number of paronomastic references to them, such as 'peer from barrel' (Joyce 1989, p. 394), which refers to how Lords Iveagh and Ardilaun have parlayed barrels of Guinness into peerages (Gifford and Seidman 1988, p. 517), as well as this quite lyrical passage on the making and brewing of Guinness:

> Terence O'Ryan heard him and straightway brought him a crystal cup full of the foamy ebon ale which the noble twin brothers Bungiveagh and Bungardilaun brew ever in their divine alevats, cunning as the sons of deathless Leda. For they garner the succulent berries of the hop and mass and sift and bruise and brew them and they mix therewith sour juices and bring the must to the sacred fire and cease not night or day from their toil, those cunning brothers, lords of the vat.
>
> (Joyce 1989, p. 224)

So there is a sense of Guinness as a signifier of Irishness already running through *Ulysses*, and it begs the question if Bloomsday is the precursor of Arthur's Day – the interesting chiasmus of one day using the forename and the other using the second name of the person in question further connects the two days. And like Guinness, *Ulysses* and Bloomsday have become global experiences, having been established in America by 'very American James Joyce Foundation' in '1967' (Derrida and Attridge 1992, p. 184). Jean Michel Rabaté asks why it is that it can be 'easier to recreate the atmosphere of Joyce's Dublin in places such as Zurich, Paris, Philadelphia?' He goes on to say that it cannot just be that there are 'more James Joyce pubs in these cities than in Dublin or that the Bloomsday celebrations have turned into mass-produced tourist attractions' (Rabaté 2001, p. 153).

The answer of course is that Bloomsday is very much an international experience, and the book has acquired a significant amount of cultural and symbolic capital around the world. In his use of the term 'capital', Bourdieu is drawing attention to the fact that capital, of any kind, is to some degree dependent 'upon social recognition', and thus it 'confers both spending power and status' (Grenfell 2008, p. 88). For Bourdieu, cultural capital referred to a 'form of value associated with culturally authorised tastes, consumption patterns, attributes, skills and awards' (Webb, Schirato and Danaher 2002, p. x). It covers a wide range of resources, such as 'verbal facility, general cultural awareness, aesthetic preferences, scientific knowledge, and educational credentials' (Swartz 1997, p. 41). Symbolic capital is 'any property (any form of capital whether physical, economic, cultural or social) when it is perceived by social agents endowed with categories of perception which cause them to know it and to recognize it, to give it value' (Bourdieu 1984, p. 47). It is a form of 'denied capital' as it is a form of power that is not perceived as power but as legitimate demands for recognition' (Swartz 1997, p. 43). It is important to note that these categories are neither fixed nor constant, as the symbolic capital of an individual is 'not only open to transformation, but is continuously fluctuating in response to changing field position and changing field structures' (Grenfell 2008, p. 132). A good summary of the relationship, and difference, between capital, cultural capital and symbolic capital has been set out as follows:

Economic capital, say one hundred dollars, can be exchanged for a night at an expensive hotel. Cultural capital, such as a university degree, can be exchanged for a desired job. And if you have symbolic capital as an expert on Bourdieu, you may be able to cash in on this by agreeing to help your fellow students with an essay using his ideas only if they grant you certain favours in return.

(Webb, Schirato and Danaher 2002, p. 110)

Both of these function by what Bourdieu terms 'the club effect', a sense of shared interests and tastes among a group of people 'which are different from the vast majority and have in common the fact that they are not common, that is, the fact that they exclude everyone who does not present all the desired attributes' (Bourdieu and Accardo 1999, p. 129).

The aesthetic is clearly one index of such a club effect, and the symbolic and cultural capital associated with *Ulysses* has been reified in global celebrations of the day on which the events of the novel are set. An example of Rabaté's point about the global nature of Bloomsday can be seen in a recent New York Bloomsday where Le Chantilly restaurant 'served kidneys and other inner organs of beasts and fowl' while actors associated with the Daedalus Theatre Company read from the book or played different characters. In addition, 'singers and musicians entertained the restaurant's patrons with songs that were featured in *Ulysses*'. The proceedings were opened by 'the General Consul of Ireland', while in another part of New York, Symphony Space staged its annual reading of portions of *Ulysses*, a twelve-hour event which was also broadcast on radio (McKenna 2002, p. 12). And of course pints of Guinness were drunk, symbolising the significance of pubs in *Ulysses*. As the narrator Bloom puts it: a 'good puzzle would be cross Dublin without passing a pub' (Joyce 1989, p. 43), and indeed, there are quite a large numbers of pubs mentioned in *Ulysses*: O'Loughlin's of Blackpitts; Conway's; Davy Byrne's; The Arch; Meagher's; The Oval; J. and T. Davy's; The Empire; Barney Kiernan's; The Ormond; Larry O'Rourke's; The Dublin Bar; Cassidy's; Andrew's; Brian Boroimhe House; Mooney's; The Scotch House; Bolton's Westmoreland House; Doran's; Daniel Bergin's; Delahunt's; Crimmins'; James and Charles Kennedy's; The Bodega; Kavanagh's; Tunney's; Mooney's *en ville*; Mooney's *sur mer*; Acky Nagle's; Jacob Halliday's; Slattery's; Donohoe's; Cormack's Corner; Mullett's; The Signal House; William Gilbey's; Findlater's; The Horse &

Tram; The Three Jolly Topers; The Bleeding Horse; Rowe's; Manning's; The Empire; The Burton Hotel; John Long's; Keogh's; Slattery's; Donohoe's; Burke's; The Moira; Larchet's; and The Old Ireland Tavern.

I would suggest that this litany of public houses is no accident as the Irish pub, and its main commodity, Guinness, has long had cultural and symbolic capital associated with it. Indeed, in *Ulysses*, barmen are called curates: 'coming up redheaded curates from the county Leitrim, rinsing empties' (Joyce 1989, p. 43), creating an association with the priesthood and the power to change the immanent bread and wine into the transcendent body and blood of Christ. This sense of an aura (a term to which we will return) about Guinness is one which was clear in the sacramental opening quotation from the Guinness website, where the action of pouring the Guinness is very like that of a curate, obeying and enacting prescribed and unchanging ritual in the sacrament of the Mass. This parallel is strengthened in the sacramental opening of *Ulysses* itself: 'For this, O dearly beloved, is the genuine Christine: body and soul and blood and ouns. Slow music, please' (Joyce 1989, p. 3). This idea of the priest as a transformer of commodities is an ongoing trope in Joyce, with the famous lines from *A Portrait of the Artist as a Young Man* telling of Stephen's wish to become 'a priest of the eternal imagination, transmuting the daily bread of experience into the radiant body of everliving life' (Joyce 1993, pp. 248–249). The symbolic capital associated with religion permeates *Ulysses*, and a parallel symbolic and cultural capital has long been associated with Guinness. As well as the sacramental double-pour, advertising has long associated Guinness with values that transcend its mere alcoholic material content.

Catherine Belsey (2002) remembers as a young girl that stout was held 'to be full of nutritional value, and was often treated as a health drink, especially by middle-aged women', but she goes on to ponder whether this was 'the whole story', as she remembers the Guinness posters which showed:

> comic cartoon animals in bright colours. Weren't these visual signifiers associating the drink with pleasure, laughter, the exchange of jokes? Weren't the adverts indicating that enjoying yourself was 'good for you', taking you out of yourself, as we might once have said? And was it the sociability of the pub, or the alcohol, that would make you see the world in the bright primary colours of the posters themselves? Either way, the

claim of the images, or the words and the images taken together, was that Guinness was 'good for' your world picture, brightening the way things looked.

(Belsey 2002, p. 22)

Belsey here is gesturing towards the cultural and symbolic capital that has long been associated with Guinness, and the sacramental ritualistic aspect is not confined to the pouring of the pint. The second part of the Guinness experience is related to how the product should be consumed: 'The Savour'. Once again, it is the master brewer Fergal Murray who is explaining the ritual:

> First of all you never look down at a pint of Guinness, you always look to the horizon, bring that elbow up, bring the glass to your lips and not you to the glass, and then break the seal as I call it, get that cream on your lips. Allow enough liquid to flow under the head to energise those taste buds, get the sweetness of the malt to the front of the tongue, the roastiness to the side and then the bitterness at the back of the throat. Get that ... savour that Guinness ... unbelievable. Hold on [*while he takes another drink*] ... Enjoy!!
>
> (<http://www.guinness.com/en-ie/thebeer-draught.html>)

So not only is there a ritualised way to pour the Guinness; there is also a ritualised and almost sacramental way to drink it. The holding up of the glass parallels the raising of the host at the consecration of the Roman Catholic mass, and the parody of this at the start of *Ulysses*: 'He held the bowl aloft and intoned: INTROIBO AD ALTARE DEI' [*capitals original*] (Joyce 1989, p. 3). This is more than just consumption – this is consumption as part of that 'club effect' of which Bourdieu spoke, where knowledge of the ritual and awareness of the processes grants cultural and symbolic capital to the act of consumption. This is because 'the realm of sacred semblances and their ascribed meanings' which still maintain 'a (veiled) hold over our cultural representations' (Dickinson 2011, p. 134) has been channelled by Guinness in order to add symbolic and cultural capital to their product, hence the idea of breaking the seal, an act which has strong religious overtones.

This may seem a large claim to make for what is, after all, a brand of beer, but a brief discussion of how cultural codes develop and change will provide the theoretical framework for an exploration of Guinness as a sacramental product, which attempts to fetishise itself as a commodity which has transcendental and quasi-religious powers in a manner similar to aspects of religion. As Karl Marx (1990, p. 165) has written: 'the products of the human brain appear as autonomous figures endowed with a life of their own', and it will become clear that Guinness, as a product, attempts to locate itself as just such an autonomous figure with life of its own. For Marx, the commodity fetish worked as a form of quasi-religious experience. In the famous table example from the first volume of *Capital: A Critique of Political Economy*, he makes this point trenchantly:

> The form of wood, for instance, is altered if a table is made out of it. Nevertheless the table continues to be wood, an ordinary, sensuous thing, but as soon as it emerges as a commodity, it changes into a thing which transcends sensuousness. It not only stands with its feet on the ground, but, in relation to all other commodities, it stands on its head, and evolves out of its wooden brain grotesque ideas, far more wonderful than if it were to begin dancing of its own free will.
>
> (Marx 1990, pp. 163–164)

The points for Marx is that the use value of the table, a four-legged raised platform at which people can sit, work and eat, has been surpassed by what he calls its exchange value. A table is not just a table, it can become a classic piece of furniture, it can become an antique, it can be exchanged for far more money than it took to purchase and manufacture because it has now attained some extra form of value.

Giorgio Agamben has made the point that Marx was in London during the first Universal Exhibition in 1851, and here he would have seen how various commodities of the Industrial Revolution were set out in Joseph Paxton's all-glass Crystal Palace, a structure which was meant to add an aura to the commodities displayed therein:

> In the galleries and the pavilions of its mystical Crystal Palace, in which from the outset a place was also reserved for works of art, the commodity is displayed to be enjoyed only through the glance at the *enchanted scene*. Thus at the Universal Exposition was celebrated, for the first time, the mystery that has now become familiar to anyone who has entered a supermarket or been exposed to the manipulation of an advertisement: the epiphany of the unattainable.
>
> (Agamben 1993, p. 38)

In capitalist culture, there needs to be more than just a value placed on the material and labour of any commodity, as otherwise the levels of profit will not be huge. Companies like Apple are classic examples of this. Apple not only met a market-demand with their iPad; they actually created the demand by making a beautiful, sleek product and then suggesting ways in which people could use it. So people bought the iPad, not to meet a challenge, solve a problem or complete a task more efficiently. They bought it because they wanted to buy this sleek and desirable object: 'the transfiguration of the commodity into *enchanted object* is the sign that the exchange value is already beginning to eclipse the use-value of the commodity' (Agamben 1993, p. 38). When it was first produced, the use-value of the iPad was non-existent: it was its exchange value that caused people to pay a large amount of money for its purchase. What was being sold was not a cutting edge technological problem-solver, but a lifestyle accessory. There is an aura (and this term is being used in a very specific context, as will become clear later in the chapter) to owning an iPad, and this same aura is at the core of the narrative of Guinness that has created an exchange value that is now world-wide. As we will see, the same process of exchange value outstripping use value is to be found in the marketing of Guinness: 'under the influence of Guinness, the sign of postmodern Dublin, we experienced the dissolution of the bonds of modernity' (Slattery 2003, p. 150).

Guinness was founded in 1759, and the stout was initially a local beer, due to distribution problems. Now the company is owned by Diageo and is a world brand with a huge distribution network. Guinness is a popular Irish dry stout that originated in the brewery of Arthur Guinness (1725–1803) at St James's Gate, Dublin. Guinness is one of the most successful beer brands worldwide. It is brewed in almost sixty countries and is available in over 100. More than 850 million litres (1.5 billion imperial or 1.8 billion US pints) are sold annually (<http://www.guinness.com/en-ie/thebeer-draught.html>). Diageo is a multinational corporation which manufactures its products at industrial scale, and Guinness, by any definition, is a mass-produced product wherein the full benefits of mechanisation, globalisation and digitisation are used in order to minimise costs and maximise profit. In short, the production is well-attuned to mass-market consumer capitalism, as it is a leisure product whose use value is enjoyment and intoxication. In summary, Guinness, as alcohol, is a legal drug which is sold for the purpose of intoxication, be that to a mild or dangerous degree, and as an intoxicant, its use is governed by laws which restrict its intake on the grounds of age and also on the grounds of set times when it can be sold and consumed in public. However, this is not the way in which the product strives to be seen in the marketplace. Rather than being marketed as an intoxicant, it is instead marketed as an object of desire.

Of course to sell it as an intoxicant would be to define it in terms of its use-value and, as Marx has noted, this would seem to be a better option, and certainly one which he favoured. However, there is a large body of research which would argue that use-value and exchange value have long been inextricably connected. Objects *qua* their material construction, have long been connected with different values. The anthropologist Marcel Mauss has discovered that complicated rituals and procedures around the giving and receiving of objects have been observed in archaic societies. He has spoken of the 'potlatch', a gathering where issues of hierarchy and position were settled through a complex form of prestation, or reciprocal and expected gift-giving and receipt. At potlatch gatherings, a family or hereditary leader hosts guests in their family's house and holds a feast for their guests. The main purpose of the potlatch is the redistribution and reciprocity of wealth. The potlatch also provided an opportunity for families to mark life occasions formally. Births, deaths, adoptions, weddings, and other major events were and are formally witnessed, so it is very much a social occasion or indeed a sacramental one, to use more Western terminology. Just as in Victorian fiction, three 'sacramental' moments were drawn on to bring down the curtain: birth, marriage and death (Sutherland 2011, p. 70). Moreover, two elements of the potlatch have in fact been attested to: 'the honour, prestige or *mana* which wealth confers; and the absolute obligation to make return gifts under the penalty of losing the *mana*, authority and wealth' (Mauss 1996, p. 6). In these social and sacramental rituals which marked the significant milestones of life – birth, death, marriage, coming to adulthood and special feasts at harvest and at various solstices, objects given as gifts had additional qualities to those of their material construction – they had exchange value which was partially created by the context of the potlatch. The material worth of the commodity was of less value than its place as a carrier of *mana*, which refers to 'the magical power of the person', and also their honour and 'one of the best translations of the word is "authority" or "wealth"' (Mauss 1996, p. 36). In a ritualistic potlatch, mana is associated with objects as they become gifts, and in a similar manner, the ritual of pouring the Guinness attempts to add this sense of authority to the drink as a commodity for consumption. Rather than just drinking it from the can or bottle, as is the case with most other beers, Guinness needs to be carefully treated in order to preserve its mana, its aura of individuality.

Before ever a drop of Guinness touches the lips of the consumer, the ritualistic pouring and the need to wait for the drink to settle, during the 119.5 seconds of 'Guinness Time', the commodity has already been made magical or special through the chip of messianic time that is created by this process. In this manner, it is similar to how, in the Exhibition in Paris in 1889, the Eiffel Tower, 'by offering a reference point visible every-where', transformed the whole city into a 'commodity that could be consumed at a single glance' (Agamben 1993, p. 40). Here Agamben has a clearer view of the duality of the commodity than Marx; Marx felt that use-value was the most significant aspect of a commodity and that exchange value was somehow a deviant quality, which allowed for the abuse of the labourer. Many would agree that capitalism does abuse labour, and that it is inherently unjust as a socio-economic system – one only has to cite the socialisation of private debt in the Irish banking and financial crisis to prove this. Nevertheless, Marx displays a flawed understanding of the semiotic value of a commodity in his analysis. As Agamben notes, while Marx alluded to the 'fetishistic character', the 'metaphysical subtleties' and 'theological witticisms' of the commodity (Agamben 1993, p. 42), he seemed to be suggesting that this came after the idea of use value (just as his own critique came twelve years after his initial one), but this belatedness is more to be found in Marx than in the semiotics of the commodity. I would argue that from the beginning of time, going back to the archaic societies of Mauss, that metaphysical or magical qualities were an important factor in the creation of any commodity.

Derrida has made the telling point that the two are in fact conjoined; he speaks of the place where 'the values of value (between use-value and exchange-value), secret, mystique, enigma, fetish, and the ideological form a chain in Marx's text', and he goes on to analyse 'the spectral movement of this chain' (Derrida 1994, p. 148). He sees use-value and exchange value are not clearly separated but 'haunted', by culture and by each other. Derrida takes this as a classic example, which has very general application, and reasserts his plea for 'hauntology' rather than the usually carefully separated and compartmentalised ontology. Exchange value haunts use-value, for example, by expressing repetition, exchange ability, and the loss of singularity (Derrida 1994, p. 161). Use-value haunts exchange value, because exchange is only possible if the commodity might be useful for others. In this sense, use value and exchange value are temporally connected: we buy a product to fill a future need – as I purchase a pint of Guinness, it is with a view to drinking it afterwards, and as such we purchase products in terms of satisfying a future desire. A desire, Derrida suggests, that is predicated on a better, more sated us in the future. Of course it is also due to a desire to be part of a club effect, to display my cultural capital and my symbolic capital. So I am not just drinking a liquid that is poured out in three seconds and plonked on the bar counter; instead, I am participating in a ritual with its own special glass, its own special double pour, its own special necessary time, Guinness Time, which is needed for it to assume its proper appearance. I am becoming part of a special group, I am demonstrating cultural and symbolic capital, as well as discernment, by choosing this product. It is less about consumption per se, and more about symbolic consumption, as I am communing with the aura of Guinness as a commodity.

The term 'aura' was first used in this sense by Walter Benjamin, when he spoke of how a religious or magical context is often what gives the work of art its aura, and by this he means that 'the earliest art works originated in the service of a ritual-first the magical, then the religious kind', and he goes on to add that the 'existence of the work of art with reference to its aura is never entirely separated from its ritual function' (Benjamin 1968, pp. 223–224). Benjamin has spoken at length of how mechanised reproductive techniques have meant that this aura is gradually lost, but Agamben has made the interesting observation that this aura does not just apply to works of art but to any commodity once, the criterion of use value has been satisfied. This means that the distinction, the borderline 'that artists from the Renaissance forward had indefatigably worked to establish, by basing the supremacy of artistic creation on the "making" of the artisan and the labourer became extremely tenuous' (Agamben 1993, p. 42). Agamben noted that the decay of the traditional idea of the aura in the work of art just meant the 'reconstitution of a new "aura" through which the object … became charged with a new value, perfectly analogous to the exchange value, whose object is doubled by the commodity' (Agamben 1993, p. 44). The Guinness website aims to develop this aura in terms of the product, and Arthur's Day is a reification of this aura in just the same way as Bloomsday is a reification of the Joycean aura of *Ulysses*.

In other words, once we decide that we need a table, then aesthetic and exchange-value considerations come into play. Thus once I have gone into a pub, and decided that I want a pint of alcohol, issues of symbolic value and the aura will help to determine my choice. If I wish to be part of the aura of Guinness, if I wish to be part of the sacramental rite of pouring and drinking, then Guinness will be my choice. The whole purpose of the website 'Guinness Experience' is to foreground this symbolic capital attached to the consumption of Guinness. The brewer and the website invariably use the singular number to refer to Guinness – it is always a single pint, a perfect pint, with little to suggest the mass-market, high-volume nature of the product. Indeed, such is the ritual and sacramentality of the pouring and the drinking experience that it would seem more like an artisanal, craft beer, brewed in a micro-brewery, rather than one of the most recognisable brand names in the world.

The sacramental nature of the Guinness experience stresses the aesthetic and the beautiful, with the classic contrast of action and stasis, as the settling process gives way to the clear black and cream solid structure of the pint, a pint which is poured into a 'branded glass', with the finger on the harp icon. The stress on the minute physical actions, and the very precise directions (the first pour brings the liquid up to the harp icon), is part of the sacramental trope of the product, as 'only the physical or material can function sacramentally, and so in the case of the incarnation it must be Christ's "flesh" that accomplishes such mediation, pointing to the divinity that lies behind the fleshly appearance' (Brown 2008, p. 52). This focus on the intricate levels of the material in order to suggest an attendant transcendence is clear in the following quote from the website:

Swirling clouds tumble as the storm begins to calm. Settle. Breathe in the moment, then break through the smooth, light head to the bittersweet reward. Unmistakeably GUINNESS, from the first velvet sip to the last, lingering drop. And every deep-dark satisfying mouthful in between. Pure beauty. Pure GUINNESS.
(<http://www.guinness.com/en-ie/thebeer-draught.html>)

The reification of this aesthetic process is in Arthur's Day, a global celebration of Guinness as a commodity replete with cultural and symbolic capital. By taking a drink and turning it into a day of celebration, which is almost deliberately not connected with the consumption of the product, is a further example of the symbolic and cultural capital that is associated with Guinness. Just as religious events have a feast day, so too does Guinness, and it is interesting that the product name is not foregrounded in the feast day. The day comprises a series of musical events and a general celebration of Guinness. It was first organised in 2009 to celebrate the 250th anniversary of the Guinness brewing company, and the events were set in Dublin, Kuala Lumpur, Lagos, New York and Yaoundé. A number of groups participate, and there are surprise gigs organised where some headline artists appear at local clubs and pubs. Guinness drinkers are expected to raise a glass to the memory of Arthur Guinness at 17:59 (5:59 pm), a reference to 1759, the year the Guinness Brewery was established, and once again, the idea of a different type of time is stressed, with the date being transposed onto the time, another way of mimicking how sacral time is morphed onto diurnal time in religious feast days. In the advertisement for the 2012 day, 'Painting the town black', the product scarcely features, as the whole add involves people painting themselves and various items of clothing as well as walls and houses black, in order to replicate the colour of Guinness.

It is another example of the symbolic nature of the consumption – people are being urged, not just to consume Guinness, but in this case, to actually 'be' Guinness, or at least to assume the colour of Guinness. An added factor is the Arthur Guinness Fund, which lends a philanthropic dimension to the day, and some €7 million has been raised to help 'social entrepreneurs deliver measurable, transformational change to communities in Ireland and worldwide' (<http://www.guinness.com/en-ie/arthursday/AGF.html>). What is most interesting about this fund is that is strengthens the associations between Guinness and the sacramental aspects of religion. Like so many sacramental and religious institutions, which offer help to the other, so Guinness, through this fund, does the same thing, and in so doing, it transforms itself once again from a commodity to a source of cultural, symbolic and now social capital, as it brings help to communities in need. Through Arthur's Day, and symbolised by the Cloud and the Clock, Guinness sets out a narrative that sets it out as a secular sacrament and a chip of messianic time. The connection between Guinness and notions of messianic time is one which has been fostered by the company, and Arthur's Day, like Bloomsday, makes the point that, just as '*Ulysses* is more than a book. It's an event' (McCourt 2004, p. xiii), so too Guinness is more than a drink – a lot more.

Works cited

Agamben, G. (1993). *Stanzas: Word and Phantasm in Western Culture*. Minneapolis: University of Minnesota Press.

Belsey, C. (2002). *Post-structuralism: A Very Short Introduction*. Oxford: Oxford University Press.

Benjamin, W. (1968). *Illuminations*. New York: Harcourt.

Bourdieu, P. (1984). *Distinction: A Social Critique of the Judgement of Taste* (trans. R. Nice). London: Routledge.

Bourdieu, P. (1991). *Language and Symbolic Power* (trans. J. B. Thompson). Cambridge, Mass.: Harvard University Press.

Bourdieu, P. and A. Accardo (1999). *The Weight of the World: Social Suffering in Contemporary Society*. Stanford: Stanford University Press.

Brown, D. (2008). *God and Mystery in Words: Experience Through Metaphor and Drama*. Oxford: Oxford University Press.

Derrida, J. (1994). *Specters of Marx: The State of the Debt, The Work of Mourning, and the New International*. P. Kamuf, trans., London: Routledge.

Derrida, J. and D. Attridge (1992). *Acts of Literature*. London: Routledge.

Dickinson, C. (2011). *Agamben and Theology*. London; New York, NY: T. & T. Clark.

Fastiggi, R. L. (2010). *New Catholic Encyclopedia Supplement 2010*. Detroit: Gale.

Ferris, D. S. (2008). *The Cambridge Introduction to Walter Benjamin*, Cambridge: Cambridge University Press.

Gifford, D. and R. J. Seidman (1988). *Ulysses Annotated: Notes for James Joyce's Ulysses.* Berkeley: University of California Press.

Grenfell, M. (2008). *Pierre Bourdieu: Key Concepts.* Stocksfield: Acumen.

Guinness Website. <http://www.guinness.com> [26 June 2013]

Guinness Website. 'Arthur's Day'. <http://www.guinness.com/en-ie/arthursday/index.html> [26 June 2013]

Guinness Website. 'The Beer'. <http://www.guinness.com/en-ie/thebeer-draught.html> [26 June 2013]

Guinness Website. 'Frequently Asked Questions'. <http://www.guinness.com/en-ie/faqs.html> [26 June 2013]

Guinness Storehouse Factsheet 1. <http://www.guinness-storehouse.com/en/pdfs/factsheets/factsheet_pdf_11.pdf> [26 June 2013]

Jennings, M. W. (1997–2003). *Walter Benjamin: Selected Writings.* Cambridge, MA: Belknap.

Joyce, J. (1989). *Ulysses.* London: Bodley Head.

Joyce, J. (1993). *A Portrait of the Artist as a Young Man.* Boston: Bedford Books of St. Martin's Press.

Marx, K. (1990). *Capital: A Critique of Political Economy Vol. 1.* B. Fowkes, trans., London: Penguin Classics.

Mauss, M. (1996). *The Gift: Forms and Functions of Exchange in Archaic Societies* (trans. I. Gunnison). London: Cohen and West.

McCourt, F. (2004). 'Foreword', in *Yes I said yes I will yes: a celebration of James Joyce, Ulysses, and 100 years of Bloomsday*, ed. N. Tully, pp. ix–xxi. New York: Vintage.

McKenna, B. (2002). *James Joyce's Ulysses: A Reference Guide.* Westport, Conn.: Greenwood.

Rabaté, J.-M. (2001). *James Joyce and the Politics of Egoism.* Cambridge: Cambridge University Press.

Slattery, D. (2003). 'Fear and Loathing in Lost Ages: Journeys through Postmodern Dublin', in *The End of Irish History?: Critical Reflections on the Celtic Tiger*, eds C. Coulter and S. Coleman, pp. 139–154. Manchester: Manchester University Press.

Sutherland, J. (2011). *How Literature Works: 50 Key Concepts.* Oxford: Oxford University Press.

Swartz, D. (1997). *Culture & Power: The Sociology of Pierre Bourdieu*, Chicago: University of Chicago Press.

The Mill Website. <http://themill.com/work/guinness/cloud.aspx> [26 June 2013]

Webb, J., Schirato, T. and G. Danaher (2002). *Understanding Bourdieu*, London: Thousand Oaks.

Notes on Contributors

DOROTHY CASHMAN is researching Irish culinary manuscripts and the culinary traditions of the landed estates and great houses of Ireland for her PhD at the Dublin Institue of Technology. She has presented papers at the inaugural Dublin Gastronomy Symposium (2012) on Dean Swift and the relationship with French culinary influence in Georgian Ireland, and to the Irish Georgian Society (2013) and the National Library of Ireland (2012) on researching the culinary manuscripts of the National Library's collection. Her continuing research is supported by research funding from Fáilte Ireland.

MARJORIE DELEUZE is working on a PhD thesis in Irish Studies entitled *Dimension identitaire des pratiques, des habitudes et des symboliques alimentaires de l'Irlande contemporaine.* She works under the supervision of Professor Catherine Maignant from Université de Lille III and lectures in French in Trinity College Dublin. She has presented papers at the inaugural Dublin Gastronomy Symposium and at the AFIS conference in Limerick.

MICHAEL FLANAGAN lectures in All Hallows College (Dublin City University) in the fields of Popular Media Culture and Irish History. He also works as a lecturer in Education and Teaching Practice in Hibernia College and St Nicholas College, Dun Laoghaire. He has presented at many conferences on the area of media and popular culture and has contributed to publications on topics related to these disciplines and related themes. He was awarded his PhD from the Dublin Institute of Technology in 2006 for his thesis entitled *True sons of Erin: Catholic / nationalist ideology and the politics of adventure in Our Boys 1914–32.*

DARRA GOLDSTEIN is Founding Editor of *Gastronomica: The Journal of Food and Culture* and the Willcox B. and Harriet M. Adsit Professor of

Russian at Williams College, USA. She is also the author of four cook-books: *A Taste of Russia* (finalist, Tastemaker Award); *The Georgian Feast* (winner of the 1994 IACP Julia Child Award for Cookbook of the Year); *The Winter Vegetarian*; and *Baking Boot Camp* (finalist, IACP Award). She has consulted for the Council of Europe as part of an international group exploring ways in which food can be used to promote tolerance and diversity, and under her editorship the volume *Culinary Cultures of Europe: Identity, Diversity and Dialogue* was published in 2005 to commemorate the fiftieth anniversary of the signing of the European Cultural Convention.

RHONA RICHMAN KENNEALLY is an Associate Professor in the Department of Design and Computation Arts at Concordia University, Canada. She is a Fellow of Concordia's School of Canadian Irish Studies and Editor of *The Canadian Journal of Irish Studies*. Her publications and teaching explore the complex dynamic of the built environment in terms of the exchanges of agency and empowerment that are continuously renegotiated and reconfigured by, and through, the practices of every-day life. Special attention is given to investigating food-related perfor-mances, both historic and present-day, and to the implications of designers' and other stakeholders' interventions affecting food-related activities. Her current, Social Sciences and Humanities Research Council of Canada (SSHRC)-funded research focuses on domestic foodscapes (the spaces in the home in which food is stored, prepared and eaten) in mid-twentieth-century households in Ireland. She is currently working on a monograph on Irish domestic food culture.

TONY KIELY is a lecturer and researcher in the College of Arts and Tourism, Dublin Institute of Technology, lecturing in the areas of business, finance, marketing and strategic management. His research interests include tradi-tional music and tourism, church tourism and the social history of Dublin. He has presented at a range of international conferences, and has published in the areas of church tourism and competency framework developments within the hospitality industry.

MÁIRTÍN MAC CON IOMAIRE is a lecturer in Culinary Arts in the Dublin Institute of Technology. He is well known as an award-winning chef, culinary historian, food writer, broadcaster and ballad singer. In 2009 he became the first Irish chef to be awarded a PhD for his thesis, *The Emergence, Development and Influence of French Haute Cuisine on public dining in Dublin Restaurants 1900–2000: An Oral History* (<http://arrow.dit.ie/tourdoc/12>). He has presented two six-part series of cookery programmes, *Aingeal sa Chistin*, for RTÉ, and has featured on numerous radio and television programmes. He is a regular contributor at the Oxford Symposium on Food and Cookery. In 2012, he chaired the inaugural Dublin Gastronomy Symposium (<www.arrow.dit.ie/dgs>), a biennial gathering of food scholars and enthusiasts. Along with his PhD candidates, Dorothy Cashman, Tara McConnell and Elaine Mahon, Máirtín is building a research cluster around Ireland's culinary past and heritage.

EAMON MAHER is Director of the National Centre for Franco-Irish Studies in IT Tallaght, where he also lectures in Humanities. Editor of the highly successful *Reimagining Ireland* book series with Peter Lang, Eamon's recent publications include *'The Church and its Spire': John McGahern and the Catholic Question* and (with Eugene O'Brien) *From Prosperity to Austerity: A Socio-Cultural Critique of the Celtic Tiger and its Aftermath*.

TARA MCCONNELL is a PhD candidate at the Dublin Institute of Technology. Food history is her area of interest, and she is currently researching period trends in gastronomy in elite households in Georgian Ireland with a particular focus on fashionable beverages and related material culture. She has presented papers at the Oxford Symposium on Food and Cookery (2010, 2013), the inaugural Dublin Gastronomy Symposium (2012), and the Eighth Annual Conference of the Association of Franco-Irish Studies (2012).

JOHN MULCAHY is Head of Food Tourism, Hospitality Education and Standards at Fáilte Ireland, the National Tourism Development Authority. He formalised his passion for food by graduating from the University of Adelaide in April 2010 with the Cordon Bleu Master of Arts in Gastronomy, adding to other academic awards from Cornell (USA), Oxford Brookes (UK), the Institute of Wine & Spirits (UK) and Dublin Institute of Technology. His dedication to food, wine and tourism stems from both a personal ardour for gastronomy and also his experience at various times over thirty years as a pub, restaurant or food service operator on three continents, as an educator, and most recently as a public servant with the National Tourism Development Authority in Ireland. He takes a particular personal interest in Irish food and how to encourage its significance for all sectors of Irish society.

BRIAN MURPHY currently lectures in hospitality, tourism and gastronomy at the Institute of Technology Tallaght, Dublin. Following his undergraduate degree, he spent a number of years working in management positions in the hospitality sector both in Ireland and abroad. He has a particular interest in wine and gastronomy research and is keen to explore the role that place and heritage can play in making wine and food products more attractive to consumers. He recently completed a PhD at the National Centre for Franco-Irish Studies (IT Tallaght) on the topic *Changing Identities in a Homogenized World: The Role of 'Place and Story' in Modern Perceptions of French Wine Culture.*

EUGENE O'BRIEN is Head of the Department of English Language and Literature in Mary Immaculate College, University of Limerick. His publications include: *Seamus Heaney – Creating Irelands of the Mind*; *Seamus Heaney and the Place of Writing*; *Seamus Heaney: Searches for Answers* and *Kicking Bishop Brennan up the Arse: Negotiating Texts and Contexts in Contemporary Irish Studies*. His latest book, *From Prosperity to Austerity: A Socio-Cultural Critique of the Celtic Tiger and its Aftermath*, co-edited with Eamon Maher, will be published in 2014.

FLICKA SMALL is a PhD candidate and tutor in the School of English, University College Cork. Her research interests centre on how food functions in contemporary literature and the semiotics of food, particularly in the writing of James Joyce. She co-authored the chapter 'The Food Culture of the Iveragh Peninsula' in *The Atlas of the Iveragh Peninsula* (2009).

She has also presented papers on the significance of food in James Joyce's *Ulysses* at Notre Dame University, Indiana; the 23rd International James Joyce Symposium, Dublin; and the 2013 Ballymaloe LitFest, Cork. Flicka has also worked as a chef, a food safety consultant and a cookery writer.

Index

Reimagining Ireland

Series Editor: Dr Eamon Maher, Institute of Technology, Tallaght

The concepts of Ireland and 'Irishness' are in constant flux in the wake of an ever-increasing reappraisal of the notion of cultural and national specificity in a world assailed from all angles by the forces of globalisation and uniformity. Reimagining Ireland interrogates Ireland's past and present and suggests possibilities for the future by looking at Ireland's literature, culture and history and subjecting them to the most up-to-date critical appraisals associated with sociology, literary theory, historiography, political science and theology.

Some of the pertinent issues include, but are not confined to, Irish writing in English and Irish, Nationalism, Unionism, the Northern 'Troubles', the Peace Process, economic development in Ireland, the impact and decline of the Celtic Tiger, Irish spirituality, the rise and fall of organised religion, the visual arts, popular cultures, sport, Irish music and dance, emigration and the Irish diaspora, immigration and multiculturalism, marginalisation, globalisation, modernity/postmodernity and postcolonialism. The series publishes monographs, comparative studies, interdisciplinary projects, conference proceedings and edited books.

Proposals should be sent either to Dr Eamon Maher at eamon.maher@ittdublin.ie or to ireland@peterlang.com.

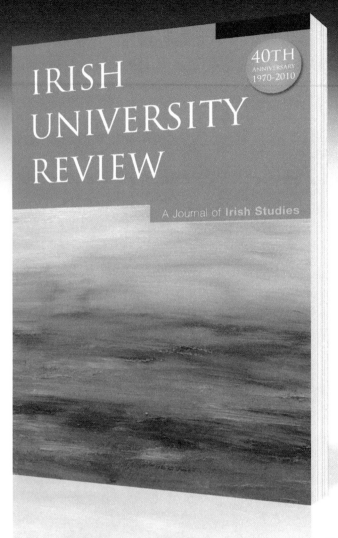